SIR WILLIAM DAVENANT

GARLAND REFERENCE LIBRARY
OF THE HUMANITIES
(Vol. 525)

Io. Grenhill pinx.   W. Faithorne Sculp.

S.ir William D'avenant K.

Figure 1. Frontispiece portrait of Sir William Davenant from *Works* (1673). Engraved by William Faithorne from a portrait by John Grenhill; see item 7.

SIR WILLIAM DAVENANT
An Annotated Bibliography
1629–1985

Sophia B. Blaydes
Philip Bordinat

GARLAND PUBLISHING, INC. · NEW YORK & LONDON
1986

Library of Congress Cataloging-in-Publication Data

Blaydes, Sophia B.
  Sir William Davenant : an annotated bibliography,
1629–1985.

  (Garland reference library of the humanities ; v. 525)
  Includes index.
  1. D'Avenant, William, Sir, 1606–1668—Bibliography.
I. Bordinat, Philip. II. Title. III. Series.
Z8218.225.B55 1986 [PR2476] 016.821′4 84-45395
ISBN 0-8240-8874-3 (alk. paper)

Printed on acid-free, 250-year-life paper
Manufactured in the United States of America

For Dave and Mary

Contents

Preface

This annotated bibliography is a comprehensive list of works by and about Sir William Davenant (1606-1668). The list of more than one thousand items has been divided into three parts and concludes with an index. Part I, "Works by Sir William Davenant," is itself divided into three parts: the first includes Davenant's collected works; the second his works that were published separately; and the third his miscellaneous works—poems that were published in the seventeenth century in miscellanies, prologues to plays by other playwrights, and commendatory poems that were published in volumes by others of his day. Part II, "Works about Sir William Davenant," is the largest part of the bibliography. It lists many of the references to Davenant and those studies that are interpretive, historical, and textual. It is arranged chronologically, divided by centuries and, for the twentieth century, divided into decades. Part III, "Bibliographies," contains a chronological list of bibliographies, long or short, that offer useful, unique, or inclusive works by and about Davenant. The final section of the volume, the index, contains an alphabetical list that enables readers to find resources by title, author, and subject.

Part I traces Davenant's works from 1629 through the twentieth century, and it includes reprints and facsimile editions. For each item in the section the following information is provided wherever appropriate: the title of the work as it appears on the publication; avenues of access through the *Short-Title Catalogue*, University Microfilms International, Greg's *Bibliography, the English and American Plays* microcard series, and the Thomason collection. Wherever applicable, each entry provides information on prefatory material, contents, and addenda, as well as pertinent dates and comments from the Stationers' Register. Each concludes with a note of explanation, description, or interpretation of the item.

The items throughout the volume are numbered consecutively; Part II continues the numbers where Part I leaves off. All of the items in Part II are listed according to the style in the 1977 edition of the *MLA Handbook*. Not only do the entries in Part II have brief comments that explain or describe the works, but they also provide cross-references to other items: some refer to

reprints or other editions, while others offer additional
debate or information.

    A bibliography of an influential and active person such
as Davenant will of necessity be broad and diffuse. He was
a theater-manager-playwright who was poet laureate, and,
during the Civil War, fought with the Royalists and found
himself in exile with them. By the Restoration, Davenant
presented the first English opera on a modern stage with the
first English actress. The entries in the bibliography
reflect those many and varied interests. The bibliography
contains the editions of his own writing--thirty or so
dramatic works, three volumes of poetry and criticism, and
other miscellaneous items--as well as the commentary and
scholarship that have accumulated over the years. Included
in the bibliography are poems, stories, plays, chapters,
notes, dissertations, and theses along with the books and
articles that touch upon Davenant. Students of the
seventeenth century, be it of literature, history, music, or
theater, will find the volume useful. Students of the
drama, especially of the seventeenth century, will find it
valuable. Studies that focus upon William Shakespeare,
Inigo Jones, Ben Jonson, John Milton, and John Dryden, among
others, may benefit from this bibliography. Indeed,
Davenant reaches so far and so wide in his life and
influence that the compilers of this bibliography have set
some limits: no reviews of books are included; books or
articles with only the occasional reference to Davenant have
been omitted. Yet, some works that do not focus on Davenant
are included, particularly if they place him in perspective
and offer illuminating commentary on his achievement. We
hope that the result of our search and our decisions is a
bibliography that will be a useful addition to the growing
library of reference guides on English literature.

Acknowledgments

We wish to acknowledge the support and the assistance
of those who contributed to the completion of this
bibliography. Through its Senate Research Grants and its
libraries, West Virginia University has provided generous
support. Dean Thomas Knight of the College of Arts and
Sciences has encouraged us in our efforts to complete our
project by extending secretarial assistance and the use of
the college's Word-Processing Center. We would especially
like to thank our typist in the English Department, Jackie
Seymour, for her patience and good humor, and Sherry Fox, in
the Word-Processing Center, whose expertise and gentle ways
helped us more than we can say. We are also indebted to
Rudolph Almasy, Chairman of the English Department, for his
continued support of our Davenant research. Finally, we
wish to acknowledge the debt we owe to the Folger
Shakespeare Library and its staff.

Introduction

From the mid-seventeenth century until our own day, Sir William Davenant has had a magnetic appeal to commentators on literature and the theater. In the seventeenth century, Thomas Hobbes and John Dryden paid tribute to him, while in the eighteenth and nineteenth centuries, anthologists Robert Anderson, Alexander Chalmers, Robert Southey, and Thomas Campbell and editors James Maidment and W. H. Logan kept Davenant's works before the reading public. In our century, significant studies of Davenant's life and works by Montague Summers, Hazelton Spencer, Alfred Harbage, Arthur Nethercot, and Douglas Bush, and editions of his works by Christopher Spencer, A. H. Gibbs, and David Gladish have enriched our understanding of his achievement. Studies of the masque, the opera, and the English theater have also proved valuable because they often include pertinent comment on Davenant.

A survey of Davenant's life and works reveals the reason for the continued attention he has received from editors and critics. In an artistic career that spanned nearly forty years, from 1629 to his death in 1668, Davenant was a major poet, critic, playwright, and theater manager. Although Davenant's poetic achievement is evident in his plays, masques, and operas, it is most clearly identified with his collected poems: *Madagascar* (1638), a volume of forty-two poems; *Gondibert* (1651), his long, unfinished epic; *Poems on Several Occasions* (1657, 1673), a volume of fifty-two poems; and three panegyrics, one to General Monck (1660) and two to Charles II (1660, 1663). The first volume, a product of his halcyon days, has some of Davenant's most celebrated poems: "For the Lady, *Olivia* Porter. A present, upon New-Yeares day" and "Jeffereidos," a mock-epic, perhaps the first of the seventeenth century. In every way a contrast to *Madagascar*, *Gondibert* was written while Davenant was awaiting execution. Instead of a celebration of court figures by the poet laureate, the epic is Davenant's response to the chaos around him. It offers a neoclassical view of the harmony, beauty, and order possible in an unsettled world. Persuasive and didactic, *Gondibert* also presents a story that depends upon the conflict of love and honor, a theme that would emerge again in *The Siege of Rhodes* and later in Dryden's heroic dramas. Davenant's didacticism and the heroic mode continue in the panegyrics that convey some of the Royalists' views of the Restoration. The first, to Monck, celebrates a temporary ruler of England early in 1660 before Charles II was restored to the throne.

The other two address the king, first as the source of
goodness and greatness for all his people and second as the
cautious patron of an aging poet laureate. The last volume,
Poems on Several Occasions was recorded in the Stationers'
Register in 1657 but it was not published until 1673 in the
magnificent folio edition of Davenant's works. Included are
some of Davenant's most memorable poems: "Song. [The Lark
now leaves his watery nest]," "The Philosopher's
Disquisition," and "The Long Vacation." From his early to
his later poetry, Davenant wrote to please and to teach; he
was, in effect, the complete poet laureate who sought to
praise and to guide his monarch and his subjects.

In 1638, at the age of thirty-two, Davenant was
appointed poet laureate. By then, however, he had already
provided the King's Men, the premier company in London, with
seven plays; in addition, he had written the scripts for two
masques and had replaced Ben Jonson as collaborator with
Inigo Jones for the lavish royal entertainments. Before the
theaters closed in 1642, Davenant gave the King's Men three
more plays and three more masques, including the most
elaborate spectacle of them all, *Salmacida Spolia*.

For over a decade, from 1629 to 1642, Davenant had been
gaining valuable experience from writing plays and masques.
From Inigo Jones he learned revolutionary scenic techniques
which in his hands would establish the nature of the stage
and of dramatic production for the next three centuries.
Though more limited than his effect on staging, Davenant's
influence on the themes of future drama was, nonetheless,
important. His plays and masques reflected the interests if
not always the tone of Queen Henrietta Maria, especially her
enthusiasm for Platonic love. Davenant focused, sometimes
satirically, on the neoplatonic ideal in his masque *The
Temple of Love* and in his play *The Platonic Lovers*.
However, in *Love and Honour*, Davenant presented the ideals
of Platonic love more seriously. In these dramas and in
Gondibert, Davenant foreshadowed the development of the
heroic drama, which held the stage until late in the
seventeenth century.

Davenant's other contributions as playwright came after
the Restoration in 1660 when he altered Shakespeare's plays
for the new stage conditions. *Macbeth*, *Hamlet*, and *The
Tempest, or the Enchanted Island* were the most successful in
their day. Yet they became most infamous in the view of
many modern critics who have been offended by what they

considered mutilations of Shakespeare's texts which included cuts, modifications of the language, and with *Macbeth* and *The Tempest* additions to the text. Most drastically altered was *The Tempest*, which after the revisions by Davenant and Dryden retained only about one-third of Shakespeare's play. Although some critics question whether the revisions constitute a contribution, the altered plays were performed, keeping Shakespeare before audiences for many years.

Although his achievements as poet and playwright were considerable, to some Davenant's greatest contribution was as theater manager. After serving the Royalist cause first as a general of ordnance, then as a privateer and royal courier, and finally as a frustrated colonizer, Davenant found himself in London with a new French wife who apparently had money to invest in his visionary theater ventures. To avoid the Parliamentary prohibition against plays, he staged a series of four entertainments. The second of these, staged in 1656 at Rutland House, was *The Siege of Rhodes*. This was a landmark production in English theater history. Although the stage was tiny and the cast small, Davenant employed the grandiose techniques of masque production which he had learned from Inigo Jones: changeable scenery, an actress, music, and *stylo recitativo*. For the first time in England, changeable scenery was used, and a woman appeared on the public stage. *The Siege of Rhodes* is now considered the first English opera.

After the Restoration, William Davenant and Thomas Killigrew were granted patents to present stage plays, an action that gave them a monopoly on theater activity in London. Davenant continued using his new production methods, providing a proscenium arch behind which scenery could be changed. In addition, he introduced machinery, modeled on that used in masque production, enabling Ariel, for example, in *The Tempest* and the Witches in *Macbeth* to fly across the stage. It was this theater with its visual magic that attracted Samuel Pepys and his friends to the playhouse. Although Davenant's production techniques would be refined, they established the picture-frame stage that dominated theaters until the mid-twentieth century. Because Davenant introduced these innovations and ideas, he is considered by many stage historians the father of the modern theater.

All of Davenant's works have been the subject of scholarly attention. From the time of their publication,

Davenant's poems, plays, and criticism have attracted
comment, but in more recent years many scholars have
directed their efforts to his contributions as theater
manager, particularly in relationship to the development of
the stage. *The Bibliography* with its chronological
arrangement highlights these trends. Even a brief survey
will reveal additional facts about Davenant, his works, and
the publishing practices of his times.

   The Bibliography, as a whole, provides information the
researcher expects to find; additionally, Part I, "Works by
Davenant," and Part II, "Works about Davenant," offer
special insights that might escape notice were it not for
the arrangement of the entries. For example, in "Works by
Davenant," the entries for the Stationers' Register for each
of the separately published plays document the complex
business transactions carried out by Henry Herringman who
gradually gained control of the canon. His efforts enabled
him to publish the handsome folio collection of Davenant's
works in 1673. Another example occurs when the entries
provide both a publication and a stage history of a play.
The Tempest is especially revealing. Between the headings
1670 and *1674, The Bibliography* lists thirty-eight editions
of the play each of which has some of the significant
Davenant-Dryden alterations. The list supports Montague
Summers' statement, "Davenant's innovations kept the stage
for well-nigh two centuries, and, however they may be
criticized from one standpoint, this fact is proof
indisputable of their theatrical effectiveness" (see item
470, p. xlix).

   The Bibliography in addition offers more conventional
evidence of the continued interest in Davenant. Part II
reveals that, in our own time, modern printing techniques
have led to reprints and facsimiles of the *Works* (1673), *The
Dramatic Works* (1872-74), *Gondibert* (1651), and many of the
plays and masques. Scholars have also provided excellent
editions of *Gondibert*, the shorter poems, the court masques,
and some of the plays.

   Turning from Part I to Part II, "Works About Davenant,"
the reader will find information of a different kind. For
example, in an overview of the seventeenth century, a reader
will note that critics whose works are most valued today,
Thomas Hobbes and John Dryden, paid tribute to Davenant, as
did Thomas Rymer, the Duchess of Newcastle, Edward Howard,
and Edward Phillips. Abraham Cowley and Edmund Waller

praised the poet in commendatory verses published with
Gondibert. On the other hand, John Denham, Davenant's
friend and fellow poet, satirized the epic, while Richard
Flecknoe bitterly attacked Davenant's poetry, lacking the
spirit of good fellowship that apparently motivated Denham.
The impression created by the serious literary critics of
these times was of respect for the man and his
achievements.

The entries for the eighteenth century indicate that
most critics continued to praise Davenant. Sir Philip
Warwick, Colley Cibber, and W. R. Chetwood were largely
favorable in their comments. Charles Gildon in his work on
Betterton observed that Davenant emphasized spectacle over
acting; Colley Cibber discussed the problems of the patent
companies after the Restoration. Though much of the
criticism focused on Davenant in his relationship to the
theater, Richard Hurd emphasized Davenant the poet and found
he was influenced too much by the French. Hurd also
lamented Davenant's need for originality, which prevented
his being "in the just rank of our poets." As the century
came to a close, the first of a group of anthologists,
Robert Anderson, published *Select British Poets* (c. 1793),
which was republished under various titles in four
subsequent editions. The section on Davenant included a
critical introduction largely favorable to the poet.

The nineteenth-century section of *The Bibliography*
reveals that critics praised and blamed Davenant.
Gondibert, its *Preface*, and the *Answer* by Thomas Hobbes were
the targets of opposing enthusiasms. Davenant's theories on
the epic, the merits of his verse, and the subject matter of
the poem were debated throughout the century, fed no doubt
by the many editions of the poem that kept it before the
reading public. At the same time, a nonliterary controversy
was revived involving Davenant's paternity. Was he
Shakespeare's illegitimate son? Although the story was
discounted by most commentators, it nonetheless added an
unpleasant note to Davenant's reputation. In 1891, F. G.
Fleay suggested that Davenant was the principal link between
the pre- and post-Restoration drama, an idea that is still
used to describe the playwright-theater-manager. Another
scholar who pointed a direction that would be followed by
others in the twentieth century was Herbert Arthur Evans
whose edition of the English masques included *Salmacida
Spolia* and valuable comment on Davenant.

The Bibliography reveals that in the twentieth century the main direction of the scholarship has been concerned with Davenant's role as playwright-manager and his impact on the development of the modern stage. Even so, the century has provided full-length studies that are major contributions and include as part of a larger picture Davenant as playwright-manager. The studies by Montague Summers, Alfred Harbage, Arthur H. Nethercot, Howard S. Collins, and Philip Bordinat and Sophia B. Blaydes provide broad surveys of the man and his achievement. The studies by Enid Welsford, Allardyce Nicoll, and Stephen Orgel and Roy Strong discuss the court masque and describe the production techniques that Davenant would later transfer to the public theater.

The studies of the Shakespeare adaptations discuss their intrinsic interest and their purpose which was to make Shakespeare fit for the new stage conditions which Davenant had introduced. Among these studies are works by Montague Summers, Allardyce Nicoll, Hazelton Spencer, Christopher Spencer, and George Robert Guffey.

Those studies which provide an overview of theater development include works by Gerald Eades Bentley, Leslie Hotson, Lily B. Campbell, and Robert D. Hume. Other subjects that have come under periodic discussion include the operas, the heroic drama, and the patent companies after the Restoration.

The subjects outlined here and many others can be explored through the use of the Index which is the key to this bibliography.

Abbreviations and Short Titles

Dramatic Works, 1872-74   *The Dramatic Works of Sir William D'Avenant, with Prefatory Memoir and Notes.* Ed. James Maidment and W. H. Logan. 5 vols. Edinburgh: William Paterson, 1872-74. See item 10.

EAP   *Three Centuries of English and American Plays, 1500-1830.* Ed. H. W. Wells. New York: Readex Microprint, c. 1952-1967.

Greg   W. W. Greg. *A Bibliography of the English Printed Drama to the Restoration.* 4 vols. London: Bibliographical Society, 1939-1959.

STC   *A Short-Title Catalogue of Books Printed in England, Scotland, and Ireland, and of English Books Printed Abroad, 1475-1640.* A. W. Pollard and G. R. Redgrave. London: Bibliographical Society, 1926.

Short-Title Catalogue of Books Printed in England, Scotland, Wales, and British America and of English Books Printed in Other Countries, 1641-1700. Donald Wing. 3 vols. New York: Columbia, 1945-51.

Stationers' Register   *A Transcript of the Registers of the Company of Stationers of London, 1554-1640 A.D.* Ed. Edward Arber. 5 vols. London: Privately Printed, 1875-1894. Rpt. New York: Peter Smith, 1950.

A Transcript of the Registers of the Worshipful Company of

	Stationers: From 1640-1708 A.D. [G.E.B. Eyre]. 3 vols. London: Privately Printed, 1913-14. Rpt. New York: Peter Smith, 1950.
Thomason	*The Thomason Tracts. 1640-1661: Microfilm Edition of the Thomason Collection at the British Library.* Ann Arbor: UMI, 1977.
UMI	University Microfilms Incorporated. Ann Arbor, 1938--.
Works, 1673	*The Works of* Sr William Davenant Kt: .... London: Printed for T. N. for *Henry Herringman* ..., 1673. See item 7.

THE
WORKS
OF
Sr William Davenant Kt

Confifting of

Thofe which were formerly Printed,

AND

Thofe which he defign'd for the Prefs:

NOW PUBLISHED

Out of the AUTHORS

Originall Copies.

LONDON:

Printed by *T. N.* for *Henry Herringman*, at the Sign of the
Blew Anchor in the Lower Walk of the *New*
Exchange. 1 6 7 3.

Figure 2. Title page of the folio edition of Davenant's collected works; see item 7.

MADAGASCAR,

With other

POEMS.

BY

S. WILLIAM D'AVENANT.

LONDON,

Printed by *T. N.* for *Henry Herringman*, and
are to be fold at his Shop at the Sign of the
Anchor in the *New Exchange,* 1672.

Figure 3. Title page of *Madagascar* that appeared in the 1673
Works but was evidently printed the preceding year; see item 7.

GONDIBERT:

AN HEROICK

POEM,

Ed WRITTEN BY *Phelips*
1755
Sʳ WILLIAM D'AVENANT.

LONDON,

Printed by *Tho. Newcomb* for *John Holden*, and are to
be fold at his Shop at the fign of the Anchor in the
NEVV-EXCHANGE, 1651.

Figure 4. Title page of *Gondibert*, 1651 edition, from the West Virginia
University Library; see item 80.

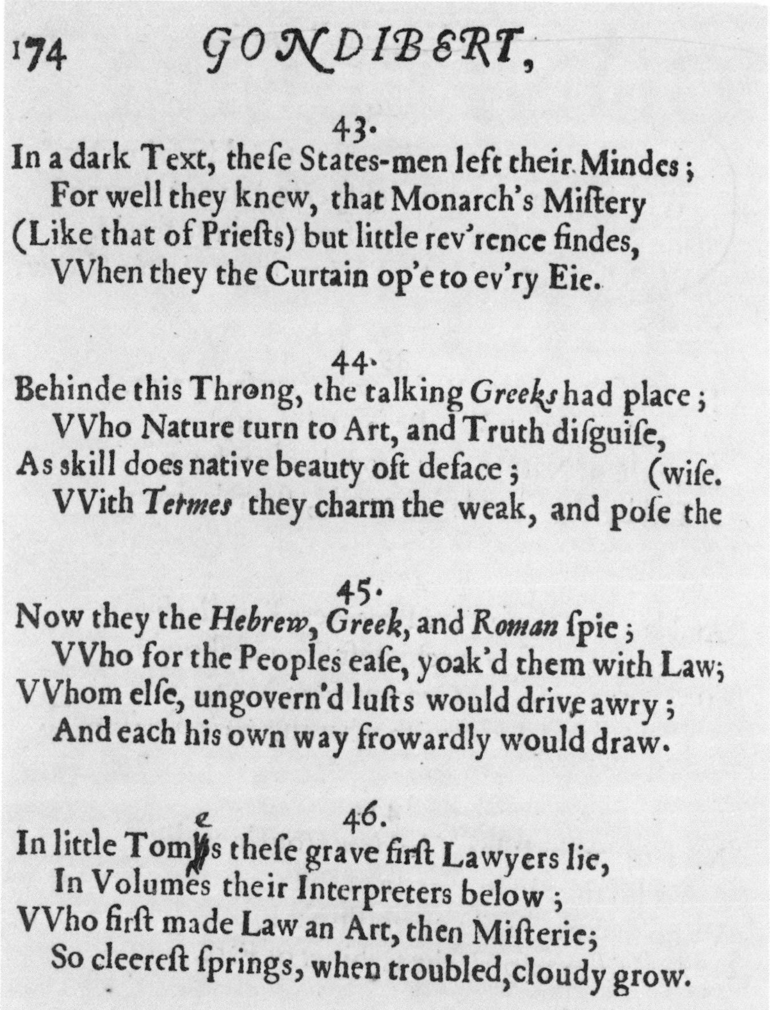

43.

In a dark Text, thefe States-men left their Mindes;
  For well they knew, that Monarch's Miftery
(Like that of Priefts) but little rev'rence findes,
  VVhen they the Curtain op'e to ev'ry Eie.

44.

Behinde this Throng, the talking *Greeks* had place;
  VVho Nature turn to Art, and Truth difguife,
As skill does native beauty oft deface;   (wife.
  VVith *Termes* they charm the weak, and pofe the

45.

Now they the *Hebrew,* *Greek,* and *Roman* fpie;
  VVho for the Peoples eafe, yoak'd them with Law;
VVhom elfe, ungovern'd lufts would drive awry;
  And each his own way frowardly would draw.

46.

In little Tombes thefe grave firft Lawyers lie,
  In Volumes their Interpreters below;
VVho firft made Law an Art, then Mifterie;
  So cleereft fprings, when troubled, cloudy grow.

47.

But here, the Souls chief Book did all precede; (ny'd;
  Our Map tow'rds Heav'n; to common Crowds de-
VVho proudly aim to teach, ere they can read;
  And all muft ftray, where each will be a Guide.

                                           About

Figure 5. A page from *Gondibert* (1651) showing a change in Book II, Canto 5, stanza 46 in a hand attributed to Davenant; see item 80.

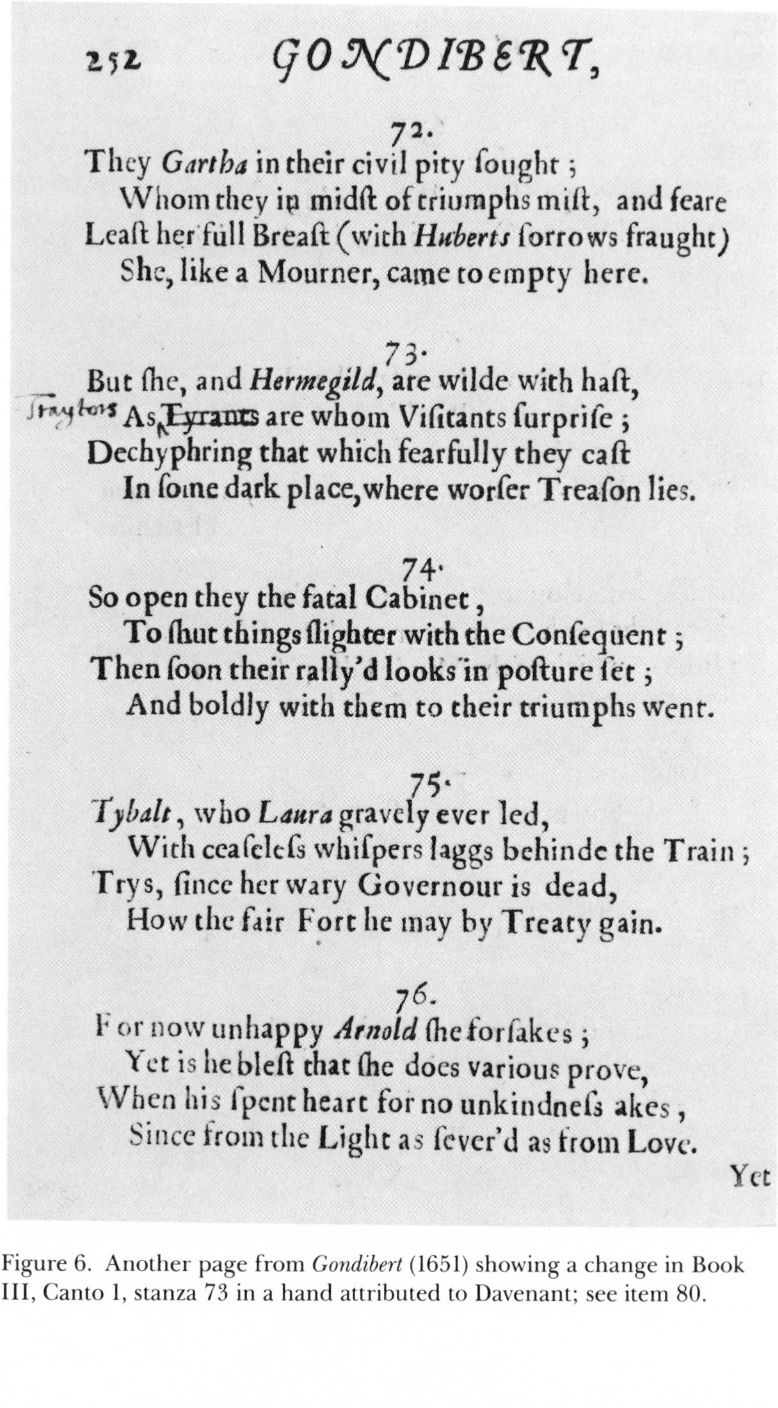

72.

They *Gartha* in their civil pity fought ;
  Whom they in midft of triumphs mift, and feare
Leaft her full Breaft (with *Huberts* forrows fraught)
  She, like a Mourner, came to empty here.

73.

But fhe, and *Hermegild*, are wilde with haft,
Traytors As Tyrants are whom Vifitants furprife ;
Dechyphring that which fearfully they caft
  In fome dark place, where worfer Treafon lies.

74.

So open they the fatal Cabinet,
  To fhut things flighter with the Confequent ;
Then foon their rally'd looks in pofture fet ;
  And boldly with them to their triumphs went.

75.

Tybalt, who *Laura* gravely ever led,
  With ceafelefs whifpers laggs behinde the Train ;
Trys, fince her wary Governour is dead,
  How the fair Fort he may by Treaty gain.

76.

For now unhappy *Arnold* fhe forfakes ;
  Yet is he bleft that fhe does various prove,
When his fpent heart for no unkindnefs akes,
  Since from the Light as fever'd as from Love.

Yet

Figure 6. Another page from *Gondibert* (1651) showing a change in Book III, Canto 1, stanza 73 in a hand attributed to Davenant; see item 80.

SIR WILLIAM DAVENANT

A. COLLECTED WORKS

Note: The section includes works from the Davenant Canon
published under separate cover or as part of major
collections of English authors.

1.   Madagascar; WITH OTHER Poems. BY W. DAVENANT.
     LONDON, Printed by *John Haviland* for *Thomas Walkly*, and
     are to be sold at his shop at the Flying Horse neare
     Yorke house, 1638. 12°. Pp. 141.

     STC 6304; UMI 954.

     Prefatory Materials:
        Imprimatur: MATTH. CLAY Feb. 26, 1637.
        Dedication: END. PORTER and H. IARMYN.
        Commendatory Poems: from Endimion Porter, I. Suckling
           (2), Thomas Carew, and William Habington.
     The Poems:
        "*Madagascar*. A POEM written to Prince RUPERT," pp.
           1-21.
        "*Elizium*. To the Duchesse of BVCKINGHAM," pp. 22-24.
        "TO the Lord *D.L.* upon his Mariage," pp. 25-26.
        "A Journey into *Worcestershire*," pp. 27-31.
        "To *Endimion* Porter," pp. 32-34.
        "TO THE QVEENE, entertain'd at night by the Countesse
           of *Anglesey*," pp. 35-36.
        "In remembrance of Master *William Shakespeare*, Ode,"
           pp. 37-38.
        "To the Lady *Bridget Kingsmill*; sent with Mellons
           after a report of my Death," pp. 39-41.
        "To the King on New-yeares day 1630," pp. 42-43.
        "TO THE QVEENE, presented with a suit, on the behalfe
           of *F.S.* directed, From *Orpheus* Prince of *Poets*, To
           the Queene of Light; In favour of a young listener
           to his *Harpe*," pp. 44-47.
        "To the Lord *B.* in performance of a vow, that night to
           write him," pp. 48-49.

"To *Endimion* Porter," pp. 50-53.

"*Ieffereidos*, Or the Captivitie of *Jeffery*," pp. 54-65.

"For the Lady, *Olivia* Porter. A present, upon a New-yeares day," pp. 66-67.

"To *I.C.* Rob'd by his man ANDREW," pp. 66-70.

"To the Earle of Portland, Lord Treasurer; on the mariage of his Sonne," pp. 71-73.

"THE QVEENE, returning to London after a long absence," pp. 74-75.

"To I.W. Vpon the death of his Mistresse," pp. 76-79.

"To *Endimion* Porter," pp. 80-81.

"Epitaph, on *I.* Walker," pp. 82-83.

"To Doctor *Cademan*, Physitian to the Queene," pp. 84-86.

"To *Endimion* Porter, When my Comedy (call'd the Wits) was presented at Black-Fryars," pp. 87-88.

"In celebration of the yearly Preserver of the Games at COTSWALD," pp. 89-91.

"On the Death of the Lady Marquesse of WINCHESTER," pp. 92-93.

"To Endimion Porter, upon his recovery from a long Sicknesse," pp. 94-95.

"Vpon the nuptials of *Charles*, Lord *Herbert*, and the Lady M. Villers," pp. 96-97.

"Prologue to a reviv'd Play of Mr Fletcher's, call'd The Woman-hater," pp. 98-99.

"To *Endimion* Porter, passing to Court to him, by water," pp. 100-02.

"Elegie on *B. Haselrick*, slaine in's youth, in a Duell," pp. 103-05.

"TO THE QVEENE, upon a New-yeares day," pp. 106-07.

"Elegie, On *Francis*, Earle of RUTLAND," pp. 108-10.

"To *Endimion* Porter," p. 111.

"To the Countesse of *Carlile*, on the death of the Earle her Husband," pp. 112-14.

"Epilogue, *TO LOVE* and *HONOR*, A Tragicomedy," p. 115.

"Epilogue, To a Vacation Play at the Globe," p. 116.

"TO THE QVEENE, upon a New-yeares day," pp. 117-18.

"TO EDWARD Earle of *Dorcet*, after his Sicknesse, and happy recovery," pp. 119-20.

"Written, When Colonell *Goring* Was beleev'd to be
  slaine, at the seige of BREDA," pp. 121-27.
"TO THE LORD Cary of Lepington, upon his
  translation of MALVEZZI," pp. 128-31.
"To *Henry Jarmin*," pp. 132-35.
"To *Tho: Carew*," pp. 136-37.
"TO Doctor *Duppa*, Deane of Christ-Church, and Tutor
  to the Prince," pp. 138-41.

Stationers' Register:
  1638 Mar. 13. For Thomas Walkley "a booke called
  Madagascar with *other Poems* by W: Davenant her
  Majesties servant."

By the year 1638, Davenant was providing plays
for the King's Men at the Blackfriars and, with Inigo
Jones, masques for their majesties at court. Thomas
Walkley's publication in 1638 of *Madagascar*, the poetry
of an established playwright, was probably good
business, especially in view of England's plans to
conquer Madagascar and of Davenant's appointment as poet
laureate in that same year.

2. Second edition: Madagascar; WITH OTHER Poems. *The
    Second Edition.* BY W. DAVENANT Knight. *LONDON,* Printed
    for *Humphrey Moseley,* and are to be sold at his shop at
    the Princes Armes in St Pauls Church-yard 1648.   12°.
    Pp. 140.

    STC D330; UMI 139:7.

    Stationers' Register:
      1648 Mar. 19. To Master Moseley "all the estate,
      right, title and interest wch said Thomas Walkeley
      hath" in *Madagascar* by William Davenant.

    The contents of the 1648 edition are the same as
    the 1638 edition, although the pagination differs
    slightly.

3. Another edition: *Madagascar.* In *Works,* 1673. Part I,
    199-254. Facs. 2 vols. New York: Benjamin Blom, 1968.

4. Another edition: *Madagascar.* William D. Walker, Jr.,
    ed. *"Madagascar with Other Poems* by Sir William
    Davenant." Thesis. Columbia 1935.   Pp. 172.

   For copy text, Walker uses the 1638 edition but
indicates significant differences from the 1648 edition
in the commentary.

5. Another edition: *Madagascar*. In A. M. Gibbs, ed. *Sir
    William Davenant*: *The Shorter Poems, and Songs From the
    Plays and Masques*. Oxford: Clarendon, 1972. Pp.
    1–80.

        Gibbs provides full discussion of the textual
    problems arising from the 1638 and 1648 editions of
    Madagascar and, in a separate appendix, sound
    commentaries on the individual poems.

6. *Two Excellent PLAYS*: The Wits, A Comedie: THE PLATONICK
    LOVERS, A Tragi-Comedie. Both presented at the Private
    House IN BLACK-FRIERS, By His Majesties Servants. *The
    Author*, Sir WILLIAM D'AVENANT, Kt *LONDON*, Printed for
    G. Bedel, and *T. Collins*, and are to be sold at their
    Shop at the Middle Temple Gate in Fleet-street, 1665.
    8°. Pp. 182.

    Greg III, 1055–56; EAP 1642–1700 (Rpts. only *The Wits*,
       pp.1–86); STC D347; UMI 378:8.

        Each play has its own title page and each its
    own dedication, *The Wits*, to Endymion Porter, *The
    Platonick Lovers* to Henry Jermyn. Pagination is
    continuous (pp. 1–182): *The Wits*, pp. 1–86; *The
    Platonick Lovers*, pp. 87–182. *The Wits* is also preceded
    by a commendatory poem by Thomas Carew.

7. THE WORKS OF Sr William D'avenant Kt: *Consisting of
    Those which were formerly Printed*. AND *Those which he
    design'd for the Press*: NOW PUBLISHED Out of the
    AUTHORS Originall Copies. LONDON: Printed for T.N.
    for *Henry Herringman*, at the Sign of the *Blew Anchor* in
    the Lower Walk of the New Exchange. 1673. Fol. Pp.
    402, 486, 111. Facs. 2 vols. New York: Benjamin Blom,
    1968.

    Greg III, 1057–58; EAP 1642–1700; STC D320; UMI 207:9.

    Prefatory Materials (without page or signature):
       Frontispiece: Portrait of Davenant, "Io.
       Grenhill pinx" and "W. Faithorne Sculp."

Title page: Cited above.
Dedications: "TO HIS Royal Highness ... [from] Mary
  D'Avenant" and to the "Reader ... [from] Henry
  Herringman."
Table of Contents: "TABLE"

Part one (402 pages):

Title page: GONDIBERT.... Printed by T.N. for *Henry
  Herringman....* 1672.
Preface to *Gondibert*, pp. 1-20.
Hobbes' "Answer ... to ... D'Avenant's Preface,"
  pp. 21-27.
Poems to Davenant by Edmund Waller, pp. 28-29, and
  Abraham Cowley, p. 30.
Gondibert, pp. 31-195.
Postscript to the *Reader*, pp. 196-98.
Title page: MADAGASCAR....Printed by T.N. for *Henry
  Herringman...,* 1672.
  Dedication to Endymion Porter.
  Poems to Davenant: By Endymion Porter, pp. 201-02,
    Sir John Suckling, pp. 202-03, Thomas Carew,
      p. 203, William Habington, pp. 203-04.
Madagascar and other poems, pp. 205-54.
Panegyrics:
  "To his Excellency the Lord General Monck,"
    pp. 255-56.
  "POEM upon His Sacred Majestie's most happy
    Return to His Dominions," pp. 256-61.
  "POEM to the Kings most Sacred Majesty," pp. 260
    [262]-71.
Title page: POEMS ON Several Occasions, Never before
  PRINTED....*Printed by* T.N. *for* Hen. Herringman
    .... 1672.
  Poems, pp. 275-340.
The First Dayes Entertainment *at* Rutland-House, *by*
  Declamations *and* Musick: *after the manner of the
  Ancients*, pp. 341-59.
Coelum Britannicum, *A Masque* at Whitehal in the
  Banquetting-House, *on* Shrove-Tuesday *night*, the
  18 of February 1633, pp. 360-82. [The masque by
  Thomas Carew was erroneously attributed to
  Davenant.]
The TEMPLE *of* LOVE, pp. 382-94.
The TRIUMPHS *of the Prince* D'AMOUR, pp. 395-402.

Part Two (486 pages):

> Title page: THE SIEGE OF RHODES: The First and
> Second Part; As they were lately Represented at His
> Highness the Duke of *YORK'S* Theatre in Lincolns-Inn
> Fields. The First Part being lately Enlarg'd. ...
> Printed by *J.M.* for *Henry Herringman*....1672.
> Dedication: To the Earl of Clarendon, sigs. A2-A2^v.
> *The Siege of Rhodes*, pp. 2-66.
> *The Play-House to be Let*, pp. 67-119 [Includes
>   *The History of Sir Francis Drake*, pp. 87-103;
>   and *The Cruelty of the Spaniards in Peru*,
>   pp. 103-14].
> *The Unfortunate Lovers*, pp. 120-65.
> *The Wits*, pp. 165-223.
> *Love and Honour*, pp. 224-72.
> *The Law Against Lovers*, pp. 272-329.
> *The Man's the Master*, pp. 329-83.
> *The Platonick Lovers*, pp. 384-414.
> *The Tragedy of Albovine*, pp. 414-40.
> *The Just Italian*, pp. 441-63.
> *The Cruel Brother*, pp. 463-86.

Part Three (111 pages):

> *News from Plimouth*, pp. 1-33.
> *The Distresses*, pp. 34-62.
> *The Siege*, pp. 63-86.
> *The Fair Favorite*, pp. 87-111.

> Stationers' Register:
> 1672 Oct. 31. For Henry Herringman by Master
> L'Estrange and Master Warden Roper "one copy of a
> booke intituled *The Workes* of *Sir* William Davenant,
> K^t, consisting of those wch were formerly printed,
> and those which he designed for the press, now
> published out of the authors originall copies."

Published five years after Davenant's death,
the handsome folio edition contains all but a few of the
plays, masques, and poems that he had written and
published earlier. It lacks *Luminalia*, which had been
printed in 1658; *Britannia Triumphans*, printed in 1638;
Salmacida Spolia, printed in 1658, and *The Rivals*,
printed in 1668. Also missing are the adaptations
clearly identified with Shakespeare, *Macbeth* and *The
Tempest, or the Enchanted Island*, although these were

later included by Maidment and Logan in *The Dramatic Works*, 1872-74. The volume contains the first publication for the plays *The Siege*, *Love and Honour*, *News from Plimouth*, *The Fair Favorite*, and *The Distresses*. It is also the first printing of the volume of poems that had appeared in the Stationers' Register in 1657 as *Severall Poems upon severall occasions* but was not printed. The volume reprints *Gondibert*, *Madagascar*, the panegyrics, *The First Dayes Entertainment*, *The Temple of Love*, *The Siege of Rhodes*, *Parts I and II*, *The Unfortunate Lovers*, *The Wits*, *The Law Against Lovers*, *The Man's the Master*, *The Platonic Lovers*, *Albovine*, *The Just Italian*, and *The Cruel Brother*. Evidently the edition was printed in three large sections, each bearing a title page and each beginning with page 1. All the title pages are dated 1672, except for the first which carries 1673.

8. *The Poetical Works of Sir William Davenant.* Edinburgh: Printed by Mundell, 1793. In *Select British Poets and Translations*, 9 vols. Ed. Robert Anderson. London: for W. Griffin ..., n.d. IV, 755-874.

      For the Davenant section, Anderson provides a separate title page and a critical introduction, which is followed by a selection from the poetry. Included are *Gondibert*, with the author's *Preface* and Hobbes' *Answer*; the poem "Madagascar"; and twenty-eight others. Among these are "The Long Vacation in London," "The Disquisition to the Dying Christian," and "The Christian's Reply," the aubade "The lark now leaves his wat'ry nest," "The Souldier going to the Field," and "In Remembrance to Master William Shakespeare. Ode." Anderson included Davenant and his work as the final section of volume 4 in a number of his editions of the British poets. Although the titles, dates, publishers, and contents, in the editions vary, each edition remains constant for Davenant and his work. The same material that appeared in 1793 is reprinted in the following editions:

> *A Complete Edition of the Poets of Great Britain.* 13 vols. London: J. & A. Arch, 1792-95.
> *A Complete Edition of the Poets of Great Britain.* 14 vols. London: J. & A. Arch, 1793-1807.
> *The Works of the British Poets.* 14 vols. London: John & Arthur Arch, 1795.

> *The Works of the British Poets.* 14 vols. London:
> J. Arch, 1795-[1807?].

9. "The Poems of Sir William Davenant." Ed. Alexander
   Chalmers. In *The Works of the English Poets, From
   Chaucer to Cowper; including the Series Edited with
   Prefaces, Biographical and Critical, By Dr. Samuel
   Johnson . . . the Additional Lives by Alexander
   Chalmers, F.S.A.* London: J. Johnson . . ., 1810. VI,
   339-435.

   > Included with the poetry are selections from
   Gondibert, with the *Preface* and Hobbes' *Answer*; "The
   Long Vacation in London"; and a good representation of
   the shorter poems, including "Song" ("The Lark"), "Song.
   The Souldier going to the Field," and "In remembrance of
   Master William Shakespeare. Ode."

10. *The Dramatic Works of Sir William D'Avenant, with
    Prefatory Memoir and Notes.* Ed. James Maidment and
    W. H. Logan. 5 vols. Edinburgh: William Paterson,
    1872-74. Rpt. New York: Russell & Russell, 1964.

    > The editors reprint all of Davenant's plays,
    including the masques and adaptations, except for
    Hamlet and *Julius Caesar*. However, they republish the
    1674 edition of *The Tempest* with the operatic
    additions by Shadwell, rather than the 1670 edition
    with alterations and additions by Davenant and Dryden.
    Useful are the reprintings of the additions made to
    some of the original texts when they reappeared in
    Works, 1673, and also the brief biographical notes on
    the courtiers and ladies who performed in the masques.

11. Tupper, James W., ed. *Love and Honour and The Siege of
    Rhodes.* Belles-Lettres Series. Boston: Heath, 1909.
    Pp. 362.

    > Prefatory Materials:
    >   Contents.
    >   Biography, pp. vii-xlvii.
    >
    > *Love and Honour*, pp. 1-178 (includes ten pages of
    >   notes).
    > *The Siege of Rhodes*, pp. 179-349 (includes fourteen
    >   pages of notes).

Addenda:
  Bibliography, pp. 350-54.
  Glossary, pp. 355-62.

      The two plays were selected because they represent Davenant's place in the development of the drama. *Love and Honour* represents the romantic drama merging into the heroic, and *The Siege of Rhodes* illustrates the fully developed heroic play, a form later used successfully by Orrery and Dryden.

12. *Selected Poems of Sir William Davenant.* Introd. Douglas Bush. Cambridge, Mass.: Willow Press, 1943. Pp. 43.

Prefatory Materials:
  Contents.
  Introduction, pp. [iii-vi].
Poems from *Madagascar*:
  "To the Queen, entertain'd at night by the Countess of Anglesey."
  "For the Lady Olivia Porter: A Present upon a New-years day."
Poems on Several Occasions Never Before Printed (*Works*, 1673): "The Countess of Anglesey lead Captive by the Rebels, at the Disforresting of Pewsam."
  "Upon the Marriage of the Lady Jane Cavendish with Mr. Cheney."
  "Song: 'The Lark now leaves his watry Nest."
  "Song: Endimion Porter, and Olivia."
  "The Philosopher and the Lover; to a Mistress dying."
  "Song: The Souldier going to the Field."
  "The Philosophers Disquisition directed to the Dying Christian."
  "The Christians Reply to the Phylosopher."
Songs from the Plays:
  "O Thou that Sleep'st like a Pigg in Straw"
  "Nights first song."
  "Chorus of Women."
  "Wake all the dead! what hoa! what hoa!"

      In his introduction, Bush surveys Davenant's life and literary achievement, emphasizing the importance of the *Preface* to *Gondibert* to seventeenth-century critical literature, the operatic *The Siege of Rhodes*, and the Shakespeare revivals.

Bush then discusses the lyric poetry, which dominates
the contents of this small volume.

13. *The Shorter Poems, and Songs from the Plays and
    Masques.* Ed. A. M. Gibbs. Oxford: Clarendon, 1972.
    Pp. 477.

        Gibbs reprints *Madagascar*; *Poems on Several
Occasions*, 1672, which, though licensed for publication
in 1657, was finally published as part of *Works*, 1673;
and the panegyrics, songs from the plays and masques,
and poems from manuscripts. Gibbs provides full
introductions, sources and textual problems, and
excellent commentaries.

B. SEPARATE WORKS

Note: The section includes the first and subsequent editions of the plays and works published with their own title pages.

14. THE TRAGEDY OF ALBOVINE, KING OF THE LOMBARDS: By W^m *D'avenant*. Printed for R. M. and are to bee sold in Saint *Dunstanes* Church-yard. 1629. 4°. Sigs. A-M4.

    Greg 422; EAP 1500-1641; STC 6307; UMI 1348.

    Prefatory Materials:
    Letter to the Earl of Somerset, sig. A2.
    Poems from Hen. Blount, sig. A2^v, Ed. Hyde, sig.
       A2^v-A3, Rich: Clerk, sig. A3, Rob. Ellice , sig.
       A3, Will: Habington, sig. A3^v, Rog: Lort, sig.
       A3^v, Tho: Ellice, sig. A4, and H. Howard, sig.
       A4.

    Stationers' Register:
    1639 July 27. Ordered that (J.) Benson have leave to
       print an impression of 1500 of the tragedy of
       Albovine by Davenant, the copy never entered and
       therefore in the disposal of the Court.
    1651 May 3. Tr. J. Marriott to R. Marriott:
       Albovine, the play.
    1653 Mar. 7. Tr. R. Marriott to (H.) Moseley: the
       tragedie of Albovine King of the Lombards, by Sir
       W^m. Davenant.
    1667 Aug. 19. Albovine King of Lombardy.

        Although not produced during Davenant's
    lifetime, *Albovine*, a revenge tragedy, was his first
    published work.

15. A possible adaptation of *Albovine*: THE REVENGEFUL
    QUEEN: the Theatre-Royal, BY His MAJESTY'S Servants.
    Written by WILLIAM PHILIPS, Esq; LONDON, Printed for
    P. Buck, at the Sign of the Temple, near the Inner
    Temple-Gate, in Fleet-street, 1698.

    STC P2118; UMI 364:10.

        In his dedicatory letter to the Duke of
    Ormond, Philips wrote, "I have followed the truth of
    the story, as any one will find, who will take the
    Pains to read it in the Fourth or Fifth Page of
    Machiavelli's History of Florence.... A considerable

time after this was Writ, I was inform'd That Sir
William Davenant had made a Play on the same Story; I
knew it not before, nor have I yet seen it: It was very
unhappy for me to happen on the same Subject with so
Ingenious a Person...." An examination of the 1674
translation of Machiavelli's *The Florentine History* (I,
16-20) reveals the Albovine-Rosamond story. There
seems little reason to doubt Philips' claim that he
depended on Machiavelli rather than Davenant.

16. Another edition of *Albovine*: In *Works*, 1673. Part II
     414-40. Facs. 2 vols. New York: Benjamin Blom, 1968.

17. Another edition of *Albovine*: In *Dramatic Works*,
     1872-74. I, 1-107. Rpt. New York: Russell & Russell,
     1964.

     Prefatory Materials:
       Introduction, pp. 3-12, and prefatory letters and
       poems, as in the first edition, pp. 13-17.

18. THE CRVELL BROTHER. A Tragedy. As it was presented,
     at the priuate House, in *Blacke-Fryers*: *By His
     Maiesties Seruants*. *LONDON*. Imprinted by *A. M.* for
     Iohn Waterson, and to bee solde at the signe of the
     Crowne in *Pauls* Church-yard. 1630. 4°. Sigs. A-K4.

     Greg 427; EAP 1500-1641; STC 6302; UMI 1170.

     Prefatory Materials:
       To Lord Weston, sigs. A3-A4.

     Stationers' Register:
       1630 Jan. 10. Ent. J. Waterson: Lic. H. Herbert: a
       play called The Crewell Brother, by Wᵐ. Davenant.
       1646 Oct. 31. Tr. (J.) Waterson to (H.) Moseley,
       plays: The Cruell Brother, by Davenant.
       1667 Aug. 19. Crewell Brother.

            The Cruel Brother was the first of Davenant's
     plays with clear evidence of production.

19. Another edition of *The Cruel Brother*: In *Works*, 1673.
     Part II, 463-86. Facs. 2 vols. New York: Benjamin
     Blom, 1968.

20. Another edition of *The Cruel Brother*: In *Dramatic
     Works*, 1872-74. I, 109-97. Rpt. New York: Russell &
     Russell, 1964.

Prefatory Materials:
   Introduction, pp. 111-16, and prefatory letter, as in
      first edition, p. 117.

21. THE IUST ITALIAN. Lately presented in the private
    house at Blacke-Friers, *By his Maiesties Seruants*.
    LONDON, Printed by *Thomas Harper* for *Iohn Waterson*,
    and are to be sold at the signe of the Crowne, in
    Paules Churchyard. 1630. 4⁰. Sigs. A-K2.

    Greg 428; EAP 1500-1641; STC 6303; UMI 1134.

    Prefatory Materials:
       Letter to the Earl of Dorset, sigs. A2-A2^V.
       Poems from Will. Hopkins, sig. A3 and Tho. Carew,
          sig. A3^V-A4.

    Stationers' Register:
       1630 Jan. 10. Ent. J. Waterson: lic. H. Herbert: a
          play called the Just Italian, by Wm. Davenant.
       1646 Oct. 31. Tr. (J) Waterson to (H.) Moseley,
          plays; The Just Italian, by Davenant.
       1667 Aug. 19. Just Italyan.

22. Another edition of *The Just Italian*: In *Works*, 1673.
    Part II, 441-63. Facs. 2 vols. New York: Benjamin
    Blom, 1968.

23. Another edition of *The Just Italian*: In *Dramatic
    Works*, 1872-74. I, 199-280. Rpt. New York: Russell &
    Russell, 1964.

    Prefatory Materials:
       Introduction, pp. 201-04, and letters and poems as in
          the first edition, pp. 205-07.

24. *The Colonel*. See *The Siege*.
    Stationers' Register:
       1630 Jan. 1. Ent.

25. THE TEMPLE OF LOVE. A Masque. Presented by the
    QUEENES Majesty, and her Ladies, at *White-hall* on
    Shrove-Tuesday, 1634. By *Inigo Iones*, Surveyor of his
    Maties. Workes, and *William Davenant*, her Maties.
    Servant. *LONDON*. Printed for *Thomas Walkley*, and are
    to be sold at his Shop neare *White-hall*. 1634. 4⁰.
    Sigs. A4-D2.

Greg 497; EAP 1500-1641; STC 14719; UMI 755.

Addenda:
The names of the masquers are given on D2.

Stationers' Register:
1658 Mar. 6.   Tr. T. Walkley to H. Moseley: The
Temple of Love, a Masque at Whitehall on Shrove
Tuesday 1634, by Sir William Davenant.
1667 Aug. 19.   Temple of Love.

26.   Another edition of *The Temple of Love*:   In *Works*, 1673.
Part I, 382-94.   Facs.   2 vols. New York: Benjamin
Blom, 1968.

27.   Another edition of *The Temple of Love*:   In *Dramatic
Works*, 1872-74.   I, 281-316.   Rpt. New York: Russell &
Russell, 1964.

Prefatory Materials:
Introduction, pp. 282-85.

Addenda:
Following the masquers' names on p. 305, the editors
present brief biographical sketches of each of the
participants, pp. 306-16.

28.   Another edition of *The Temple of Love*:   In Daniel
Joseph Steible, ed. "A Critical Edition of Sir William
Davenant's *The Temple of Love* and *The Platonic Lovers*."
Diss. Cincinnati 1939.   Pp. 1-21.

Steible includes in his introduction a
biographical sketch of Davenant and a discussion of
Platonic love. The edition is carefully annotated, and
there is a bibliography.

29.   Another edition of *The Temple of Love*:   In Stephen
Orgel and Roy Strong, eds. *Inigo Jones: The Theatre of
the Stuart Court*.   London: Sotheby Parke Bernet, 1973.
II,   598-629.

Prefatory Materials:
Background information including costs, contemporary
opinions, and modern commentaries, p.   599.

Addenda:
Jones' drawings of scenery and costumes, pp. 598,

604-29, include descriptions of each drawing by the
editors.

30. Selections from *The Temple of Love*: In Allardyce
     Nicoll, ed., *Readings From British Drama: Extracts From
     British and Irish Plays.* New York: Crowell, 1928. Pp.
     162-66.

          The passage included is by Indamora, acted by
     the queen, who with her beautiful followers, "raise
     strange doctrines, and new sects of Love:

                Which must not woo or court the person, but
                The mind: and practice generation not
                Of bodies but of souls."

31. THE TRIUMPHS OF THE PRINCE D'AMOVR. A Masque PRESENTED
     BY HIS Highnesse at His Pallace in the Middle Temple,
     the 24th of Februarie 1635 LONDON, Printed for *Richard
     Meighen*, next to the Middle Temple Gate in Fleetstreet.
     1635, 4°. Pp. [17].

     Greg 502; EAP 1500-1641; STC 6308; UMI 1134.

     Prefatory Materials:
       Letter to Every Reader.

     Addenda:
       Names of the Masquers, p. [17].

     Stationers' Register:
       1636 Feb. 19. Ent. (R.) Meighen: lic. Mr. Thomas
         Maunsell Master of the Revells in the Temple: a
         maske called The Triumphs of the Prince d'Amour, by
         W. D.
       1646 Nov. 7. Tr. Mercie, wid. of (R.), Meighen to
         herself and G. Beadell: The Triumphes of Prince
         Damour, by Davenant.

32. Another edition of *The Triumphs of the Prince D'Amour*:
     In *Works*, 1673. I, 395-402. Facs. 2 vols. New York:
     Benjamin Blom, 1968.

33. Another edition of *The Triumphs of the Prince D'Amour*:
     In *Dramatic Works*, 1872-74. I, 317-40. Rpt. New York:
     Russell & Russell, 1964.

Prefatory Materials:
   Introduction, pp. 319-26, and Letter To Every Reader,
   p. 327.

Addenda:
   Names of the Masquers, p. 340.

34. Another edition of *The Triumphs of the Prince D'Amour*:
     In *Trois Masques a la cour de Charles 1er d'Angleterre*.
     Ed. Murray Lefkowitz. Paris: Editions Centre National
     de la Recherche Scientifique, 1970. Pp. 111-69.

     Prefatory Material:
        Introduction, pp. 111-23.

     Addenda:
        Musical settings by H. & W. Lawes, pp. 139-69.

            Lefkowitz has written an introduction in
     French in which he comments on the stage history, the
     story, the actors, the music, and the scenery of *The
     Triumphs of the Prince d'Amour*.

35. THE PLATONICK LOVERS. A Tragaecomedy. Presented in
     the private House in the *BLACK-FRYERS, BY his Majesties
     Servants*. The Authour WILLIAM D'AVENANT, Servant to
     her Majestie. LONDON, Printed for *Richard Meighen*,
     next to the Middle Temple in Fleetstreet. 1636. 4°.
     Sigs. A-L^V.

     Greg 506; EAP 1500-1641; STC 6305; UMI 1122.

     Prefatory Materials:
        Letter to Henry Iermyn, sig. A2.

     Stationers' Register:
        1636 Feb. 4. Ent. (R.) Meighen: lic. H. Herbert: a
           play called The Platonicke Lovers, by Wm.
           Davenant.
        1646 Nov. 7. Tr. Mercie wid. (R.) Meighen to herself
           and G. Beadell: The Platonick Lovers, by
           Davenant.

36. Another edition of *The Platonic Lovers*: In *Two
     Excellent PLAYS*: The Wits, A Comedie: THE *PLATONICK*
     LOVERS, A Tragi-Comedie. Both presented at the Private
     House in BLACK-FRIERS, By His Majesties Servants. *The*

Author, SIR WILLIAM D'AVENANT, Kt *LONDON*. Printed for
G. Bedel, *T. Collins*, and are to be sold at their Shop
at the Middle Temple Gate in Fleet-street 1665. Pp.
87-182.

EAP 1642-1700; STC D347; UMI 378:9.

37. Another edition of *The Platonic Lovers*: In *Works*,
1673. Part II, 384-414. Facs. 2 vols. New York:
Benjamin Blom, 1968.

38. Another edition of *The Platonic Lovers*: In *Dramatic
Works*, 1872-74. II, 1-105. Rpt. New York: Russell &
Russell, 1964.

Prefatory Materials:
  Introduction, pp. 3-5.

39. Another edition of *The Platonic Lovers*: In Daniel
Joseph Steible, ed. "A Critical Edition of Sir William
Davenant's *The Temple of Love* and *The Platonic Lovers*."
Diss. Cincinnati 1939. Pp. 22-128.

Steible uses the second edition (1665),
rather than the first (1636), "because it is the last
with which Davenant is likely to have had anything to
do." Steible includes in his introduction a
biographical sketch of Davenant and a discussion of
Platonic love. The edition is carefully annotated, and
there is a bibliography.

40. Another edition of *The Platonic Lovers*: Wendell
Wright Broom, Jr., ed. "An Old-Spelling Critical
Edition of William Davenant's *The Platonick Lovers*."
Diss. Texas Tech 1984.

Broom depends on the 1636 quarto edition at
the Bodleian for the copy-text, for the 1636 is the
only substantive edition which was probably from the
author's manuscript, and the Bodelian copy contains
none of the altered accidentals of the quarto's three
corrected forms. In his discussion, Broom focuses on
"the establishment of the genealogy of the text and of
the nature and authority of the revisions made in two
of the three seventeenth-century editions."

41. THE WITTS. A Comedie, PRESENTED AT THE Private House
in Blacke Fryers, by his Majesties Servants. The

Authour WILLIAM D'AVENANT, *Servant to Her Majestie*.
LONDON, Printed for RICHARD MEIGHEN, next to the Middle
Temple in Fleetstreet. 1636. 4⁰. Sigs. A-K4.

Greg 507; EAP 1500-1641; STC 6309; UMI 1134.

Prefatory Materials:
  Letter to Endymion Porter, sig. A3.
  Poem by T. Carew, sig. A3^V.

Stationers' Register:
  1636 Feb. 4. Ent. (R.) Meighen: lic. H. Herbert: a
    play called The Witts, by Wm. Davenant.
  1646 Nov. 7. Tr. Mercie wid. of (R.) Meighen to
    herself and G. Beadell: The Witts, by Davenant.

42. Another edition of *The Wits*: In *Two Excellent PLAYS*:
     The Wits, A Comedie: THE *PLATONICK* LOVERS, A
     Tragi-Comedie. Both presented at the Private House IN
     BLACK-FRIERS, By His Majesties Servants. *The Authour*,
     Sir WILLIAM D'AVENANT, KT *LONDON*. Printed for *G.
     Bedel*, and *T. Collins*, and are to be sold at their shop
     at the Middle Temple Gate in Fleet-street, 1665. Pp.
     1-86.

     EAP 1642-1700; STC D347; UMI 378:9.

43. Another edition of *The Wits*: In *Works*, 1673. Part II,
     165-223. Facs. 2 vols. New York: Benjamin Blom,
     1968.

44. Another edition of *The Wits*: THE WITS. In R. Dodsley,
     ed. A SELECT COLLECTION OF OLD PLAYS. IN TWELVE
     VOLUMES. THE SECOND EDITION, CORRECTED AND COLLATED
     WITH THE OLD COPIES, WITH NOTES CRITICAL AND
     EXPLANATORY. LONDON. PRINTED BY J. NICHOLS: FOR J.
     DODSLEY, PALL MALL. MDCCLXXX. VIII, 397-514. Rpt.
     London: S. Prowett, 1825-27.

     Prefatory Materials:
       Biographical introduction, pp. 399-400.
       List of Davenant's plays, pp. 401-02.
       Dedication to Endymion Porter, p. 403.
       Poem from T. Carew, p. 404.

     Addenda:
       Rpt. title page of 1636 edition, p. 514.

45. Another edition of *The Wits*: In *The Ancient British Drama*. 3 vols. [Ed. Sir Walter Scott.] London: William Miller, 1810. I, 280-317.

   Prefatory Materials:
   Introduction, pp. 280-81.

   The notes are usually limited to identifying obscure or archaic words.

46. Another edition of *The Wits*: In *Dramatic Works*, 1872-74. II, 107-244. Rpt. New York: Russell & Russell, 1964.

   Prefatory Materials:
   Introduction, pp. 109-15.
   Poem to Endymion Porter, pp. 113-14.
   Poem by T. Carew, p. 116.

   Addenda:
   Alterations and additions which occur in the folio of 1673.

   More than five hundred lines have been added including the new prologue and epilogue spoken at the Duke's Theatre.

47. Another edition of *The Wits*: THE WITTS. A Comedie. In *Six Caroline Plays*. The World's Classics 583. Ed. A. S. Knowland. London: Oxford Univ. Press, 1962. Pp. 345-432.

   For the text, Knowland uses the 1636 edition. He includes a facsimile of the title page and reprints the dedicatory letter to Endymion Porter and the commendatory verse from Thomas Carew.

48. BRITANNIA TRIUMPHANS. A Masque, Presented at White Hall, by the Kings Majestie and his Lords, on the Sunday after Twelfth-night, 1637. BY *Inigo Iones* Surveyor of his Majesties workes, *William Davenant* her Majesties servant. LONDON. Printed by *Iohn Haviland* for *Thomas Walkley*, and are to be sold at his shop at the flying Horse neere Yorke house, 1637. 4°. Pp. [28].

   Greg 526; EAP 1500-1641; STC 14718; UMI 755.

Addenda:
   The names of the masquers are given on p. [28].

Stationers' Register:
   1658 Mar. 6.   Tr. T. Walkley to H. Moseley: Brittania
      Triumphans, a masque at Whitehall at Twelth Night
      1637, by Sir William Davenant.
   1667 Aug. 19.   Brittannia Triumphans.

         Britannia Triumphans is not included in
   Works, 1673.

49.   Another edition of *Britannia Triumphans*:   In *Dramatic
      Works*, 1872-74.   II, 245-300.   Rpt. New York: Russell
      & Russell, 1964.

      Prefatory Materials:
         Introduction, pp. 247-64.

      Addenda:
         The names of the masquers are given on p.   290.
         Brief character sketches of the masquers are
         presented, pp. 291-300.

50.   Another edition of *Britannia Triumphans*:   In *Trois
      Masques a la cour de Charles 1er d'Angleterre*.   Ed.
      Murray Lefkowitz.   Paris: Editions Centre National de
      la Recherche Scientifique, 1970.   Pp. 171-243.

      Prefatory Materials:
         Introduction, pp. 171-85.
         Inigo Jones' designs for costumes and scenery,
            Figures 18-36, between pp. 26 and 27.

      Addenda:
         Musical settings by William Lawes, pp. 211-43.

            Lefkowitz has written an introduction in
      French in which he comments on the stage history, the
      story, the actors, the music, and the scenery of
      Britannia Triumphans.

51.   Another edition of *Britannia Triumphans*:   In Stephen
      Orgel and Roy Strong, eds.   *Inigo Jones: The Theatre
      of the Stuart Court*.   London: Sotheby Parke Bernet,
      1973.   II, 660-703.

Prefatory Materials:
Background information including costs and modern
commentaries, p. 661.

Addenda:
Jones' drawings of scenery and costumes, pp. 660,
668-703 includes descriptions of each drawing by the
editors.

52. LVMINALIA, OR The Festivall of Light. Performed in a
Masque at Court, By the Queenes Majestie, and her
Ladies. On *Shrove-tuesday* Night, 1637. LONDON.
Printed by *Iohn Haviland* for *Thomas Walkley*, and are to
be sold at his shop at the flying Horse neere Yorke
house, 1637. 4°. Pp. 21.

Greg 527; EAP 1500-1641; STC 16923; UMI 847.

Addenda:
The names of the masquers are given on p. 21.

Stationers' Register:
1658 Mar. 6. Tr. T. Walkley to H. Moseley: Luminalia
or the Festivall of Light, a masque at Court on
Shrove Tuesday night 1637, by Sir William
Davenant.
1667 Aug. 19. Luminalia.

Though no name appears on the title page, the
entry in the Stationers' Register for 6 Mar. 1658,
indicates that Davenant is the author. *Luminalia* is
not included in *Works*, 1673.

53. Another edition of *Luminalia*: In *Miscellanies of the
Fuller Worthies' Library*. 4 vols. Ed. A. B. Grosart.
Blackburn, Lancs.: Privately Printed, 1872-76. IV,
613-30.

The masque first appeared separately in
pamphlet form and was later bound with volume IV.
Grosart reproduced the title page of the 1637 edition
and reprinted the masque.

54. Another edition of *Luminalia*: In Stephen Orgel and Roy
Strong, eds, *Inigo Jones: The Theatre of the Stuart
Court*. London: Sotheby Parke Bernet, 1973. II,
704-23.

Prefatory Materials:
Background information including costs and modern
commentaries, p. 705.

Addenda:
Jones' drawings of scenery and costumes, pp. 704,
710-23, includes descriptions of each drawing by the
editors.

55. *The Spanish Lovers.* See *The Distresses*, item 162.
Licensed for performance by Sir Henry Herbert, Nov. 30,
1639.

56. SALMACIDA SPOLIA. *A MASQUE.* Presented by the King and
Queenes Majesties, at White-hall, On *Tuesday* the 21.
day of *January* 1639. *LONDON.* Printed by *T. H.* for
Thomas Walkley, and are to be sold at the signe of the
flying Horse neere Yorke house, 1639. 4⁰. Sigs.
A-D4ᵛ.

Greg 571; EAP 1500-1641; STC 6306; UMI 1348.

Addenda:
The names of the masquers appear on sig. D4ᵛ.

Stationers' Register:
1658 Mar. 6. Tr. T. Walkley to H. Moseley: Salmatida
[sic] Spolia, a masque at Whitehall on Tuesday the
21th day of January 1639, by Sir William Davenant.
1667 Aug. 19. Salmacida Tholia [sic].

        This was the last of the masques that graced
the court of Charles I. It was not included in *Works*,
1673.

57. Another edition of *Salmacida Spolia*: In *Dramatic
Works*, 1872-74. II, 301-31. Rpt. New York: Russell
& Russell, 1964.

Prefatory Materials:
Introduction, pp. 303-07.

Addenda:
The names of the masquers are given on p. 327.
Brief character sketches of the masquers appear on
pp. 328-31.

58. Another edition of *Salmacida Spolia*:   In *English
     Masques*.   Ed. Herbert Arthur Evans.   London: Blackie,
     1897.   Pp. 229–45.

59. Another edition of *Salmacida Spolia*:   In *A Book of
     Masques*:   *In Honour of Allardyce Nicoll*.   Ed.   T. B. J.
     Spencer and Stanley Wells.   Cambridge: Cambridge Univ.
     Press, 1967.

60. Another edition of *Salmacida Spolia*:   In Stephen Orgel
     and Roy Strong, eds. *Inigo Jones: The Theatre of the
     Stuart Court*.   London: Sotheby Parke Bernet, 1973.   II,
     728–85.

     Prefatory Materials:
       Background information including costs and modern
       commentaries, p. 729.

     Addenda:
       Jones' drawings of scenery and costumes, pp. 728,
       735–85, includes descriptions of each drawing by the
       editors.

61. TO THE HONORABLE KNIGHTS, CITIZENS, AND BURGESSES OF
     THE HOVSE OF *COMMONS*, ASSEMBLED IN PARLIAMENT.   The
     Humble Remonstrance of William Davenant, Anno 1641.
     Broadside.

     STC D345; UMI 1255.

             Davenant, having been captured by officers of
     Parliament for his part in the Army Plot, asked
     Parliament's pardon for anything he might inadvertently
     have said or written against them.   He further affirmed
     that Jermyn and Suckling, who were also under
     accusation, had no designs "against your glorious and
     happy proceedings"; on the contrary, they had extolled
     "the natural necessity of Parliament" and had scorned
     "any that should perswade the KING he could be
     fortunate without them."   His *Remonstrance* was
     successful to the degree that he avoided punishment
     and was freed on bail.

62. TO THE HONOVRABLE, KNIGHTS, CITIZENS AND BVRGESSES, OF
     the Court of Commons assembled In Parliament, 1641.
     The humble Petition of *William Davenant*.   London
     printed, 1641.   Broadside.

STC D344.

   "The humble Petition" resembles the "Humble
Remonstrance" in its purpose and its arguments. Here
Davenant confesses "it is possible I may be guiltie of
some mis-becomming words, yet not words made dangerous
Principles and Maximes, but lose Arguments: disputed at
Table perhaps with too much fancie and heat...." His
argument apparently prevailed, for he was released on
bail.

63. LONDON, KING CHARLES *HIS* AUGUSTA, OR, CITY ROYAL, Of
     the Founders, the Names, and oldest Honours of that
     CITY. An Historicall and Antiquarian Work. Written at
     first in Heroicall Latin Verse, according to Greek,
     Roman, British, English, and other Antiquities and
     Authorities, and now translated into English Couplets,
     with Annotations. PSAL. 142. 5. *Memor fuidierum
     antiquorum.* Imprimatur. Na. Brent. LONDON. Printed
     for William Leybourn, 1648 4°.

     STC D328.

     Prefatory Material:
       To the Reader, sigs. A2-A2^V.

          No author or translator is mentioned on the
     title page; however, the prefatory note to the reader
     carries the following attribution: *"it came from the*
     Studie of that accomplished Poet of our Time, Sir Will.
     Davenant, whose Ingenious *Fancy hath spun him such a
     woofe, of immortal praise, that shall never be eaten
     through, with the all-else endevouring teeth of Time,
     or blasted by the* poysonous breath of envy." However,
     Thomas H. Blackburn presents evidence which suggests
     that Endymion Porter's brother-in-law, Edmund Boulton,
     was the author. See *1962:*Blackburn.

64. THE VNFORTUNATE LOVERS: A Tragedie; As it was lately
     Acted with great applause at the private House in
     Black-Fryers; By His Majesties Servants. The Author
     William Davenant, Servant to Her Majestie. *LONDON,*
     Printed by *R. H.* and are to be sold by *Francis Coles* at
     his Shop in the Old Bailey, Anno Dom. 1643. 4°. Pp.
     [48].

     Greg 624; EAP 1642-1700; STC D348; UMI 179:3.

Prefatory Material:
  To Philip Earle of Pembroke and Montgomery, sig. A2.

Stationers' Register:
  1646 Mar. 7. Ent. (H.) Moseley by consent of (R.?)
    Heiron: lic. Sir Nath. Brent: a tragedy called The
    Unfortunate Lovers &c., by Wm. Davenant.
  1667 Aug. 19. Unfortunat Lovers.

65. Another edition: THE UNFORTUNATE LOVERS: A Tragedy.
  As it was lately Acted with great applause at the
  private House in *Black-Fryers, By His Majesties
  Servants*. The Author *William Davenant* K^t Servant to
  Hir Majestie. *LONDON*, Printed for Humphrey Moseley,
  and are to be sold at his Shop at the Princes Armes in
  St. *Paul's* Church-yard. 1649. 4⁰. Pp. [48].

  Greg 624(ii); STC D349; UMI 1090.

  Prefatory Material:
    As in the first edition.

66. Another edition of *The Unfortunate Lovers*: In *Works*,
  1673. Part II, 120-65. Facs. 2 vols. New York:
  Benjamin Blom, 1968.

          About 150 lines have been added in five
  places to this edition, including two songs and some
  low humor. The five additions vary in length from
  fifteen to over fifty lines and are scattered over the
  last four acts.

67. Another edition of *The Unfortunate Lovers*: In *Dramatic
  Works*, 1872-74. III, 1-90. Rpt. New York: Russell &
  Russell, 1964.

  Prefatory Materials:
    Editors' introduction, pp. 3-10.
    Letter To Philip, Earl of Pembroke and Montgomery, p.
      11.

          The editors include as addenda the 1673
  additions, pp. 87-90. See item 66.

68. A possible adaptation of *The Unfortunate Lovers*:
  INJUR'D INNOCENCE: A TRAGEDY. As it is ACTED At the
  THEATRE-ROYAL IN *DRURY-LANE*. *Si quid inexpertum scenae*

committis, *& audes Personam formare novam*; servetur and
imum Qualis ab incaepto processerit. Hor. de Arte
Poet. *LONDON*: Printed for J. BRINDLEY, at the
King's-Arms in New-Bond Street. M.DCCXXXII.

Prefatory Materials:
  Dedication to His Royal Highness the Prince, sigs.
  A2-A3.
  Preface, sig. A3^V.

      Playwright Fettiplace Bellers may have
depended on *The Unfortunate Lovers* for his plot,
although Nethercot argues against this possibility.
See *1938*:Nethercot, p. 165, n. 37.

69. LOVE AND HONOVR, Written by W. DAVENANT Knight
    Presented by His Majesties Servants at the
    Black-Fryers. *LONDON*, Printed for *Hum: Robinson* at the
    Three Pidgeons and *Hum: Moseley* at the *Princes Armes* in
    St. *Pauls* Church-yard. 1649. 4°. Pp. 35.

    Greg 684; EAP 1642-1700; STC D329; UMI 275:10, 451:24.

    Stationers' Register:
      1646 Sept. 4 (?). Ent. (H.) Robinson and (H.)
        Mozeley, several tragedies and comedies: lic.
        Langley: Love and Honor, by Sir Wm. Davenant.
      1667 Aug. 19. Tr. Ann wid. of H. Moseley to H.
        Herringman: Love and Honor, by Sir William
        Davenant, one halfe.
      1673 Jan. 30. Tr. exor. of H. Robinson to J. Martin
        and H. Herringman: Davenants Love and Honour,
        halfe.
      1683 Aug. 21. Tr. wid. of J. Martin to R. Scott:
        Davenants Love and Hon^r., a fourth.

      One of Davenant's most successful plays, *Love
and Honor* pleased both Caroline and Restoration
audiences, and, with the theme of love and honor, it
anticipated the heroic drama, which remained popular
until the 1670s. On January 11, 1720, Charles Malloy
resurrected a portion of the play, which he joined with
comic sections of Shakspeare's *Henry V* and Shirley's
The Wedding to form a farce called *The Half-pay
Officers*. For an account, see *1872*:Maidment, III,
94-98. See item 72.

70. Another edition of *Love and Honor*: In *Works*, 1673.
     Part II, 224-72. Facs. 2 vols. New York: Benjamin
     Blom, 1968.

71. Another edition of *Love and Honor*: In *Dramatic Works*,
     1872-74. III, 91-192. Rpt. New York: Russell &
     Russell, 1964.

     Prefatory Materials:
       Introduction, pp. 93-98.

     Addenda:
       Alterations introduced in *Works*, 1673, pp. 186-92.

72. Adaptation of underplot of *Love and Honor*: THE
     Half-Pay Officers; A COMEDY: As it is ACTED By His
     Majesty's Servants.... *LONDON*: Printed for A.
     Betteworth, and *W. Boreham*, in *Pater-Noster-Row*, *T.
     Jauncy*, at the *Angel* without *Temple-Bar*, and *J.
     Brotherton* and *W. Meadows* on Cornhill. 1720. 8⁰· Pp.
     79. Facs. London: Cornmarket, 1969.

          The connection with Davenant arises from the
     following remark in the Preface: "The Part of Mrs.
     Fryer is in an Old Play, call'd *Love and Honour*, which
     she acted when she was young, and which was so
     imprinted in her Memory, she could repeat it every
     Word; and it was to an accidental Conversation with
     her, this Farce ow'd its Being." Later the play was
     published with its own title page and pagination in
     Francis Longe, *Collection of Plays*. 327 vols.
     1748-1812. CLXXV, 1-79.

73. Another edition of *Love and Honor*: In *Love and Honour
     and The Siege of Rhodes*. Ed. James W. Tupper. Boston:
     Heath, 1909. Pp. 1-77.

          In addition to a brief biography, a
     bibliography, a glossary, and a general introduction,
     Tupper provides comments on sources and on the text; he
     also provides informative notes. Although published in
     1909, the edition is still useful.

74. Another edition of *Love and Honor*: In *Early
     Seventeenth-Century Plays, 1600-1642*. Ed. Harold
     Reinoehl Walley and John Harold Wilson. New York:
     Harcourt, 1920. Pp. 917-81.

The brief introduction places *Love and Honor*
as an early play in the continuum from the romantic
drama of Beaumont and Fletcher to the heroic play
popular in the reign of Charles II.

75. THE PREFACE TO GONDIBERT, AN HEROICK POEM WRITTEN BY
    SIR WILLIAM D'AVENANT: WITH AN ANSWER TO THE PREFACE BY
    Mr HOBBES. A PARIS, Chez MATTHIEV GVILLEMOT, rue
    Sainct Iacques au coin de la rue Parcheminerie, a
    l'Enseigne de la Bibliotheque. M.DC.L. 8°. Pp. 164.

    STC D335; UMI 24:29.

    Prefatory Materials:
      Author's Preface, pp. 1–127.
      Hobbes' Answer, pp. 128–60.

    Addenda:
      Poems from Ed. Waller, pp. 161–62, and from Ab.
        Cowley, pp. 163–64.

76. A DISCOURSE UPON GONDIBERT. An Heroick *POEM* Written by
    Sr *WILLIAM D'AVENANT* With an Answer to it by Mr HOBBS.
    A PARIS, Chez MATTHIEV GVILLEMOT, rue Sainct Jacques au
    Coin de la Parcheminerie, a l'Enseigne de la
    Bibliotheque, M.DC.L. 12°. Pp. 145.

    STC D322; UMI 413:13.

    Prefatory Material:
      To Sir WILLIAM D'AVENANT, upon his first two Books of
        GONDIBERT, finished before his Voyage to America,
        Poem by Edmund Waller, sigs. A2–A2^v.
      Commendatory poem by Abraham Cowley, sigs. A3–A3^v.

77. Another edition of *The Preface*...: In *The Poetical
    Works of Sir William Davenant*. In *Select British Poets
    and Translations*. Vol. IV. Ed. Robert Anderson.
    London: W. Griffin ...[1793?].

78. Another edition of *The Preface*: In "Poems of Sir
    William Davenant." In *Works of the English Poets, From
    Chaucer to Cowper*. . . . Vol. V. Ed. Alexander
    Chalmers. London: J. Johnson..., 1810. Pp. 349–72.

79. Another edition of *The Preface*: In *Critical Essays of
    the Seventeenth Century*. Ed. J. E. Spingarn. Oxford:
    Clarendon, 1908. II, 1–67.

In his general introduction, Spingarn
discusses Davenant and Hobbes, especially the latter,
as precursors of "the New Aesthetics."

80. GONDIBERT: AN HEROICK POEM, WRITTEN BY Sr *WILLIAM*
D'AVENANT. Printed by *Tho. Newcomb* for *John Holden*,
and are to be sold at his Shop at the sign of the
Anchor in the NEW-EXCHANGE, 1651. 4°. Pp. [350].
Facs. Menston: Scolar, 1970. Rpt. London: British Book
Centre, 1975.

STC D325; UMI 24:18.

Prefatory Materials:
    Davenant's Preface to Thomas Hobbes, pp. 1-70.
    Hobbes' Answer, pp. 71-88.
    Commendatory Poem from Ed. Waller, sigs. M3-M3^v.
    Commendatory Poem from Ab. Cowley, sigs. M4-M4^v.

Addenda:
    Davenant's Postscript, sig. kkk-Kkk3^v.

Stationers' Register:
    1650/51 Mar. 17. Assigned to John Holden by Thomas
    Newcombe "a booke called *Gondibert*, An heroick
    poem, written by Sr Wm Davenant."

        Gladish identifies this as the first edition.
Copies of this edition contain manuscript corrections,
apparently by the author. See item 89 below.

81. GONDIBERT: AN HEROICK POEM; WRITTEN BY Sir *WILLIAM*
D'AVENANT. *LONDON*, Printed for *John Holden*, and are to
be sold at his Shop at the sign of the Anchor in the
New-Exchange, 1651. 8°. Pp. 248.

STC D326; UMI 735:5.

Prefatory Materials:
    Davenant's Preface to Hobbes, pp. 1-51.
    Hobbes' Answer, pp. 52-64.
    Poem from Ed. Waller, sigs. E2-E2^v.
    Poem from Ab. Cowley, sigs. E3-E3^v.

Addenda:
    Davenant's Postscript, pp. 243-[48].

Dowlin argues convincingly that the octavo
was set from the quarto and, therefore, is the second
edition. See *1939*:Dowlin.

82. Another edition of *Gondibert*: In *Works*, 1673. Part I,
1-198. Facs. 2 vols. New York: Benjamin Blom, 1968.

83. Adaptation of *Gondibert*: GONDIBERT AND BIRTHA. A
TRAGEDY. *Scibere jussit Amor*. *Ovid*. *OXFORD*, Printed at
the THEATRE, MDCCLI. In William Thompson's *Poems on
Several Occasions, To which is added Gondibert and
Birtha, A Tragedy*. Oxford: Printed at the Theatre,
1757. 4º. Pp. 218-444.

Thompson has written a five-act revenge
tragedy in blank verse based loosely on the
Gondibert-Rhodolinda-Birtha love triangle.

84. Another edition of *Gondibert*: In *The Poetical Works of
Sir William Davenant*. In *Select British Poets and
Translations*. Vol. IV. Ed. Robert Anderson. London:
W. Griffin ..., [1793?].

85. Selections from *Gondibert*: In "The Poems of Sir
William Davenant." In *Works of the English Poets, From
Chaucer to Cowper* .... Vol. VI. Ed. Alexander
Chalmers. London: J. Johnson, 1810. Pp. 349-431.

Chalmers includes Davenant's *Preface* and
Hobbes' *Answer*, plus an introduction.

86. Selections from *Gondibert*: In *Specimens of the British
Poets: with Biographical and Critical Notices, and An
Essay on English Poetry by Thomas Campbell*. 7 vols.
London: John Murray, 1819. IV, 96-107.

Prefatory Material:
  Biographical Note, pp. 96-98.

87. Selections from *Gondibert*: In *Select Works of the
British Poets, From Chaucer to Jonson, with
Biographical Sketches*. Ed. Robert Southey. London:
Longman, Rees, Orme, Brown, and Green, 1831. Pp.
912-74.

Prefatory Material:
  "Sir William Davenant," pp. 912-13.

88. Another edition of *Gondibert*: GONDIBERT: AN HEROICK
POEM, WRITTEN BY Sr WILLIAM D'AVENANT. Menston:
Scolar, 1970.

> Prefatory Material:
> Introduction.

> Addenda:
> "The Philosophers Disquisition to the Dying
> Christian" and "The Christians Reply to the
> Philosopher" (reduced size).
> *The Seventh and Last Canto to the Third Book of
> Gondibert.*

> This is a facsimile of the 1651 quarto
edition of *Gondibert.* In the two-page introduction,
there is an account of Davenant's experiences during
the years 1646-50, with comment on his exile, capture,
and imprisonment. Information is also provided on the
various editions of the three works presented in the
book.

89. Another edition of *Gondibert*: In *Sir William
Davenant's Gondibert.* Ed. David F. Gladish. Oxford:
Clarendon, 1971. Pp. 253-65.

> Prefatory Materials:
> Introduction, including comment on the backgrounds
> and texts of *Gondibert*, Davenant's *Preface* and
> Hobbes' *Answer*, and *The Seventh Canto of The Third
> Book*, pp. ix-xlv.

> Addenda:
> Commendatory poems by Waller and Cowley, pp. 269-71.
> *Certain Verses written by several of the Author's
> Friends*, pp. 272-86.
> Charles Cotton's poem to Davenant, p. 287.
> Commentary, pp. 289-312.

> Gladish includes the 1651 4° edition,
Davenant's *Preface* and Hobbes' *Answer*, the commendatory
poems by Waller and Cowley, *The Seventh Canto of the
Third Book*, *Certain Verses* by the court wits, and
Charles Cotton's poem to Davenant.

90. THE SIEGE OF RHODES Made a Representation by the Art
of Prospective in Scenes, And the Story sung in

Recitative Musick. At the back part of *Rutland*-House
in the upper end of *Aldersgate*-Street, *LONDON*. *LONDON*,
Printed by *J. M.* for Henry Herringman, and are to be
sold at his Shop, at the Sign of the *Anchor*, on the
Lower-Walk in the New-Exchange, 1656. 4º. Pp. [41].

Greg 763(a1); EAP 1642-1700; STC D339; Thom.
    E.498.(6.).

Prefatory Materials:
    To the Reader, sigs. A2-A3^V·

Addenda:
    List of performers and composers, p. [41].

Stationers' Register:
    1656 Aug. 27. Ent. H. Herringman: a maske called The
        Siege of Rhodes, made a representation by the art
        of prospective in scenes, and the story sung in
        recitative musicke, by Sir William Davenant, acted
        at the back part of Rutland House at the upper end
        of Aldersgatestreet.

            Though fifteen years later it would be the
object of Buckingham's satire in *The Rehearsal*, this
is the landmark play that introduced the first actress,
changeable scenery, and the opera to the English public
stage.

91.   Another edition: THE SIEGE OF RHODES. Made a
       Representation by the Art of Prospective in Scenes, and
       the story sung in *Recitative* Musick. At the Cock-Pit
       in *Drury* Lane. *LONDON*, Printed by J. M. for *Henry*
       Herringman, and are to be sold at his Shop, at the Sign
       of the *Anchor*, on the Lower-walk in the *New-Exchange*,
       1659. 4º. Sigs. A-F4.

       Greg 763(b1); STC D341; UMI 1439:31.

92.   THE SIEGE OF RHODES: The First and Second Part; As
       they were lately represented at His Highness the Duke
       of *YORK'S Theatre in Lincolns-Inn Fields*. The first
       Part being lately enlarg'd. Written by Sir WILLIAM
       D'AVENANT. *LONDON*, Printed for *Henry Herringman*, and
       are to be sold at his Shop, at the Sign of the *Anchor*,
       on the Lower-walk in the *New-Exchange*. 1663. 4º.
       Part I. Pp. 46. Part II. Pp. [63].

Greg 827a; EAP 1642-1700; STC D342; UMI 709:27.

Prefatory Materials:
  To the Earl of Clarendon, sigs. A2-A3^v.
  Part II title page.

Stationers' Register:
  1659 May 30. Ent. H. Herringman: a booke The Second
    Part of the Seige of Rhodes, made a representation
    by the art of prospective in scenes, and the story
    sung in recitative musicke, by Sir William
    Davenant.

      Greg notes that some copies incorporated a
doctored version of the 1659 edition as Part I in an
apparent attempt to dispose of remaindered copies while
other copies were altered much more substantially.
These alterations are discussed in detail by Hedback
(item 100) in her edition of the plays (pp. xiv-xxii)
and by Philip R. Wikelund in his review of Hedback's
edition, *Philological Quarterly*, 53 (1974), 681-83.

93. Another edition: THE SIEGE OF RHODES: The First and
    Second Parts; As they were lately Represented at His
    Highness the Duke of *YORK's* Theatre in *Lincolns-Inne*
    Fields. The First Part being lately Enlarg'd. Written
    by Sir *WILLIAM D'AVENANT*. *LONDON*, Printed for *Henry*
    Herringman, and are to be sold at his Shop, at the Sign
    of the *Anchor*, in the Lower Walk of the *New-Exchange*.
    1670. 4°. Pp. 101.

    Greg 827(b); STC D343; UMI 709:28.

    Prefatory Materials:
      To the Earl of Clarendon, sigs. A2-A3^v.

94. Another edition of *The Siege of Rhodes, I and II*: In
    Works, 1673. Part II, 1-66. Facs. 2 vols. New York:
    Benjamin Blom, 1968.

95. Another edition of *The Siege of Rhodes, I and II*: In
    Dramatic Works, 1872-74. III, 231-365. Rpt. New York:
    Russell & Russell, 1964.

    Prefatory Materials:
      Editors' Introduction, pp. 233-55.

96. Another edition: THE SIEGE OF RHODES: The First and
    Second Part. In *Love and Honour and The Siege of
    Rhodes*. Ed. James W. Tupper. Boston: Heath, 1909.
    Pp. 179-354.

       In addition to a brief biography, a
    bibliography, a glossary, and a general introduction,
    Tupper comments on sources and on the text; he also
    provides informative notes. Although published in
    1909, the edition is still useful.

97. Selections from *The Siege of Rhodes, Part I*: In
    Allardyce Nicoll, ed. *Readings From British Drama:
    Extracts From British and Irish Plays*. New York:
    Crowell, 1928. Pp. 168-70.

       The selection is from the Third Entry of
    Part I.

98. Another edition of *The Siege of Rhodes, Part I*: In
    *Plays of the Restoration and Eighteenth Century as They
    Were Acted at the Theatres-Royal by Their Majesties
    Servants*. Ed. Dougald MacMillan and Howard Mumford
    Jones. New York: Holt, 1931. Pp. 3-26. Rpt. 1959.

    Prefatory Materials:
      Introduction, pp. 3-4.

       The edition is well annotated; the final note
    on page twenty-five is a detailed resume of Part II.

99. Another edition of *The Siege of Rhodes*: Andrew
    Anthony Tadie, ed. "Sir William Davenant's 'The Siege
    of Rhodes': A Critical Old-Style Spelling Edition."
    Diss. Saint Louis 1972.

100. Another edition: *The Siege of Rhodes: A Critical
     Edition*. Studia Anglistica Upsaliensia 14. Ann-Mari
     Hedback. Uppsala: Acta universitatis Upsaliensia,
     1973.

        Hedback includes both textual and
     historical-literary introductions. In the former, she
     illustrates effectively the variations among the
     editions of the plays and comments on the Douai
     Manuscript of Part Two. In the latter, she indicates
     possible Turkish sources in both England and France

and shows how Davenant was a part of a vigorous
dramatic tradition in his use of Turkish history as
background for his plays. She also discusses the
plays in terms of their structures, their connections
with French classicism and the theme of love and
honour, and their political ideas. Under "Works
Quoted ..." she provides a bibliography.

101. THE FIRST DAYS Entertainment AT Rutland-House, By
Declamations and *Musick*: After the manner of the
ANCIENTS. *by* Sr *W. D. LONDON*, Printed by *J. M.* for *H.*
Herringman, and sold at his Shop at the *Anchor*, in the
New-Exchange, in the Lower Walk. 1657. 8°. Pp.
[91].

Greg 770; EAP 1642-1700; STC D323; Thom. E.1648.(2.).

Addenda:
Composers named, sig. G3.

Stationers' Register:
1656 Sept. 9. Ent. H. Herringman: a booke entituled
The First Dayes Entertainment at Rutland Howse, by
declamations and musicke after the manner of the
ancients, by Sir Wm. Davenant.

Not a play, but two debates with musical
interludes, *The First Days Entertainment* opens with a
verse prologue, continues with prose debates between
Diogenes and Aristophanes on the merits of public
entertainment and between a Londoner and a Parisian on
the merits of their cities, and it closes with a verse
epilogue. Using this unique form, Davenant was able
to initiate dramatic activity, despite the prohibition
against plays under the Commonwealth.

102. Another edition of *The First Days Entertainment*: In
Works, 1673. Part II, 341-59. Facs. 2 vols. New
York: Benjamin Blom, 1968.

103. Another edition of *The First Days Entertainment*: In
Dramatic Works, 1872-74. III, 192-230. Rpt. New
York: Russell & Russell, 1964.

Prefatory Materials:
Introduction, pp. 195-96.

104. The Cruelty of the SPANIARDS IN PERU. Exprest by
      Instrumentall and Vocall Musick, and by the Art of
      Perspective in Scenes, &c. Represented daily at the
      Cockpit in DRURY-LANE, At three after noone
      punctually, *LONDON*, Printed for *Henry Herringman*, and
      are to be sold at his Shop at the *Anchor* in the Lower
      walk in the *New-Exchange*. 1658. 4º. Pp. 27.

      Greg 787; EAP 1642-1700; STC D321.

      Stationers' Register:
         1658 Nov. 30. Ent. H. Herringman: a booke called The
         Cruelty of the Spaniards in Peru, exprest by
         instrumentall and vocall musicke and by the art of
         prospective in scenes, &c., represented dayly at
         the Cockpit in Drury Lane, by Sir William
         Davenant.

              Though no playwright is mentioned on the
      title page, the entry in the Stationers' Register for
      30 Nov. 1658 indicates that Davenant was the author.

105. Another edition of *The Cruelty of the Spaniards in
      Peru*: The Fourth ACT. THE Play-house to be Let. In
      Works, 1673. Part II, 103-14. Facs. 2 vols. New
      York: Benjamin Blom, 1968.

106. Another edition of *The Cruelty of the Spaniards in
      Peru*: The Fourth Act, *The Play-House to Be Let*. In
      Dramatic Works, 1872-74. IV, 76-94. Rpt. New York:
      Russell & Russell, 1964.

107. THE HISTORY OF Sʳ Francis Drake. Exprest by
      Instrumentall and Vocall Musick, and by Art of
      Perspective in Scenes, &c. *The First Part*.
      Represented daily at the *Cockpit* in Drury-*Lane* at
      Three Afternoon Punctually. *LONDON*, Printed for *Henry
      Herringman*, and are to be sold at his shop at the
      Anchor in the Lower walk in the *New-Exchange*. 1659.
      4º. Pp. 37.

      Greg 798; EAP 1642-1700; STC D327; Thom. E.764.(1.)

      Stationers' Register:
         1659 Jan. 20. Ent. H. Herringman: a booke called
         the history of Sir Francis Drake, exprest by
         instrumentall and vocall musick and by art of

perspective in scenes, &c., the First Parte, By
Sir Will. Davenant.

Although "First Part" appears on the
title page, no second part has been located. An entry
in the Stationers' Register for Jan. 20, 1659,
establishes Davenant as the author. As he had done
with *The Siege of Rhodes*, he used changeable scenery
and instrumental and vocal music to create an opera,
thereby circumventing the Commonwealth prohibition
against stage plays.

108. Another edition: THE HISTORY of Sr *FRANCIS DRAKE*.
The Third ACT. THE Play-house to be Let. In *Works*,
1673. Part III, 87-103. Facs. 2 vols. New York:
Benjamin Blom, 1968.

109. Another edition: THE HISTORY OF SIR FRANCIS DRAKE.
ACT 3. THE PLAYHOUSE TO BE LET. In *Dramatic Works*,
1872-74. IV, 49-76. Rpt. New York: Russell &
Russell, 1964.

Prefatory Materials:
Introduction, pp. 3-13.

110. POEM, UPON HIS SACRED MAJESTIES MOST HAPPY RETURN TO
HIS DOMINIONS. Written by Sr William Davenant.
LONDON, Printed for *Henry Herringman*, and are to be
sold at his Shop at the signe of the *Anchor* on the
Lower walk in the *New Exchange*. 1660. 4°. Pp. 22.

STC D334; UMI 257; Thomason E.184.(2.).

111. Another edition of *Poem*...: In *Works*, 1673. Part I,
256-61. Facs. 2 vols. New York: Benjamin Blom,
1968.

112. Another edition of *Poem*...: In A. M. Gibbs, ed. *The
Shorter Poems, and Songs from the Plays and Masques*.
Oxford: Clarendon, 1972. Pp. 82-90.

113. POEM, TO THE KING'S MOST Sacred Majesty. By S^r
WILLIAM D'AVENANT. LONDON, Printed for *Henry
Herringman*, at the *Anchor* in the Lower Walk in the New
Exchange. 1663. 4°. Pp. 34.

STC D333; UMI 207:10.

114. Another edition of *Poem*...: In *Works*, 1673. Part I,
     260 [262]-71. Facs. 2 vols. New York: Benjamin
     Blom, 1968.

115. Another edition of *Poem*...: In A. M. Gibbs, ed. *The
     Shorter Poems, and Songs from the Plays and Masques.*
     Oxford: Clarendon, 1972. Pp. 90-103.

116. THE RIVALS. A COMEDY. Acted by His Highness the Duke
     of York's Servants. Licensed September 19. 1668.
     Roger L'Estrange *LONDON*, Printed for *William Cademan*,
     at the *Pope's Head* in the Lower Walk of the New
     Exchange. 1668. 4⁰. Pp. 56. Facs. London:
     Cornmarket, 1970.

     STC D336; EAP 1642-1700; UMI 451:26.

          Although no playwright is indicated on the
     title page, both Downes and Langbaine attribute *The
     Rivals* to Davenant. The play is an adaptation of *The
     Two Noble Kinsmen*, which is a dramatization of
     Chaucer's "The Knight's Tale." Reducing drastically
     the time covered by the story and the number of
     speaking parts, Davenant contrived a play with a happy
     ending and a full measure of moral instruction.

117. Another edition: THE RIVALS. A COMEDY. Acted by His
     Highnes the Duke of York's Servants. Licensed
     September 19, 1668. *Roger L'Estrange LONDON*, Printed
     for *William Cademan*, at the *Popes Head* in the Lower
     Walk of the *New-Exchange*. 1669. 4⁰. Pp. 56.

     Prefatory Materials:
       Actors Names, sig. A4.

          This appears to be a reissue of the 1668
     edition with a new title page.

118. Another edition of *The Rivals*: In Francis Longe, ed.
     Collection of Plays. 327 vols. 1748-1812, CVI,
     1-56.

          This is the 1669 edition bound with ten
     other plays to form volume CVI.

119. Another edition of *The Rivals*: In *Dramatic Works*,
     1872-74. V, 213-93. Rpt. New York: Russell &
     Russell, 1964.

Prefatory Materials:
   Introduction, pp. 215-20.

120. THE Man's the Master: A COMEDY. WRITTEN BY Sir
WILLIAM D'AVENANT, KNIGHT. In the SAVOY. Printed for
Henry Herringman, at the *Blew-Anchor*, in the Lower
Walk of the New-Exchange. 1669. 4⁰. Pp. 77.

STC D331; EAP 1642-1700; UMI 451:25.

Stationers' Register:
   1669 Jun. 8. Ent. Henry Herringman, A Comody
    Intituled, The Man is the Master, by Sr Willm
    Davenant.

    The Man's the Master, Davenant's last play,
is an adaptation of Scarron's *Jodelet ou Le Maitre
Valet*, which was based on a Spanish play by Rojas
Varilla. To an already complicated plot, Davenant
added a burlesque subplot. After its initial
production, it was thrice revived in 1673, 1726, and
1775.

121. Another edition of *The Man's the Master*: In *Works*,
1673. Part II, 329-83. Facs. 2 vols. New York:
Benjamin Blom, 1968.

122. Another edition: THE MAN's THE MASTER: A COMEDY, IN
FIVE ACTS, AS NOW PERFORMED AT THE THEATRE-ROYAL,
COVENT-GARDEN. WRITTEN BY Sir WILLIAM DAVENANT.
LONDON: Printed for T. EVANS, in the *Strand*, near
York Buildings. MDCCLXXV. 4⁰. Pp. 66.

    Maidment and Logan footnote the differences
between this edition and the 1669 edition and suggest
that the changes were made by Woodward, who acted
Jodelet in 1775. Three cuts were made totaling about
five pages, a song was changed from a part-song to a
solo, and several sentences were altered to suit the
times. The portions cut involved low humor and did
not further the plot. The Prologue and Epilogue were
not reprinted in 1775.

123. Another edition of *The Man's the Master*: In *Dramatic
Works*, 1872-74. V, 1-107. Rpt. New York: Russell &
Russell, 1964.

Prefatory Materials:
Introduction, pp. 3-6.

124.   THE TEMPEST, OR THE Enchanted Island. A COMEDY. As
       it is now Acted at his Highness the Duke of *York's*
       THEATRE *LONDON*, Printed by *J. M.* for *Henry Herringmen*
       at the *Blew Anchor* in the *Lower-walk* of the
       New-Exchange. MDCLXX. 4°. Pp. 83. Facs. London:
       Cornmarket, 1969. Facs. In *After the Tempest*.
       Introd. George Robert Guffey. Los Angeles: Clark
       Memorial Library, 1969.

       Greg 538; EAP 1642-1700; STC S2944; UMI 297:37.

       Prefatory Material:
       Preface by John Dryden, sigs. A2-A3^v.

       Stationers' Register:
       1669/70 Jan. 9. Ent [for Hen. Herringman]... under
          the hands of Master L'Estrange and Warden Smith a
          copie of a booke intituled *The Tempest, or the
          enchanted island*. A Trage-Comedy. As it is acted
          at his Royall Highnes the Duke of Yorks Theatre
          &c

              The Davenant-Dryden *Tempest*, which,
       according to Montague Summers, held the stage for over
       two centuries, retained only about one-third of
       Shakespeare's play. Some characters were cut, and
       others were added, most notably Hippolyto, who had
       never seen a woman, and Dorinda, who had never seen a
       man, while much of Prospero's best poetry was lost.
       Yet, the long stage history testifies to the
       adaptation's theatrical effectiveness.

125.   Another edition: THE TEMPEST OR THE Enchanted Island.
       A COMEDY As it is now Acted at his Highness the Duke
       of York's THEATRE. *LONDON*, Printed by *T. N.* for *Henry
       Herringman*, at the *Blew Anchor* in the *Lower Walk* of
       the *New-Exchange*. MDCLXXIV. 4°. Pp. 82. Facs. In
       After the Tempest. Introd. George Robert Guffey. Los
       Angeles: Clark Memorial Library, 1969.

       STC S2945; UMI 160:2.

       Prefatory Materials:
       Preface by John Dryden, sigs. A2-A3^v.

This version, based on the 1670
Davenant-Dryden edition, contains elaborate directions
for staging and music added by Shadwell for production
at the well-equipped Dorset Garden Theatre.

126. Another edition: THE TEMPEST, OR THE Enchanted Island.
A COMEDY: As it is now Acted AT HIS HIGHNESS THE *Duke
of York's Theatre*. LONDON, Printed by *J.* Macock, for
Henry Herringman at the Sign of the *Blew Anchor* in the
Lower Walk of the *New-Exchange*. M.DC.LXXVI. 4⁰. Pp.
82.

STC S2946; UMI 297:38.

This is another edition of the 1674
Davenant-Dryden version with additions by Shadwell.

127. Another edition: THE TEMPEST: OR THE Enchanted
Island. A COMEDY: As it is now Acted AT HIS HIGHNESS
THE *Duke of York's Theatre*. *LONDON*, Priented by J.
Macock, for *Henry Herringman* at the Sign of the
Blew-Anchor in the Lower Walk of the *New-Exchange*.
M.DC.LXXVI. 4⁰. Pp. [58].

STC S2946.

Although the title page is almost identical
with that of the 1676 edition and it carries that
date, this is a new setting, having only fifty-eight
instead of eighty-two pages. The new setting of the
title page has introduced a misspelling "Priented" for
"Printed" and hyphens separating "Blew Anchor" and
"New Exchange." A note in the Folger Catalogue
suggests a printing date about 1692 because quarto
sets of Dryden's works were being prepared at that
time.

128. Another edition: THE TEMPEST, OR THE Enchanted
Island. A COMEDY. As it is now Acted At Their
Majesties Theatre IN DORSET-GARDEN. *LONDON*, Printed
by *J. M.* for *H. Herringman*; and sold by *R. Bentley*,
at the Post-House in *Russell-street, Covent-Garden*.
1690. 4⁰. Pp. 62.

STC S2947; UMI 297:30.

This is another edition of the 1674
Davenant-Dryden version with additions by Shadwell.

129.   Another edition: THE TEMPEST, OR THE Enchanted
       Island.   A COMEDY.   As it is now Acted At Their
       Majesties Theatre IN *DORSET-GARDEN*.   *LONDON*.   Printed
       by *J. M.* for *H. Herringman*; and sold by *R.* Bentley,
       at the Post-House in Russel-street, Covent-Garden.
       1690.   4⁰.   Pp. 62.   In THE WORKS of Mr. John Dryden,
       . . . LONDON, Printed, and are to be Sold by *Jacob
       Tonson*, at the Sign of the *Judge's Head* in
       Chancery-Lane, near *Fleet-street*, 1691.

       STC D2207; UMI 208.

       Prefatory Materials:
         Preface by Dryden, as in the 1670 edition, sigs.
         A-A2ᵛ.

130.   Another edition: THE TEMPEST, OR THE Enchanted
       Island.   A COMEDY.   As it is now Acted At Their
       Majesties Theatre IN *DORSET-GARDEN*.   LONDON, Printed
       by J.M. for H. Herringman; and sold by *R. Bentley*, at
       the Post-House in Russel-street, Covent-Garden.   1690.
       Sigs. [A-A3ᵛ]; pp. [1-62].   In THE WORKS OF Mr. John
       Dryden.   *In Four Volumes*.   CONTAINING [Contents of all
       four volumes given in double columns on the title page
       of this first volume].   *LONDON*, Printed for *Jacob
       Tonson* at the Sign of the *Judge's Head* in
       Chancery-Lane, near *Fleet*-street, 1693.   4⁰.

       STC D2208; UMI 1382:4.

       Prefatory Materials:
         Preface by John Driden, sigs. A2-A2ᵛ.

             This edition, which is a reprint of the 1674
       Shadwell operatic version of the Davenant-Dryden
       adaptation, appears in volume I with *An Essay of
       Dramatick Poesy* and eight other plays, each with its
       own title page, pagination, and signature.   The dates
       on the title pages range from 1675 to 1692.   An
       advertisement on the final unnumbered page lists
       "Plays Printed for Henry Herringman" and includes
       fifteen titles by Davenant.

131.   Another edition: THE TEMPEST, OR THE Enchanted
       Island.   A COMEDY.   As it is now Acted By His
       MAJESTIES SERVANTS.   *LONDON*, Printed by *Tho. Warren*,
       for *Henry* Herringman, and Sold by *R. Bentley, J.*

Tonson, F. Saunders, and *T.* *Bennet*, M DC XCV. 4°.
Pp. 61.

STC S2948; UMI 334:13.

This is another edition of the 1674
Davenant-Dryden version with additions by Shadwell.

132. Another edition: THE TEMPEST, OR, THE Enchanted
Island. A COMEDY. As it is now Acted by His
MAJESTIES SERVANTS. *LONDON*, Printed by *Tho.* *Warren*,
for *Henry Herringman*, and Sold by R. Bentley, J.
Tonson, *F. Saunders*, and *T.* *Bennet*, MDCXCV. Pp. 60.
In THE Dramatic Works of Mr. JOHN DRYDEN. In Three
Volumes. VOL. I. ... *LONDON*: Printed for *R. Bentley*,
at the Post House in Russel-Street in *Covent-Garden*.
1695. 4°.

Prefatory Materials:
  Separate title page for the play, sig. A.
  Dryden's preface, sigs. A2-A2^V.

This is a reprint of Shadwell's 1674
operatic version of the Davenant-Dryden *Tempest*.

133. Another edition: THE TEMPEST: OR, THE Enchanted
Island. A COMEDY: As it is now Acted, By His
MAJESTIES SERVANTS. *LONDON*, Printed for J. Tonson,
and T. Bennet, and Sold by *R. Wellington*, at the
Dolphin and *Crown* at the West-end of S. *Paul's*
Church-yard. *G. Strahan*, over against the Royal
Exchange in *Cornhil*, and *B*. Lintott, at the Post-house
next the Middle-Temple Gate in Fleet-street, MDCCI.
4°. Pp. [61].

This is another edition of the Shadwell
operatic version of the Davenant-Dryden *Tempest*.

134. Another edition: THE TEMPEST, OR, THE Enchanted
Island. In THE COMEDIES, TRAGEDIES, AND OPERAS
Written by *JOHN DRYDEN*, Esq; Now first Collected
together, and Corrected from the Originals. In Two
Volumes. *LONDON*, Printed for *Jacob Tonson*, at
Gray's-Inn-Gate in Gray's-Inn-Lane; *Thomas Bennet*, at
the *Half-Moon*; and *Richard Wellington*, at the Lute in
St. *Paul's* Church-yard. MDCCI. Fol. pp. [226]-274.

Prefatory Materials:
     Driden's Preface, pp. [226]-227.

          The 1701 folio reprints the 1670 edition for
the first time. According to Montague Summers, this
was the only reprinting of the 1670 edition until
Summers himself did so in *Shakespeare Adaptations*
(1922). Summers apparently had not seen the beautiful
limited edition published by the Rowfant Club in 1911
(See item 155).

135. Another edition: THE TEMPEST: OR, THE *ENCHANTED
      ISLAND*. A COMEDY. First written by *Mr. WILLIAM
      SHAKESPEAR*. & since altered by *S^r*. *WILLIAM DAVENANT*,
      AND Mr. *JOHN DRYDEN*. LONDON, Printed in the Year
      1710. 8⁰. Pp. 112.

      Prefatory Materials:
         Dryden's Preface, pp. 3-6.

136. Another edition: THE TEMPEST: OR, THE *Enchanted
      Island*. A COMEDY As it is Acted at His HIGHNESS the
      DUKE of *YORK's* THEATRE. Printed in the YEAR
      MDCCXVII. In The DRAMATICK WORKS OF *John Dryden*, Esq;
      VOLUME *the* SECOND. Printed for JACOB TONSON at
      Shakespeare's Head over-against Katherine-Street in
      the *Strand*. MDCCXVII. 12⁰. pp. [162]-254.

      Prefatory Materials:
         Dryden's preface, pp. 165-68.

          This is a reprint of Shadwell's 1674
      operatic version of the Davenant-Dryden *Tempest*.

137. Another edition: THE TEMPEST: OR THE *ENCHANTED
      ISLAND*. A COMEDY. First written by *Mr. William
      Shakespear*. & since altered by *S^r*. *WILLIAM DAVENANT*
      AND *Mr. JOHN DRYDEN* LONDON, Printed for the Company
      [n.d.]. 8⁰. Pp. 103.

      Prefatory Materials:
         Dryden's preface, pp. 3-5.

          This is a reprint of the 1710 edition. A
      note in the Folger Catalogue suggests a publication
      date c.1721.

138. Another edition: THE TEMPEST: OR, THE *Enchanted Island*. A COMEDY. As it is Acted at His HIGHNESS *the* DUKE of *YORK'S* THEATER. Printed in the YEAR MDCCXXV. In The DRAMATICK WORKS OF *John Dryden*, Esq; *LONDON:* Printed for JACOB TONSON at *Shakespeare's Head*, over-against Katherine-Street in the Strand. MDCCXXV. 12°. Pp. 163-254.

   This edition, which reprints the Shadwell operatic version of the Davenant-Dryden *Tempest*, follows closely that of the 1717 edition, although the head ornaments differ.

139. Another edition: THE TEMPEST: OR, THE *Enchanted Island*. A COMEDY. As it is Acted at His HIGHNESS the Duke of *YORK'S* THEATRE. LONDON: Printed for *J. Tonson*. And Sold by W. FEALES at *Rowe's* Head, at the Corner of *Essex-Street*, in the *Strand*. MDCCXXXIII. 12°. Pp. [94].

   Prefatory Materials:
     Frontispiece: DuGuernier engraving.
     Dryden's preface, sigs. A3-A4ᵛ.

   This is another edition of the Shadwell operatic version of the Davenant-Dryden *Tempest*.

140. Another edition: THE TEMPEST: OR, THE ENCHANTED ISLAND. A COMEDY. By Mr. *DRYDEN*. *LONDON:* Printed for JACOB TONSON in the *Strand*. MDCCXXXV. In THE DRAMATICK WORKS OF *JOHN DRYDEN*, Esq; IN SIX VOLUMES. *LONDON:* Printed for JACOB TONSON in the *Strand*. MDCCXXXV. 12°.

   Prefatory Materials:
     Engraving of a scene from the play by G. van der Gucht after Gravelot.

   The play has its own title page in black and red ink.

141. Another edition: THE TEMPEST: OR, THE ENCHANTED ISLAND. A COMEDY. In THE DRAMATICK WORKS OF JOHN DRYDEN, Esq. VOLUME the SECOND. LONDON: Printed for J. and R. TONSON in the Strand. MDCCLXII. 12°. Pp. 171-263.

Prefatory Materials:
Dryden's preface, pp. 172-76.

This is a reprint of Shadwell's 1674
operatic version of the Davenant-Dryden *Tempest*.

142. Another edition: THE TEMPEST: OR, THE *ENCHANTED
ISLAND*. A COMEDY, As it is performed at the
THEATRE-ROYAL, SMOCK-ALLEY. *DUBLIN*: Printed for
THOMAS WALKER, at CICERO'S-HEAD, No. 79, Dame-street.
1775. 8º.

This is another edition of the Shadwell
operatic version of the Davenant-Dryden *Tempest*.

143. Another edition: THE TEMPEST; OR, THE ENCHANTED
ISLAND. WRITTEN BY SHAKESPEARE; WITH ADDITIONS FROM
DRYDEN: AS COMPILED BY J. P. KEMBLE. AND ACTED FIRST
AT THE THEATRE ROYAL, DRURY LANE, OCTOBER 13TH, 1789
LONDON: Printed for J. DEBRETT, opposite BURLINGTON
HOUSE, PICCADILLY. M,DCC,LXXXIX. 8º. Pp. 56.

Prefatory Materials:
Dramatis Personae.

Addenda:
Epilogue by General Burgoyne.

Kemble moved the storm to the beginning of
Act II, restored some of Prospero's lines, but
retained Hippolyto and Dorinda from the
Davenant-Dryden version.

144. Another edition: THE TEMPEST; OR, THE ENCHANTED
ISLAND. WRITTEN BY SHAKESPEARE; WITH ADDITIONS FROM
DRYDEN; AS COMPILED BY J. P. KEMBLE. AND FIRST ACTED
AT THE THEATRE ROYAL, DRURY LANE. October 13th 1789.
In A Collection of Much-Esteemed *DRAMATIC PIECES* As
Performed at the Theatres Royal, *DRURY LANE* and *COVENT
GARDEN*. 2 vols. London: Printed for J. DEBRETT,
opposite Burlington House, Piccadilly. 1795, 12º. I,
233-84.

This is a reprint of the 1789 edition.

145. Another edition: *Shakespeare's* TEMPEST; OR, *THE
ENCHANTED ISLAND*, A PLAY, ADAPTED TO THE STAGE, WITH

ADDITIONS FROM DRYDEN AND DAVENANT, BY J. P. KEMBLE;
AND NOW FIRST PUBLISHED AS IT IS ACTED AT THE *THEATRE
ROYAL* IN *COVENT-GARDEN.* LONDON: PRINTED FOR LONGMAN,
HURST, REES, AND ORME, PATERNOSTER ROW; AND SOLD IN
THE THEATRE. 1806. 4°. Pp. 62.

Prefatory Material:
  Persons Represented, sig. A2.

      This is an inexpensive edition, printed on
cheap paper. Kemble was cast as Prospero, although he
was listed second in the cast, which included a woman,
Miss Logan, as Hippolyto, the young man who has never
seen a woman. In his adaptation, Kemble moved the
storm to the opening of Act II, restored some of
Prospero's lines, and retained Dorinda and Hippolyto
from the Davenant-Dryden version.

146. Another edition: Shakespeare's TEMPEST; OR *THE
ENCHANTED ISLAND.* A PLAY, ADAPTED TO THE STAGE, WITH
ADDITIONS FROM DRYDEN AND DAVENANT, BY J. P. KEMBLE;
AND NOW FIRST PUBLISHED AS IT IS ACTED AT THE *THEATRE
ROYAL* IN *COVENT-GARDEN.* A NEW EDITION. LONDON:
PRINTED FOR LONGMAN, HURST, REES, AND ORME. 1807.
8°. Pp. 57.

Prefatory Material:
  Persons Represented, sig. A2.

      This is an inexpensive edition, printed on
cheap paper. Unlike the 1806 edition in which he
appeared second among the "Persons Represented,"
Kemble was listed first in this edition. Miss Logan
was again assigned to act Hippolyto and three Sea
Nymphs were added to the cast. In this adaptation,
Kemble moved the storm to the opening of Act II,
restored some of Prospero's lines, and retained
Dorinda and Hippolyto from the Davenant-Dryden
version.

147. Another edition: *The Tempest; or, the Enchanted
Island. A Comedy.* In *The Works of John Dryden,* ...
Ed. Walter Scott, Esq., vol. III. London: William
Miller, 1808. 8°. Pp. 95-205.

Prefatory Materials:
  Introduction, pp. 97-98.
  Dryden's preface, pp. 99-102.

In his introduction, Scott presents a
sympathetic account of Davenant's life, discounting,
in process, the Shakespeare paternity story.   Scott
describes *Gondibert* as Davenant's "greatest
performance" which "incurred, when first published,
more ridicule, and in latter times more neglect, than
its merit deserves."   Regarding authorship, Scott
follows Dryden's lead and assigns much of the
adaptation to Davenant.

148.   Another edition: THE TEMPEST; OR; THE ENCHANTED
ISLAND; A PLAY, IN FIVE ACTS; BY WILLIAM SHAKESPEARE.
ADAPTED TO THE STAGE WITH ADDITIONS FROM DRYDEN AND
DAVENANT, BY J. P. KEMBLE. AS PERFORMED AT THE
THEATRE ROYAL, COVENT GARDEN. PRINTED UNDER THE
AUTHORITY OF THE MANAGERS FROM THE PROMPT BOOK.   WITH
REMARKS BY MRS. INCHBALD. LONDON: PRINTED FOR
LONGMAN, HURST, REES, ORME, AND BROWN,
PATERNOSTER-ROW.   1808.   12⁰.   Pp. 72.

Prefatory Material:
Frontispiece engraving by Warren of a painting by
Howard depicting Prospero, Ferdinand, and Miranda
asleep.

Kemble's *Tempest* is more an adaptation of
both the Shakespeare and the Davenant-Dryden versions.
He restored some of Prospero's lines from the
Shakespeare, retained Hippolyto and Dorinda from the
Davenant-Dryden, and shifted the storm to the opening
of Act II.   In additon, he retained the songs, but cut
the masques.   This edition is included in *The British
Theatre; or a Collection of Plays, Which are Acted at
the Theatres Royal ... With Biographical and Critical
Remarks by Mrs. Inchbald*. Vol. V.   London: Longman,
Hurst, Rees, Orme, 1808.

149.   Another edition: *Shakespeare's* TEMPEST; OR, THE
ENCHANTED ISLAND, A PLAY; ADAPTED TO THE STAGE WITH
ADDITIONS FROM DRYDEN AND DAVENANT, BY J.P. KEMBLE;
AND NOW PUBLISHED AS IT IS PERFORMED AT THE THEATRES
ROYAL.   *LONDON*:   PRINTED FOR JOHN MILLER, 25,
BOW-STREET, COVENT GARDEN; AND SOLD IN THE THEATRES.
London: Miller, 1815.   12⁰.   Pp. 61.

Prefatory Material:
Persons Represented, p. [3].

Another cheap edition, the 1815 follows
closely the earlier Kemble adaptations with the storm
opening Act II, Prospero recovering some lines from
Shakespeare, and Dorinda and Hippolyto of the
Davenant-Dryden version continuing as balancing
characters. Kemble and Young were both cast as
Prospero.

150.   Another edition: THE TEMPEST, *A PLAY*, IN FIVE ACTS,
BY W. SHAKESPEARE. Printed from the Acting Edition
with Remarks. TO WHICH ARE ADDED, A DESCRIPTION OF
THE COSTUME, CAST OF THE CHARACTERS, SIDES OF ENTRANCE
AND EXIT, RELATIVE POSITIONS OF THE PERFORMERS ON THE
STAGE, AND THE WHOLE OF THE STAGE BUSINESS, AS NOW
PERFORMED AT THE THEATRES-ROYAL, LONDON. Embellished
with a Wood Engraving from an original Drawing made
expressly for this Work, by I.R. CRUIKSHANK, and
executed by Mr. WHITE. London: PRINTED AND PUBLISHED
BY T. DOLBY, BRITANNIA 17 CATHERINE-STREET, STRAND;
AND SOLD BY ALL BOOKSELLERS. 1824. Pp. 50.

Prefatory Materials:
  Engraving, p. [1].
  Costume descriptions, p. [4].
  Cast, p. [5].
  Stage directions discussed, p. [6].

Addenda:
  Position of the Characters at the Fall of the
    Curtain diagram, p. 51.

This is a commercial acting edition, roughly
resembling Barron's *Theatre Classics for the Modern
Reader*, with costumes, positions of actors, and stage
business all described. The text is the Kemble
adaptation, which retains Dorinda and Hippolyto of the
Davenant-Dryden version. Macready was cast as
Prospero.

151.   Another edition: THE TEMPEST; OR; THE ENCHANTED
ISLAND; A PLAY, IN FIVE ACTS; BY WILLIAM SHAKESPEARE.
ADAPTED TO THE STAGE WITH ADDITIONS FROM DRYDEN AND
DAVENANT, BY J. P. KEMBLE. AS PERFORMED AT THEATRE
ROYAL, COVENT GARDEN. PRINTED UNDER THE AUTHORITY OF
THE MANAGERS FROM THE PROMPT BOOK. WITH REMARKS BY
MRS. INCHBALD. LONDON: Printed FOR HURST, ROBINSON,
AND CO. 90 CHEAPSIDE. [c. 1816]. 12⁰. Pp. 72.

Prefatory Materials:
  Remarks, pp. 3-5.
  Dramatis Personae.

152. Another edition of *The Tempest*: In *Dramatic Works*,
      1872-74. V, 395-521. Rpt. New York: Russell &
      Russell, 1964.

      Prefatory Material:
        Introduction, pp. 397-412.

            This is a reprint of the 1674 edition, which
      is the Shadwell operatic version of the
      Davenant-Dryden *Tempest*.

153. Another edition of *The Tempest*: In *The Dramatic Works
      of John Dryden With a Life of the Author by Sir
      Walter Scott, Bart.* Vol. III. Ed. George Saintsbury.
      Edinburgh: William Paterson, 1882. Pp. 99-226.

            Though Saintsbury cites as his source the
      1670 edition, he reprints the 1674 edition with the
      operatic additions by Shadwell. In his introduction,
      Saintsbury cites Scott, who reviews Davenant's life
      and comments on *Gondibert*, "his greatest performance,
      [which] incurred, when first published, more ridicule,
      and in latter times more neglect, than its merit
      deserves." Saintsbury then discusses this version of
      The Tempest, being careful to indicate "that very
      little of this Shakespeare travesty is Dryden's."

154. Another edition: *The Tempest. In Plays of Mr.
      William Shakespeare As Re-written or Re-arranged by
      His Successors of the Restoration Period. As
      presented at the Duke's Theatre and elsewhere circa
      1664-1669.* The Bankside Restoration Shakespeare. Ed.
      Appleton Morgan. Introd. Frederick W. Kilbourne. New
      York: New York Shakespeare Society, 1908. Pp. 5-237.

      Prefatory Material:
        Introduction, pp. vii-xi.

            In the Bankside Restoration Shakespeare,
      which was limited to two-hundred-fifty copies, the
      Davenant-Dryden *Tempest* was printed on odd-numbered
      pages, facing equivalent scenes from Shakespeare's
      play on the even-numbered pages. Because the

adaptation retains only about one-third of the
original, many blank pages are scattered through the
two plays.

155.   Another edition: *The Tempest: A Comedy By William
        Shakespeare [Reprinted from the Folio of 1623]
        Together with the Text Revised and Rewritten By John
        Dryden and William D'Avenant* .... Introd. Sir Sidney
        Lee. Ed. Willis Vickery. Cleveland: Rowfant Club,
        1911. Pp. 75-180.

        Prefatory Materials:
          Portrait of Dryden, facing p. 77.
          Title page of 1670 edition, p. 77.

                This beautiful, leather-bound volume
        presents the Davenant-Dryden adaptation. Probably
        because it was a limited edition published in
        Cleveland, it was unknown to Montague Summers, who
        stated that his reprint of the 1670 edition in
        Shakespeare Adaptations (1922) was the first since
        1701. In Section VI of the introduction, Sir Sidney
        Lee discusses the Davenant-Dryden adaptation and that
        of Shadwell (1674), as these relate to Shakespeare's
        original play, and he attributes the various changes
        to the new theater conditions of the Restoration.
        Both Lee and Vickery, the editor, respect Davenant,
        Lee describing him as "an accomplished poet and
        dramatist," and Vickery praising him as "a brilliant
        dramatist." Yet, both refer to the adaptation as
        vandalism.

156.   Another edition of *The Tempest*: In *Shakespeare
        Adaptations*. Ed. Montague Summers. 1922. Rpt. New
        York: Benjamin Blom, 1966.

                Summers reprints the 1670 edition, claiming
        it is now available for the first time since Tonson
        published the two-volume Dryden in 1701. His claim
        fails to consider the Rowfant Edition of 1911. See
        item 155. In his introduction, Summers describes the
        development of Restoration theater, especially as it
        relates to Shakespeare, Davenant's adaptations, and
        The Tempest, or the Enchanted Island. He gives
        special attention to the contributions of Davenant,
        Dryden, and later Shadwell, and to the stage history
        until Macready.

157.   Another edition of *The Tempest*: In *The Complete Works
        of Thomas Shadwell*. Ed. Montague Summers. London:
        Fortune, 1927. II, 183-269.

            Summers reprints the 1674 edition, which is
        the Shadwell operatic version of the Davenant-Dryden
        Tempest. In his introduction, he presents a general
        statement about the 1670 and 1674 editions and directs
        the reader to his *Shakespeare Adaptations*. He follows
        with a stage history of the adaptation from 1667 until
        the early nineteenth century.

158.   Another edition: *The Tempest or the Enchanted Island*.
        In *Dryden: The Dramatic Works*, vol. II. Ed. Montague
        Summers. London: Nonesuch, 1931. Pp. 143-229.

        Prefatory Materials:
          Source, pp. 145-47.
          Theatrical history, pp. 148-51.

            Summers reprints the Shadwell operatic
        edition of 1674, which is an adaptation of the
        Davenant-Dryden *Tempest*. In his introductory
        comments, he details the differences between these
        versions and surveys their stage history until
        Macready returned the play to Shakespeare in 1838.

159.   Another edition of *The Tempest*: In *Five Restoration
        Adaptations of Shakespeare*. Ed. Christopher Spencer.
        Urbana: Univ. of Illinois Press, 1965. Pp. 109-99.

            Spencer reprints the 1674 edition of *The
        Tempest, or the Enchanted Island*, which is the
        Davenant-Dryden text with the operatic alterations and
        additions by Shadwell. Spencer provides full notes
        and a discussion of the relevant texts.

160.   Another edition of *The Tempest*: In *The Works of John
        Dryden*. Vol X. Ed. Maximillian E. Novak and George
        Robert Guffey. Berkeley: Univ. of California Press,
        1970. Pp. 1-104.

            The editors present a full commentary on
        details surrounding the play, including stage history,
        the relationship between Davenant and Dryden, and
        their alterations to the play. The editors also
        provide detailed notes.

161. Adaptation of *The Tempest*: Vivian Summers, ed. *The Tempest: A Performing Script from Shakespeare's Play and the 1674 Adaptation.* Sevenoaks: Novello, 1974. Pp. 40.

     Summers's adaptation of Shadwell's 1674 version of the Davenant-Dryden *Tempest* substitutes as much of Shakespeare's original text as possible and retains appropriate dramatic settings for Purcell's music.

162. *The Distresses* [Perhaps *The Spanish Lovers*; see item 55]. In *Works*, 1673. Part III, 34-62. Facs. 2 vols. New York: Benjamin Blom, 1968.

     Greg 832; EAP 1642-1700 [*Works*, 1673]; STC D320 [*Works*, 1673]; UMI 207:9 [*Works*, 1673].

     Stationers' Register:
       1646 Sept. 4. Ent. for Robinson and Mozeley "these sevrall Tragedies & Comedies ..." Distresses by William Davenant.
       1658 Feb. 12. Ent. J. Crooke ... *The Distresses*.
       1672 Oct. 14. Assigned by Ann Moseley, wid. of Humphrey Moseley, "right and tytle" to *The Distresses*.
       1673 Jan. 30. Assigned from the estate of the late Humphrey Robinson to J. Martyn and H. Herringmen *The Distresses*.
       1683 Aug. 21. Assigned by wid. of J. Martin to R. Scott, Davenant's *The Distresses*.

     The Distresses may be *The Spanish Lovers*, which was licensed for performance by Sir Henry Herbert, Nov. 30, 1639. See Greg, II, p. 926,n.

163. Another edition of *The Distresses*: In *Dramatic Works*, 1872-74. IV, 281-363. Rpt. New York: Russell & Russell, 1964.

     Prefatory Material:
     Introductory note, p. 283.

164. *The Fair Favorite.* In *Works*, 1673. Part III, 87-111. Facs. 2 vols. New York: Benjamin Blom, 1968.

     Greg 834; EAP 1642-1700 [*Works*, 1673]; STC D320 [*Works*, 1673]; UMI 207:9 [*Works*, 1673].

Stationers' Register:
  1646 Sept. 4.   Ent. (H.) Robinson and (H.) Mozeley,
    several tragedies and comedies: lic.   Langley:
    Fair Favourite, by Sir Wm. Davenant.
  1672 Oct. 14.   Tr. wid. of H. Moseley to H.
    Herringman, saluo iure cuilibet: The Faire
    Favourite.
  1673 Jan. 30.   Tr. exor. H. Robinson to J. Martyn
    and H. Herringman: Davenants Fair Favourite,
    halfe.
  1683 Aug. 21.   Tr. wid. of J. Martin to R. Scott,
    saluo iure cuiuscunque: Davenants Faire Favorite,
    a fourth.

165.   Another edition of *The Fair Favorite*:   In *Dramatic
       Works*, 1872-74.   IV, 201-80.   Rpt. New York: Russell
       & Russell, 1964.

       Prefatory Material:
       Introduction, p. 203.

166.   *THE Law against Lovers*.   In *Works*, 1673.   Part II,
       272-329.   Facs. 2 vols. New York: Benjamin Blom,
       1968.   Rpt. with introd. by A.M. Gibbs.   London:
       Cornmarket, 1970.

       EAP 1642-1700 [*Works*, 1673]; STC D320 [*Works*, 1673];
         UMI 207:9 [*Works*, 1673].

             The Law Against Lovers is Davenant's altered
       version of Shakespeare's *Measure for Measure*
       intermingled with the Beatrice and Benedick plot from
       Much Ado About Nothing.   In an apparent effort to
       eliminate objectionable material, he cut Mistress
       Overdone and changed the emphasis of Angelo's
       propositioning of Isabella so that it becomes a test
       of her virtue, not an attempted seduction.

167.   Another edition of *The Law Against Lovers*:   In
       Dramatic Works, 1872-74.   V, 109-211.   Rpt. New York:
       Russell & Russell, 1964.

       Prefatory Material:
       Introduction, pp. 111-14.

168.   Another edition of *The Law Against Lovers*:   With
       Measure for Measure. *In Plays of Mr. William*

*Shakespeare As Re-written or Re-arranged by His
Successors of the Restoration Period. As presented at
the Duke's Theatre and elsewhere circa 1664-1669.* The
Bankside Restoration Shakespeare. Ed. Appleton
Morgan. Introd. Frank Carpenter. New York: New York
Shakespeare Society, 1908. Pp. 3-91.

Prefatory Material:
  Introduction, pp. vii-xii.

          In the Bankside Restoration Shakespeare,
which was limited to two-hundred-fifty copies, *The Law
Against Lovers* was printed on odd-numbered pages,
facing equivalent scenes from *Measure for Measure* on
even-numbered pages. Because the adaptation also
includes scenes from *Much Ado About Nothing*, which are
not reprinted, and because there are substantial
alterations from Shakespeare's *Measure for Measure*,
many blank pages are found in this volume.

169. Another edition of *The Law Against Lovers*: In "Sir
      William Davenant's *The Law Against Lovers*." Ed. J. H.
      Gellert. Diss. Birmingham 1976.

170. *News from Plimouth.* In *Works*, 1673. Part III, 1-33. Facs.
      2 vols. New York: Benjamin Blom, 1968.

      Greg 831; EAP 1642-1700 [*Works*, 1673]; STC D320
      [*Works*, 1673]; UMI 207:9 [*Works*, 1673].

      Stationers' Register:
        1646 Sept. 4. Ent. (H.) Robinson and (H.)
          Moseley, several tragedies and comedies: lic.
          Langley: News from Plymouth, by Sir Wm. Davenant.
        1672 Oct. 14. Tr. wid. of H. Moseley to H.
          Herringman, saluo iure cuilibet: Newes from
          Plymouth.
        1673 Jan. 30. Tr. exor. of H. Robinson to J. Martyn
          and H. Herringman: Davenants Newes from Plymouth,
          halfe.
        1683 Aug. 21. Tr. wid. of J. Martin to R. Scott,
          saluo iure cuiuscunque: Davenants News from
          Plymouth, a fourth.

          Davenant probably wrote this Jonsonian
satire as a "Vacation Play" for the vigorous audience
of the Globe. He focused on a group of lively sailors

ashore at Portsmouth, not Plymouth, where they seek
fun and fortune with women, drink, and song. Davenant
aims his satire at dueling, marriage, the provinces,
and his Blackfriars' audience, which had left the City
to avoid the summer's heat.

171.   Another edition of *News from Plymouth*: In *Dramatic
        Works*, 1872-74. IV, 105-99. Rpt. New York: Russell &
        Russell, 1964.

        Prefatory Material:
          Introductory note, p. 107.

172.   Another edition: *News From Plymouth. Commedia*: Testo
        inglese e traduzione italiana a fronte a cura di.
        Trans. Anna Maria Crino. Verona: Fiorini, 1972. Pp.
        173.

        Prefatory Material:
          Introduction, pp. 1-13.

            Crino reprints the Maidment and Logan text
        and, on facing pages, her own translation into
        Italian. In her introduction, she presents the few
        available facts on the stage history, a bibliographic
        note, and a review of Davenant's life and works
        including comment on the operas and the adaptations.
        She concludes with further comment on *News from
        Plymouth*.

173.   *THE Play-house to be Let*. In *Works*, 1673. Part II,
        67-119. Facs. 2 vols. New York: Benjamin Blom,
        1968.

        EAP 1642-1700 [*Works*, 1673]; STC D320 [*Works*, 1673];
          UMI 207:9 [*Works*, 1673].

            Langbaine described *A Playhouse to be Let* as
        "several Pieces of different kinds handsomely tackt
        together." Act I, set in Davenant's own playhouse
        during the summer, depicts the company determining
        what they will stage to attract an audience to relieve
        the seasonal financial problems. The remaining acts
        are the results of the auditions. Act II, a farce, is
        a translation of Moliere's *Sganarelle, ou le Cocu
        imaginarie*, acted by a company of French actors; Acts
        III and IV are revivals of two of Davenant's

Interregnum operas, *The History of Sir Francis Drake*
and *The Cruelty of the Spaniards in Peru*; and Act V is
a burlesque of Mrs. Katherine Philips' *Pompey, a
Tragedy*, which had been produced elaborately at the
Smock Alley Theatre in Dublin.

174. Another edition of *The Playhouse to be Let*: In
      Dramatic Works, 1872-74. IV, 1-104. Rpt. New York:
      Russell & Russell, 1964.

      Prefatory Material:
        Introduction, pp. 3-13.

175. *The Siege* [Perhaps *The Colonel*]. In *Works*, 1673.
      Part III, 63-86. Facs. 2 vols. New York: Benjamin
      Blom, 1968.

      Greg 833; EAP 1642-1700 [*Works*, 1673]; STC D320
        [*Works*, 1673]; UMI 207:9 [*Works*, 1673].

      Stationers' Register:
        1653 Sept. 9. Ent. (H.) Moseley: includes
          Davenant's *The Siege* in a list of about forty
          plays.
        1672 Oct. 14. Assigned by Ann Moseley, widow of
          Humphrey Moseley, "right and tytle" to *The Siege*.

              The Siege is believed to be the same play as
      The Colonel, which was licensed for performance by Sir
      Henry Herbert on July 22, 1629; yet this
      identification is doubtful. See Greg, 927.

176. Another edition of *The Siege*: In *Dramatic Works*,
      1872-74. IV, 365-437. Rpt. New York: Russell &
      Russell, 1964.

      Prefatory Material:
        Introduction, p. 367.

177. Songs from *Macbeth*: "Speak, Sister, speak; is the
      deed done?" and "Let's have a Dance upon the Heath."
      In Macbeth: A TRAGEDY. ACTED At the *DUKES THEATRE
      LONDON*, Printed for *William Cademan* at the *Popes-Head*
      in the *New Exchange*, in the Strand. 1673. 4º. Pp.
      67. Facs. London: Cornmarket, 1969.

      STC S2929.

Although the text is Shakespeare's, not
Davenant's, the two songs which are printed in Act II
probably are by Davenant. For a discussion of the
authorship of the songs, see *1972*:Gibbs, p. lxxvii.

178. *Macbeth*: Reprint of the Songs (with music by Matthew
      Locke). In The Original *Songs Airs & Choruses* which
      were introduced in the *TRAGEDY of* MACBETH in Score
      Composed by *MATTHEW LOCKE* Chapel Organist to *Queen
      Catherine* Consort to *King Charles* II. Revised &
      Corrected by *Dr Boyce*, Dedicated to DAVID GARRICK
      Esqr. LONDON Printed and Sold by IOHN IOHNSTON at No
      11 York street COVENT GARDEN [1770].

      Prefatory Material:
        Dedicatory letter to David Garrick from John
        Johnston.

179. MACBETH, A TRAGAEDY. With all the ALTERATIONS,
      AMENDMENTS, ADDITIONS AND NEW SONGS. *As it is now
      Acted at the* Dukes Theatre. *LONDON.* Printed for *P.
      Chetwin*, and are to be Sold by most Booksellers, 1674.
      4⁰. Pp. 66.

      Gregg 356, n.; STC S2930; UMI 297:28; EAP
      1642-1700.

      Prefatory Materials:
        The Argument, sig. A2.
        The Persons' Names, sig. A2^v.

      This is Davenant's version that was the
      Macbeth generally performed from the mid-1660s until
      1744 when Garrick restored Shakespeare's text to the
      stage.

180. Another edition: MACBETH, A TRAGEDY: With all the
      ALTERATIONS, AMENDMENTS, ADDITIONS, AND NEW SONGS. *As
      it is now Acted at the Dukes Theatre, LONDON*: Printed
      for *A. Clark*, and are to be sold by most Booksellers,
      1674. 4⁰. Pp. 60. Facs. London: Cornmarket,
      1969.

      STC S2931.

181. Another edition: MACBETH, A TRAGEDY: With all the
      ALTERATIONS: AMENDMENTS, ADDITIONS, AND NEW SONGS.
      As it is now Acted at the Theatre Royal. LONDON,

Printed for *Hen. Herringman*, and are to be sold by
Jos. Knight and *Fra. Saunders*, at the *Blue Anchor* in
the Lower Walk of the New-Exchange, 1687. 4⁰. Pp.
60.

STC S2932; UMI 297:29.

182. Another edition: MACBETH, A TRAGEDY: With all the
ALTERATIONS, AMENDMENTS, ADDITIONS AND NEW SONGS. *As
it is now Acted at the Theatre Royal*. LONDON, Printed
for *H. Herringman*, and *R. Bentley*, and are to be sold
by Thomas Chapman at the *Chyrugeons Arms* over against
the *Mewse* near Charing-Cross. 1687. 4⁰. Pp. 60.

STC S2987.

183. Another edition: MACBETH, A TRAGEDY With all the
ALTERATIONS, AMENDMENTS, ADDITIONS, AND NEW SONGS. As
it is now Acted at the Theatre Royal. *LONDON*.
Printed for *H. Herringman*, and *R. Bentley*; and sold
by *R. Bentley, J. Tonson*, and *F*. Sanders. 1695. 4⁰.
Pp. 60.

STC S2935; UMI 297:30.

184. Another edition: MACBETH. A TRAGEDY. With all the
ALTERATIONS, AMENDMENTS, ADDITIONS, AND *NEW SONGS*. As
it is now Acted at the QUEEN'S-THEATRE. *LONDON*:
Printed for *J. Tonson*: And Sold by *John Phillips* at
the *Black Bull* over-against the *Royal Exchange* in
Cornhill. 1710. 4⁰. Pp. 52.

Prefatory Material:
  Dramatis Personae, sig. A2ᵛ.

        The cast included Betterton as Macbeth, and
Wilks as Macduff.

185. Another edition: MACBETH. A TRAGEDY. With all the
ALTERATIONS, *AMENDMENTS*, ADDITIONS, AND *NEW SONGS*. As
it is now Acted at the QUEEN'S-THEATRE. LONDON:
Printed for *J. Tonson: And Sold by John Philips* at
the *Black Bull* over-against the *Royal Exchange* in
Cornhill. 1710. 4⁰. Pp. 52.

        This edition resembles closely the preceding
entry. However, the title pages differ because

"Phillips" becomes "Philips" in this edition, and the hyphen separating "QUEEN'S-THEATRE" is shorter and placed lower than in the preceding entry. Also, on three occasions, pages are misnumbered in this edition, and there are numerous misprints.

186. Another edition: MACBETH A TRAGEDY. With all the Alterations and New Songs, As it was Acted at the Theatre-Royal In DRURY-LANE. [Dramatis Personae are listed on the title page.] Printed in the Year 1710. Pp. 24.

   A manuscript note on the Folger Library copy terms this a "Unique copy of *Macbeth*."

187. Another edition: MACBETH: A TRAGEDY; As it is now Acted at the New Theatre of EDINBURGH. *Written by* Mr. SHAKESPEAR, *with Alterations* by Mr. TATE. EDINBURGH: Printed by T. and W. RUDDIMANS for ALLAN RAMSAY, and sold at his Shop, 1731. Pp. 72.

   Prefatory Material:
     Dramatis Personae.

   The Folger Catalogue notes, "Although Tate's name appears on the title page, this is the Davenant version, and Tate had nothing to do with it."

188. Another edition of *Macbeth*: In *Dramatic Works*, 1872-74. V, 295-394. Rpt. New York: Russell & Russell, 1964.

   Prefatory Materials:
     Introduction, pp. 297-313.
     The Persons' Names, p. 314.

189. Another edition: *Macbeth*. In *A New Variorum Edition of Shakespeare*, vol. II. Ed. Horace Howard Furness. Philadelphia: Lippincott, 1874. Pp. 303-55.

   As part of his extensive explanatory material following Shakespeare's text, Furness reprints the 1674 edition, which contains Davenant's additions and alterations. In subsequent editions, Furness reprints only Davenant's additions, with line references from the First Folio.

190. Another edition: In *Davenant's Macbeth from the Yale Manuscript: An Edition with a Discussion of the Relation of Davenant's Text to Shakespeare's*. Ed. Christopher Spencer. New Haven: Yale Univ. Press, 1961. Pp. 226.

      Spencer argues effectively that the Yale manuscript was copied from Davenant's first draft of the adaptation of *Macbeth*, which consisted of a copy of the 1623 folio edition of the play with words crossed out and additions made in the margins or, in the case of the four new scenes, on separate sheets. Spencer provides an extensive introduction in which he discusses the manuscript and the printed texts by both Shakespeare and Davenant, and he provides lists of variants among the editions and the manuscript.

191. Another edition of *Macbeth*: In *Five Restoration Adaptations of Shakespeare*. Ed. Christopher Spencer. Urbana: Univ. Illinois Press, 1965. Pp. 33–107.

      Spencer reprints the 1674 edition of Davenant's *Macbeth*. In addition, he provides notes and a discussion of the relevant texts.

192. *Hamlet*: THE TRAGEDY OF HAMLET Prince of Denmark. As it is now Acted at his Highness the Duke of York's Theatre. By WILLIAM SHAKESPEARE. LONDON: Printed by *Andr. Clark*, for *J. Martyn*, and *H. Herringman*, at the Bell in St. *Paul's* Church-Yard, and at the Blue Anchor in the lower Walk of the New-Exchange, 1676. 4°. Pp. 88.

Greg 197i; STC S2950; UMI 297:41.

      Davenant believed Shakespeare's version "too long to be conveniently Acted" and cut about twenty percent, including Hamlet's advice to the players and the characters Cornelius, Voltimand, and Reynaldo. He also cut the soliloquies severely. Yet, Pepys, who saw the play six times in seven years, praised it and its leading actor, Betterton, while Downes, the prompter, testified to the play's financial and popular success when he wrote, "No succeeding Tragedy for several Years got more Reputation, or Money to the Company than this."

193. Another edition of *Hamlet*: THE TRAGEDY OF HAMLET
      Prince of Denmark. As it is now Acted at his Highness
      the Duke of York's Theatre. By WILLIAM SHAKESPEARE.
      LONDON: Printed by Andr. Clark, for J. Martyn, and H.
      Herringman, at the Bell in St. Paul's Church-Yard,
      and at the Blue Anchor in the lower Walk of the New
      Exchange, 1676. 4°. Pp. 88.

      Greg 197j; STC S2951; UMI 823:5.

              This is, with three variations, a
      line-by-line reprint of the other 1676 edition. The
      most obvious variation is that the reprint requires
      four rather than three lines for the imprint.
      Pagination and signatures are identical, although the
      compositor of the reprint has introduced a
      considerable number of accidentals.

194. Another edition of *Hamlet*: THE TRAGEDY OF HAMLET
      Prince of Denmark. As it is now Acted at his Highness
      the Duke of *York's* Theatre. BY *WILLIAM SHAKESPEARE*.
      LONDON: Printed for *H. Heringman* and *R. Bentley*, at
      the Blew Anchor the *New* Exchange, and in
      Russel-street in *Covent-Garden*. 1683. 4°. Pp. 88.

      STC S2952; UMI 297:42.

195. Another edition of *Hamlet*: THE TRAGEDY OF HAMLET
      Prince of Denmark. As it is now Acted at the Theatre
      Royal, by their Majesties Servants. BY *WILLIAM
      SHAKESPEARE*. *LONDON*: Printed for *H. Herringman*, and
      R. Bentley, and are sold by *R. Bentley, J. Tonson, T.
      Bennet*, and *F. Sanders*. MDCXCV. 4°. Pp. 82.

      STC S2954.

              This is a reprint with only slight changes
      of the 1676 edition.

196. Another edition of *Hamlet*: THE TRAGEDY OF HAMLET
      Prince of Denmark. As it is now Acted at the Theatre
      Royal, by their Majesties Servants. BY *WILLIAM
      SHAKESPEARE*. *LONDON*: Printed for *R. Bentley*, in
      Russel-street in Covent-Garden. MDCXCV. 4°. Pp.
      82.

      STC S2955.

197.   Another edition of *Hamlet*: THE TRAGEDY OF HAMLET
       Prince of Denmark. As it is now Acted by Her
       MAJESTIES Servants. BY *WILLIAM SHAKESPEARE*. LONDON:
       Printed for *Rich. Wellington*, at the *Dolphin* and
       Crown in *Paul's* Church-Yard, and *E. Rumball* in
       Covent-Garden. 1703. 4⁰. Pp. 82. Facs. London:
       Cornmarket, 1969.

       Prefatory Material:
          Contains Davenant's note to the reader that the
          play is too long to be conveniently acted.

198.   THE SEVENTH And Last CANTO OF THE THIRD BOOK OF
       GONDIBERT, Never yet Printed. By Sir *William
       Davenant. LONDON*, Printed for *William Miller* and
       Joseph Watts at the *Gilded Acorn* in St. Paul's
       Church-Yard, over against the little North Door, 1685.
       8⁰. Pp. 45. Facs. In *Gondibert: An Heroick Poem,
       Written by Sr. William D'Avenant.* Menston: Scolar,
       1970.

       STC D338.

       Prefatory Materials:
          Introductory note, sigs. A2–A2ᵛ.
          To Sir William Davenant, in Answer to the Seventh
             Canto of the Third Book of His Gondibert,
             Dedicated to my Father, pp. 4–8.
          Dedicated to Charles Cotton, Esq., p. 9.

                    See *1940*: McManaway.

199.   THE TRAGEDY OF JULIUS CAESAR: With the DEATH of
       Brutus and *Cassius*; Written Originally by SHAKSPEAR,
       And since alter'd by Sir WILLIAM DAVENANT and JOHN
       DRYDEN, late Poets Laureat. As it is now Acted by His
       Majesty's Company of Comedians at the Theatre-Royal.
       To which is prefix'd, The Life of JULIUS CAESAR,
       abstracted from *Plutarch* and *Suetonius*. *London*,
       Printed for W. CHETWOOD at *Cato's* Head in
       Russel-Court, near the *Theatre-Royal*, and R. FRANCKLIN
       at the *Sun* over-against St. Dunstan's Church in
       Fleet-street. MDCCXIX. 4⁰. Pp. 77.

       Prefatory Materials:
          To Robert Wilks, Esq. From W. Chetwood, pp. [v–vi].
          Life of Caesar, pp. vii–ix.
          Dramatis Personae, p. [x].

The text is close to Shakespeare's in the
First Folio. Fewer than one hundred lines have been
cut, although these include the assassination of
Cinna, a poet (III.iii). Stage directions for
thunder, lightning, and shouting have been added and,
most significantly, Caesar's Ghost has been
reintroduced in Act V, after the lines, "O Julius
Caesar, thou art mighty yet!/Thy spirit walks
abroad..." (V. iii.94-95). Van Lennep doubts that
Davenant had anything to do with these alterations
because *Julius Caesar* was the property of Killigrew's
rival company. See *1946*: Van Lennep. The Folger
copy with the price on the title page appears to have
been a separate publication. The play was also
included in *A Collection of Plays by Eminent Hands; in
four volumes*. London: W. Mears, 1719. I, 1-77.

C. MISCELLANEOUS WORKS

Note: The section includes poems from seventeenth-century miscellanies, prologues to plays by other playwrights, and commendatory poems. See *1972*: Gibbs, "Index of Titles."

200. THE FAITHFVLL SHEPHERDESSE. ACTED AT SOMERSET House before the KING and QVEENE on Twelfe night last, 1633. And divers times since with great applause at the Private House in Black-Friers, by his Majesties Servants. *Written by* IOHN FLETCHER. The third Edition, with Addition. LONDON, Printed by *A. M.* for *Richard Meighen*, next to the Middle Temple in Fleet-street. 1634. 4°.

Poetry by Davenant:
   "A Broyling Lambe on Paris chiefe altar lies," sig. A3ᵛ.

   The poem was reprinted in the 1656 and 1665 editions of the play and in *Works*, 1673. The lines were introduced with the following brief note: "This Dialogue newly added, was spoken by way of Prologue to both their Majesties at the first acting of this Pastoral at *Somerset-house* on Twelfe-night 1633."

201. ANNALIA DVBRENSIA. *LONDON*, Printed by Robert Raworth, for Matthew Walbancke. 1636. 4°.

Poetry by Davenant:
   "Vpon the yeerely celebration of Mr. ROBERT DOVERS Olimpick Games vpon *Cotswold-Hills*."

   Not all copies of the 1636 edition include the unsigned poem by Davenant, which is the last poem among the thirty-five that comprise this strange book. The poem is attributed to Davenant because it was included in *Madagascar* (1638). Among the poets who pay tribute to Dover are Ben Jonson, Michael Drayton, Thomas Randolph, and Thomas Heywood. Subsequent editions which include the Davenant poem are by A.B. Grosart (1877), E.R. Vyvyan (1878), and Christopher Whitfield (*Robert Dover and the Cotswold Games: Annalia Dubrensia*. London: Sotheran, 1962).

202. ROMVLVS AND TARQVIN *First Written in Italian* By the *Marques Virgilio Malvezzi*: And now *taught English* by *H: Lᵈ Cary. of Lepingto[n] the second Edition.* LONDON Printed *by I. H.* for Iohn Benson, *and are to be*

sould at his Shopp under St *Dunstons* Church Fleet
street. 1638. 12⁰.

STC 17220; UMI 851.

Poetry by Davenant:
  "To the Right Honourable his much esteemed friend,
    Lord CARY of Lepington, upon his Translation of
    Malvezzi," sigs. A5ᵛ-A6.

        Davenant's was the third of six commendatory
poems included in this second edition of Carey's
translation. The others were by Suckling, Carew,
Townshend, Thomas Wortley, and Robert Stapylton. The
poem was included in *Madagascar*.

203. THE ACADEMY OF Complements. Wherein, *Ladies,*
      Gentlewomen, Schollers, and *Strangers* may accommodate
      with gentile Ceremonies, Complementall amorous high
      expressions, and forms of speaking or writing of
      Letters most in fashion ... The seventh Edition, ...
      1646. 12⁰.

      STC G1401B

      Poetry by Davenant:
        "The Philosopher and the Lover; to a Mistress
          dying."

        The poem appeared in 1630 in the fifth act
of Davenant's *The Just Italian* as "A Song betweene two
Boyes." It was reprinted with this title in the 1650
edition of *The Academy of Complements* and again as
"The Philosopher and the Lover; to a Mistress dying,"
in *Works*, 1673. The 1646 edition is attributed to
John Gough.

204. The foure Ages OF ENGLAND: OR, The Iron Age. *With*
      other select POEMS. Written by Mʳ. A. Cowley. ...
      Printed in the Yeere 1648.

      STC C6671; UMI 935:17.

      Poetry by Davenant:
        "To my Lord Lieutenant of Ireland," pp. 61-62.

        The poem was included in the editions of
1675 and 1705, and in *Poems on Several Occasions* in
Works, 1673.

205. THE WOMAN HATER, OR THE Hungry courtier. A Comedy, As
it hath been Acted by his Majesties Servants with
great Applause. Written by FRANCIS BEAUMONT AND JOHN
FLETCHER. Gent. ... *LONDON*, Printed for *Humphrey*
Moseley, and are to be sold at his Shop at the *Princes*
Arms in St. *Pauls* Church-yard. 1649. 4°.

STC B1619; UMI 857:21.

Poetry by Davenant:
"The Prologue to the *Woman-hater*, or the Hungry
Courtier."

In *Madagascar*, the poem is entitled
"Prologue to a reviv'd Play of Mr. Fletcher's."
Gibbs describes the poem from the third edition, while
the title page recorded here is from the "Second
Edition-Second Issue," according to a manuscript entry
above the imprint. The title page of the third
edition differs from this "Second Issue" because the
word "lately" has been added before "Acted."

206. THE FABLES OF AESOP Paraphras'd in Verse, and adorn'd
with Sculpture, *By* JOHN OGILBY LONDON, Printed by
Thomas Warren for Andrew Crook, at the Green Dragon in
St. *Pauls* Church-yard. 1651. 4°.

STC A689.

Poetry by Davenant:
"To my Friend Mr. Ogilby."

An unmarked signature with commendatory
poems by Davenant and James Shirley was apparently
inserted in signature A after Ogilby's dedicatory
letter to Lord Beauchamp. In his letter Davenant
praises Aesop whose "Satyric strain Doth spare the
Person though the Vice is slain" and Ogilby in whose
"Verse, methinks, I Aesop see Lesse bound than when
his Master made him free."

207. THEOPHILA, OR LOVES SACRIFICE. A Divine Poem.
WRITTEN BY E[dward]. B[enlowes]. Esq; Several *Parts*
thereof set to fit Aires by Mr J. *JENKENS*. ... LONDON:
Printed by *R. N.* Sold by *Henry Seile* in *Fleetstreet*,
and *Humphrey Moseley* at the Princes Arms in *S. Pauls*
Church-yard. 1652. Fol.

STC B1879; UMI 306.

Poetry by Davenant:
   "TO THE AUTHOR Upon His Divine Poem," signed "WILL.
   DAVENANT, Tower, May 13, 1652," sigs. (c)-(d)^v.

         Davenant's poem was inserted with a letter
by W. Dennie between sigs. C and C2. The insert,
which was marked (c) and (d), consisted of one full
signature (c) and one half signature, or single leaf
(d), allowing for a total of six folio pages. Dennie
used two, Davenant four. A valuable comment on
Davenant is found in the same volume in Th. Pestill's
commendatory poem. The key passage follows:

   Beaumont and *Fletcher* coyn'd a golden *Way*,
   T'expresse, suspend, and passionate a *Play*.
   Nimble and Pleasant are all Nations there,
   For two *Intelligences* rul'd the *Spheare*.

   Both *Sock* and *Buskin* sunk with them, and then
   Davenant and *Denham* buoy'd them up agen,
   Beyond these *Pillers* Some think nothing is:
   Great BRITAINS *Wit* stands in a Precipice.

208.   WIT AND DROLLERY, JOVIAL POEMS. Never before Printed.
       by Sir *J*[*ohn*]. M[ennis]. *Ja*[*mes*]: *S*[*mith*]. Sir
       W[*illiam*]. *D*[*avenant*]. *J*[*ohn*]. *D*[*onne*]. And other
       admirable Wits. London: *For Nath*: Brook, 1656. 4o.

STC W3131.

Poetry by Davenant:
   "The Long Vacation."

         "The Long Vacation" was first published in
this 1656 edition and was reprinted in the 1661 and
1682 editions. The version that appears in *Works*,
1673, has been altered considerably. The poem, a
poetic burlesque of a London gambler, starving
prostitute, and penniless actor, also depicts a
destitute writer, perhaps Davenant himself, whose
audience had fled to the country to escape the
summer's heat.

209.   Another edition of "The Long Vacation": Wit and
       Drollery, *JOVIALL POEMS* Corrected and much amended,

with ADDITIONS, By Sir J[ohn]. M[ennis]. Ja[mes]:
S[mith]. Sir W[illiam] D[avenant]. J[ohn] D[onne],
the most refined Wits of the Age. *LONDON*, Printed for
Nath. Brook, at the Angel in Cornhil, 1661. 8⁰.

STC W3132; UMI 1112:2.

Poetry by Davenant:
  "The Long Vacation," pp. 87-93.

210. Another edition of "The Long Vacation": WIT AND
DROLLERY. Jovial Poems. Corrected and Amended, with
New Additions. *Ut Nector Ingenium*. *LONDON*, Printed
for *Obadiah Blagrave*, at the *Bear* in St. *Pauls
Church-Yard*, 1682. 8⁰.

STC W3133; UMI 993:12.

Poetry by Davenant:
  "The Long Vacation," pp. 225-31.

211. POEMS CONSISTING OF EPISTLES & EPIGRAMS, SATYRS,
EPITAPHS and ELOGIES, SONGS, and SONNETS. With
variety of other drolling Verses upon several Subjects
Composed by no body must know whom, and are to be had
every body knows where, and for somebody knows what.
LONDON, Printed for *Henry Brome* at the *Gin* in *Ivy
Lane*. 1658. 8⁰.

STC E524.

Poetry by Davenant:
  "For Mistress Porter on a New years day," p. 25.

        The volume is listed under John Eliot in the
British Museum. Under the title "For the Lady, *Olivia*
Porter. A present, upon a new-yeares day," the poem
had appeared twenty years earlier in *Madagascar*, pp.
66-67.

212. WITS INTERPRETER, THE *ENGLISH PARNASSUS*. OR, A Sure
Guide to those Admirable Accomplishments that compleat
our English Gentry.... The 2d Edition, with many new
Additions, By I[ohn]. C[otgrave].... *London*, Printed
for *N. Brook*, at the Angel in Cornhill, near the Royal
Exchange. 1662. 8⁰.

STC C6371; UMI 683:18.

Poetry by Davenant:
"A Farewell to his Mistresse, on his going to the
    Wars [Song. The Souldier going to the Field],"
    p. 200.

213. Another edition of "A Farewell to his Mistresse":
      WITS INTERPRETER. THE *ENGLISH PARNASSUS*. OR, A sure
      Guide to those Admirable Accomplishments that compleat
      our English Gentry.... The 3d Edition with many new
      Additions, By *J.C.* ... LONDON, Printed for N. Brook,
      at the *Angel* in *Cornhill*, and *Obadiah Blagrave*, at the
      Printing Press in *Little Britain*. MDCLXXI. 8⁰.

      STC C6372; UMI 683:19.

      Poetry by Davenant:
      "A Farewell to his Mistresse, on his going to the
          Wars [Song. The Souldier going to the Field],"
          p. 200.

214. THE NEW Academy OF COMPLEMENTS, ERECTED For Ladies,
      Gentlewomen, Courtiers, Gentlemen, Scholars,
      Souldiers, Citizens, Country-men, and all persons, of
      what degree soever, of both Sexes, Stored with Variety
      of Courtly and Civil Complements, Eloquent Letters of
      Love and Friendship WITH An Exact COLLECTION of the
      Newest and Choicest *SONGS* a la Mode, Both Amorous and
      Jovial, COMPILED *By the most refined Wits of the Age*.
      London: Printed for Samuel Speed, neer the
      Inner-Temple-gate in Fleetstreet. 1669. 12⁰.

      STC N529; UMI 326:4.

      Poetry by Davenant:
      "Dear Love, let me this ev'ning die," p. 253.
      "He deserved much better than so," p. 147.
      "Let's have a dance upon the heath," p. 201.
      "My Lodging it is on the cold ground," p. 146.
      "Our ruler hath got the Vertigo of State," p. 170.
      "Wake all ye dead, what Ho, what ho," p. 168.
      "Ye Fiends and Furies come along," p. 206.

              All of these but the first, "Dear Love,"
      came from Davenant's plays. "My Lodging it is on the
      cold ground" and "He deserved much better than so,"

both from *The Rivals,* were sung by Moll Davis with
such appeal that she attracted the amorous attentions
of the king.

215. Another edition of "Dear Love...," "He deserved...,"
"Let's have...," "My Lodging...," "Our ruler...,"
"Wake all...," and "Ye Fiends...": THE NEW ACADEMY OF
COMPLEMENTS ERECTED for Ladies, Gentlemen, Scholars,
Souldiers, Citizens, Countrey-men, and all persons, of
what degree soever, of both Sexes. Stored with a
variety of Courtly and Civil Complements, Eloquent
Letters of Love and Friendship. WITH An Exact
Collection of the Newest and Choicest *SONGS* a la Mode,
Both Amorous and Jovial. COMPILED By L[ord]
B[uckhurst]. *Sir* C[harles] S[edley]. *Sir* W[illiam]
D[avenant]. *and others, the most refined Wits of this
Age. London,* Printed for Tho. Rooks, at the
Ink-Bottle in *Threadneedle*-Street. 1671. 12°.

STC N530; UMI 363:9.

Poetry by Davenant:
"Dear Love, let me this ev'ning die," pp. 267-68.
"He deserved much better than so," p. 160.
"Let's have a dance upon the heath," p. 216.
"My Lodging it is on the cold ground," p. 159.
"Our ruler hath got the Vertigo of State," p.   183.
"Wake all ye dead, what Ho, what ho," p. 181.
"Ye Fiends and Furies come along," p. 200.

Although the 1671 edition is longer than the
1669 edition, the Davenant material is the same except
for the altered pagination.

216. Another edition of "Dear Love...," "He deserved...,"
"Let's have...," "My Lodging...," "Our ruler...,"
"Wake all...," and "Ye Fiends...": THE NEW ACADEMY OF
COMPLEMENTS, ERECTED For Ladies, Gentlewomen,
Courtiers, Scholars, Souldiers, Citizens, Country-men,
and all persons of what degree soever, of both Sexes.
Stored with variety of Courtly and Civil Complements,
Eloquent Letters of Love and Friendship. WITH An
Exact Collection of the Newest and Choicest SONGS *a la
Mode.* Both Amorous and Jovial. COMPILED *By* L[ord]
B[uckhurst]. *Sir* C[harles] S[edley]. *Sir* W[illiam]
D[avenant]. *and others, the most refined Wits of this
Age. London*: Printed for *George Sawbridge,* at the
Bible on Ludgate-Hill. 1681. 12°.

STC N531; UMI 611:7.

Poetry by Davenant:
  "DEar Love, let me this Ev'ning die," pp. 267-68.
  "HE deserved much better than so," p. 160.
  "LEts have a Dance upon the Heath," p. 216.
  "My Lodging it is on the cold ground," p. 159.
  "OUr Ruler hath got the Vertigo of State," pp.
    183-84.
  "Wake, all ye dead, what Ho, what Ho," pp. 181-82.
  "YOu Fiends and Furies, come along," pp. 220-21.

         The Davenant selections are the same as
those in the 1671 edition with minor changes.

217.   THE HISTORY OF THE WARRS OF FLANDERS: WRITTEN in
       ITALIAN BY THAT LEARNED AND FAMOUS Cardinal
       BENTIVOGLIO; ENGLISHED By the Right Honourable HENRY
       Earl of *MONMOUTH*, THE WHOLE WORK.   ILLUSTRATED ...
       LONDON, Printed for *D. Newman, T. Cockerill, S.
       Heydrick, C. Smith*, and *J. Edwin*, MDCLXXVIII.   Fol.

       STC B1912.

       Poetry by Davenant:
         "To the EARL of MONMOUTH: On his Translation of
           BENTIVOGLIO."

               This is one of three commendatory poems, the
       other two by Edmund Waller and Ph. Frowde.   Davenant
       praises Monmouth for his kindness in informing
       "un-languag'd Men" and for his judgment "in the choice
       of Authors" to translate.

218.   THE ACADEMY OF COMPLEMENTS WITH MANY New Additions OF
       Songs and Catches *A-la-mode* ... Composed for the use
       of *Ladies* and *Gentlewomen. By the most refined Wits
       of this Age.* London: Printed for *P. Parker* at the
       Leg and *Star* in Cornhil, 1684.   12⁰.

       STC G1406.

       Poetry by Davenant:
         "Come ye termagant Turks," p. 302.
         "Dear Love let me this Evening dy," p. 262.
         "Go thy way," p. 192.
         "My Lodging is on the cold ground," p. 268.

"Our Ruler hath got the vertigo of State," pp.
  334-35.
"Run to Loves Lott'ry! Run, Maids, and rejoyce,"
  p. 370.
"Under the Willow Shades they were," p. 240.
"Wake all ye dead what ho, what ho," p. 227.
"Ye Fiends and Furies Come Along," p. 258.

A.   SEVENTEENTH-CENTURY STUDIES: 1639-1699

1639

219.   *Conceits, Clinches, Flashes, and Whimzies; A Jest-Book of the Seventeenth Century.*   1639.

See *1640*:   Chamberlain; *1660*:   [Armstrong]; *1860*: Halliwell; *1864*:   Hazlitt; *1866*:   Hazlitt.

1640

220.   Chamberlain, Robert.   *Jocabella, or, A cabinet of Conceits.*...London: Donald Frere, 1640.   Pp. A6, B-I12, K6.

The volume contains the following joke that is based on the 1636 quarto edition of *The Wits*: "One, having a play book called the Wits which he much valued, by chance lost it: but while he was chafing and swearing about the losse of his book, in comes one of his friends, who asking the cause of his distemper, it was answered that he had lost his wits." See *1639: Conceits*; *1660*:   [Armstrong]; *1860*:   Halliwell; *1864*: Hazlitt; *1866*:   Hazlitt.

1645

221.   *The Great Assizes Holden in Parnassus By Apollo And His Assessours at Which Sessions are arraigned Mercurius Britanicus.*   London: E. Husbands, 1645.   Pp. A-F4, G1.

Davenant is rejected in the comic poem as a juryman in the trial that is to determine his literary merit.   The reason: he lacks a nose:

Hee him assur'd that all the world might know,
His art was high, although his nose was low.

See *1967: The Great*

1651

222.   Cowley, Abraham.   "To SIr William D'Avenant, Upon his two first Books of *Gondibert*, Finish'd before his Voyage to America." In *Gondibert: An Heroick Poem.* Sir

William D'Avenant. London: Thomas Newcomb for John
Holden, 1651. Pp. [91-92]. Rpt. David Gladish, ed.
Oxford: Clarendon, 1971, pp. 270-71.

The poem is forty lines of heroic couplets in
which Cowley praises and blesses Davenant before the
ill-fated voyage to the New World.

223.   Hobbes, Thomas. "The Answer of Mr. Hobbes to Sr Will.
D'avenant's *Preface* Before *Gondibert*." In *Gondibert:
An Heroick Poem*. Sr William D'avenant. London: John
Holden, 1651, pp. 71-88.

The work is the philosopher's response to
Davenant's "Preface." In it, Hobbes praises *Gondibert*:
"I never yet saw Poem, that had so much shape of Art,
health of Morality, and vigour of beauty of Expression
as this of yours."

224.   Sheppard, Samuel. *Epigrams, Theological,
Philosophical, and Romantick....* London: T.
Bucknell, 1651. Pp. 98.

The volume includes an epigram "*On Mr.*
Davenants *most excellent Tragedy of* Albovinek *of*
Lombards" (No. 30, p. 98) which places the play with
Shakespeare's *Othello* and Jonson's *Cataline*:

> *SHakespeares' Othello, Johnsons Cataline*
> Would lose their luster, were thy *Albovine*
> Placed betwixt them,
> . . . .
> This Tragedy (let who list dare dissent)
> Shall be thy everlasting Monument.

225.   Waller, Edmund. "To Sr. Will. D'Avenant, upon his two
first Books of *Gondibert*. Finish'd before his Voyage
to America." In *Gondibert: An Heroick Poem*. Sir
William Davenant. London: Thomas Newcomb for John
Holden, 1651. Pp. [89-90]. Rpt. David Gladish, ed.
Oxford: Clarendon, 1971, pp. 269-70.

The poem is forty-two lines of heroic couplets
in which Waller praises Davenant and laments his leaving
for America.

1653

26. Calvert, Cecil, Second Baron Baltimore. *The Lord
     Baltimore's Case, Concerning the Province of
     Maryland....Unto which is also annexed, a true Copy of
     a Commission from the late King's Eldest Son, to Mr.
     William Davenant, to dispossess the Lord Baltemore of
     the said Province, because of his adherence to this
     Commonwealth.* London, 1653.

         The pamphlet contains a restatement of
     Davenant's commission. It is reprinted in *Narratives of
     Early Maryland.* See *1910:* Hall.

27. *Certain Verses Written by Severall of the Authours
     Friends: to be Reprinted with the Second Edition of
     Gondibert. With Hero and Leander, the mock poem.*
     London, 1653. Rpt. *Sir William Davenant's Gondibert.*
     Ed. David F. Gladish. Oxford: Clarendon, 1971, pp.
     272-86.

         The volume is a satiric response to Davenant's
     Gondibert by the court wits. On p. 7, Denham is named
     in the poem, "Upon the Author," in the first line:
     "Denham come help me to laugh...." On page 15 another
     title page is printed as follows: "The Incomparable
     Poem Gondibert Vindicated from the Wit-Combats of Four
     Esquires, Clinias, Dametas, Sancho, and Jack Pudding.
     1653."

228. [Denham, John.] *Certain Verses Written by severall of
     the Authour's Friends; To Be Reprinted with the Second
     Edition of Gondibert. With Hero and Leander the mock
     Poem.* London: n. p., 1653. Pp. 24.

         The volume contains comic, obscene, and
     scatological poems that satirize Davenant's heroic poem.
     A number of the court wits wrote for it but two are
     identified, Denham and Jack Donne.

1656

229. M[ennes], Sir J[ohn] and J[ames] S[mith]. *Musarum
     Deliciae: Or, The Muses Recreation. Conteining
     Severall Pieces of Poetique Wit.* The second Edition.
     London: Henry Herringman, 1656. Pp. A3, 101.

The work is a collection of poems with
scatological wit. Two of them refer to Davenant.

1659

230.   Pecke, Thomas. *Parnassi Puerperium: or, Some
       well-wishes to ingenuity .... to which is annext a
       century of heroick epigrams.* London: T. Bassett,
       1659. Pp. 184.

       On p. 180 in the thirtieth epigram, Pecke
praises Davenant in *"To the Egregious Poet, Sir* Will.
Davenant," who is "more than *Atlas,* to the fainting
Stage."

1660

231.   [Armstrong, Archibald]. *A Choice Banquet of Witty
       Tests.* London, 1660. Sigs. B-K12, L6.

       The duodecimo volume contains the joke based
on the 1636 edition of *The Witts.* Another octavo edition was published in 1660 by "T. J. to be sold by Peter
Dring," which was published again in 1665 as the "second
edition." See *1639: Conceits; 1640:* Chamberlain;
1860: Halliwell; *1864:* Hazlitt; *1866:* Hazlitt.

1664

232.   Cavendish, Margaret. Princess, The Lady Marchioness
       of Newcastle. *CCXI Sociable Letters.* London: William
       Wilson, 1664. Pp. 453.

       Margaret Cavendish judges *Gondibert* to be
superior to the Homeric epics because it is "Most and
Nearest to the Natures, Humours, Actions ... and Natural
Powers, and Abilities of Men ... wherefore most of the
Heroick Poets make their chief Heroes to have the
Assistance of particular Gods and Goddesses, so as to
Impower them above the Effects of Nature...." However,
she does criticize Davenant's overwriting, which makes
the meaning difficult to discover "without often
Perusal, and Strict Examination ..." (p. 258). See
1969: Cavendish.

233. Cavendish, Margaret Lucas, Duchess of Newcastle. *The*
      Life of The Thrice Noble, High, and Puissant Prince
      William Cavendishe, Duke, Marquess, and Earl of
      Newcastle .... 1667; rpt. London: A. Maxwell, 1675.
      Pp. A3-F, 259.

         The biography of the Duke of Newcastle by his
      wife, Margaret Lucas Cavendish, was originally published
      in 1667. In the life of her husband, the Duchess writes
      of his relationship to Davenant and to Hobbes. During
      the Civil War, Newcastle was the commander in chief of
      the Royalist forces and his lieutenant-general of the
      ordnance was Davenant. See *1886*: Firth.

1668

234. Flecknoe, Richard. *Sr William D'avenant's Voyage To*
      The Other World: With His Adventures in the Poets
      Elizium. A Poetical Fiction. London: Richard
      Flecknoe, 1668. Sigs. A8. Rpt. in Edmond Malone's *The*
      Plays and Poems of William Shakespeare.... Vol. III.
      London, 1790, pp. 340-44; rpt. in A. K. Croston's
      Theatre Miscellany: Six Pieces Connected with the
      Seventeenth-Century Stage. Oxford: Basil Blackwell,
      1953, pp. 59-67.

         In his satirical attack on Davenant, Flecknoe
      incorporates others' views of the manager-playwright.
      Having been spurned by both Davenant and his players,
      Flecknoe warns the company against Davenant in the last
      lines: "Take heed hereafter how you disoblige Him, who
      can not onely write for you, but against you too." See
      1953: Flecknoe.

1669

235. Howard, Edward. "The Preface to the Reader." *The*
      Brittish Princes. London: H. Herringman, 1669, sigs.
      A4-a2.

         Howard lauds Homer and Virgil, of the past,
      and Spenser, Sir William Davenant, and Drayton, "of our
      own Country," as poets who are justly dignified by the
      "Heroick Muse." Howard praises *"Gondibert*, in which
      there are many remote and excellent thoughts, with apt

and perspicious expressions, the essential dignities of
the Muses."

1670

236. Dryden, John. "Preface to the Enchanted Island." *The
      Tempest, or The Enchanted Island. A Comedy. As It Is
      Now Acted at His Highness the Duke of York's Theatre.*
      London: Henry Herringman, 1670. Pp. A3, 84.

       Dryden praises Davenant for "so quick a
fancy....He borrowed not of any other....His corrections
were sober and judicious....I am satisfied I could never
have receiv'd so much honour in being thought the Author
of any Poem how excellent soever, as I shall from the
joining my imperfections with the merit and name of
Shakespear and Sir *William Davenant.*" Dated December 1,
1669.

1674

237. Rymer, Thomas. "The Preface of the Translator." In
      Rene Rapin. *Reflections on Aristotle's Treatise of
      Poesie, Containing The Necessary, Rational, and
      Universal Rules for the Epick, Dramatick, and other
      sorts of Poetry. With Reflections on the Works of the
      Ancient and Modern Poets, And their Faults Noted.*
      London: Herringman, 1674, sigs. A3-b2v. Rpt. in
      Critical Essays of the Seventeenth Century. Ed. J.E.
      Spingarn. Oxford: Clarendon, 1908-09, II, 168-70.

       Rymer's assessment of Davenant and his epic
poem *Gondibert* affirms the poet's position "next after
Spenser" for his wit and "extraordinary judgement."
While Rymer finds some weaknesses in Davenant's poem, he
states that "had he been pleased to finish it,
[*Gondibert*] would doubtless not have been left so open
to the attack of Criticks."

1675

238. Phillips, Edward. *Theatrum Poetarum, or A Compleat
      Collection of the Poets, Especially The Most Eminent
      of all Ages.* London: Smith, 1675. Pp. 261.

       Edward's encyclopedic survey of modern poets
and poetesses provides a flattering tribute to Davenant
shortly after the poet's death.

1676

239. Suckling, Sir John. *The Poems, Plays, Letters, etc.*
      London: H. Herringman, 1676. Pp. 558.

          The volume contains eight separate title pages
      that include works seen through press by Suckling but
      not published until after his death by his friends.
      Included are about five poems directed to Davenant, his
      close friend.

1682

240. Whitelocke, Sir Bulstrode. *Memorials of the English
      Affairs from the Beginning of the Reign of King
      Charles the First to the Happy Restauration of King
      Charles the Second.* 4 vols. London: Nathaniel
      Ponder, 1682.

          The volume provides letters and commentary on
      Davenant that enable us to fill in some of the gaps
      surrounding the poet's imprisonment in the Tower, his
      trial date, and his release.

1687

241. Langbaine, Gerard. *Momus Triumphans: Or, The
      Plagiaries of the English Stage and The Lives and
      Characters of the English Dramatick Poets.* London:
      N.C., 1687. Pp. 7, 182, [208].

          The book lists known authors alphabetically
      and gives information on plays, reputation, and other
      works by them. Davenant's is an early biographical
      account. The brief article contains some errors, but it
      offers a bibliography, some source studies, and perfor-
      mance history. *1691*: Langbaine; See *1973*: Langbaine.

242. Winstanley, William. *The Lives of the Most Famous
      Poets, or the Honour of Parnassus; in a Brief Essay of
      the Works and Writings of Above Two Hundred of them,
      from the Time of King William the Conqueror to the
      Reign of His Present Majesty, King James II.* London:
      S. Manship, 1687. Pp. a3, 221.

          On pp. 185-86, Winstanley provides an account
      of Davenant as "one of the Chiefest of *Apollo's* Sons,

for the great fluency of his Wit and Fancy." Suckling's
poem "Sessions" is quoted and readers are encouraged to
read the 1673 folio collection of Davenant's work. See
1860: Halliwell, *A Dictionary*.

1691

243.   Langbaine, Gerard. *An Account of the English
       Dramatick Poets, or, Some Observations and Remarks on
       the Lives and Writings, of All Those That Have
       Publish'd Either Comedies, Tragedies, Tragi-Comedies,
       Pastorals, Masques, Interludes, Farces, or Opera's in
       the English Tongue.* Oxford: L. L., 1691. Pp. 556.

            The 1691 volume is based upon Langbaine's *New
       Catalogue of English Plays* (London, 1688 [December
       1687]. An unauthorized edition of the *New Catalogue* had
       appeared one month earlier as *Momus Triumphans*, and a
       new revised edition by Charles Gildon was published in
       1699 with the title *The Lives and Characters of the
       English Dramatick Poets*. See *1687*: Langbaine; see *1973*:
       Langbaine.

244.   Wood, Anthony a. *Athenae Oxonienses. An Exact
       History of All the Writers and Bishops Who Have Had
       Their Education in the University of Oxford:
       1500-1690.* 2 vols. London: Thomas Bennet,
       1691-1692.

            The work is a contemporary source of
       biographical material, not only on Davenant, who is
       treated in a main entry, but also on others who touched
       his life. There are included details and stories about
       Davenant, some of them taken from Aubrey. See *1860*:
       Halliwell, *A Dictionary*.

1692

245.   Ashmole, Elias (1617-1692). See *1966*: Josten.

1694

246.   Blount, Sir Thomas Pope. *De Re Poetica; or, Remarks
       upon Poetry. With Characters and Censures of the Most
       Considerable Poets, Whether Ancient or Modern.
       Extracted Out of the Best and Choicest Criticks.*
       London: R. Bently, 1694. Pp. 377.

Pages 1-129 contain "Remarks upon Poetry."
The section on "Characters and Censures" is separately
numbered. Among the dramatists considered is Davenant
(pp. 58-65) in a biographical account with errors but in
general a favorable comment that draws and quotes
heavily from Dryden, Wood, Winstanley, Hobbes, Cowley,
and Rimer, who is more adversely critical. The account
concludes with Suckling's joke concerning Davenant's
nose from "The Sessions of the Poets."

1698

247.   Ridpath, George.   *The Stage Condemn'd*.   London: John
       Salusbury, 1698.   Pp. 216.

Ridpath, a Whig, in an attack on Davenant's
Britannia Triumphans, intersperses his detailed summary
of the masque with denunciations of the poet for
glorifying the sacreligious monarch, and of Charles I
for celebrating himself on a Sunday when he should have
been celebrating God. Ridpath also criticizes Davenant
for representing "the Graver sort" as imposters and
cheats. See *1972*: Ridpath.

1699

248.   Wright, James.   *Historia Histrionica: An Historical*
       Account of the English-Stage. Shewing the Ancient
       Use, Improvement, and Perfection. With A Short
       Discourse of the English Stage, by Richard Flecknoe.
       London: G. Groom, 1699.   Pp. 52.   Rpt.   New York and
       London: Garland, 1974.

Wright mentions scenes that Davenant
introduced and that Betterton continued.

1701

249. Warwick, Sir Philip. *Memoirs of the Reign of King Charles I with a Continuation to the Happy Restauration of King Charles II.* London: Ri. Chitwell, 1701. Pp. 437.

       The work offers an authentic account of Davenant through the commentary on the then Earl of Newcastle. Warwick considers the personality and competence of Newcastle who chose "Sir William Davenant, an eminent good Poet, and loyall Gentleman, to be Lieutenant-Generall of his Ordnance. This inclination of his own, and such kind of witty society (to be modest in the expression of it) diverted many counsels, and lost many opportunities; which the nature of that affair, this great man had now entred into, required" (pp. 235-36).

1702

250. Brown, Thomas, ed. *Miscellanea Aulica: or, A Collection of State-treatises, never before Publish'd ... Collected from their originals.* London: J. Hartley, Rob. Gibson, and Tho. Hodgson, 1702. Pp. A8, 440.

       The volume includes in the collection two letters from Abraham Cowley to Henry Bennet who speaks of Davenant's ill-fated trip to the New World.

1705

251. Philips, Katherine. *Letters from Orinda to Poliarchus.* London: Bernard Lintott, 1705. Pp. 246.

       The letters from Mrs. Philips to Sir Charles Cotterell offer explanation of Davenant's burlesque of Philips' treatment of *Pompey*, a play that she translated from Corneille and produced in Dublin with great pomp.

1710

252. Gildon, Charles. *The Life of Mr. Thomas Betterton, the Late Eminent Tragedian. Wherein the Action and Utterance of the Stage, Bar, and Pulpit, are*

      distinctly consider'd. With the Judgment of the Late
Ingenious Monsieur de St. Evremond, upon the Italian
and French Music and Opera's...To Which is Added the
Amorous Widow...A Comedy...By Mr. Betterton. London:
R. Gosling, 1710. Sigs. A-M8, A-E8, F4.

      Gildon's biography provides us with commentary
on Davenant and the controversy that arose between
acting and spectacle. Early in the book he discusses
The Siege of Rhodes and the actresses, especially Mrs.
Saunderson who lived with the Davenants prior to her
marriage to Betterton.

1719

253.   Jacob, Giles. *The Poetical Register: or, The Lives*
     and Characters of the English Dramatick Poets. 2
     vols. London: E. Curle, 1719.

      The first volume contains a brief biography of
Davenant that suggests Shakespeare's relationship with
Davenant's mother. It closes with Davenant's epitaph.

1721

254.   Rushworth, John. *Historical Collections of Private*
     Passages of State, Weighty Matters in Law, Remarkable
     Proceedings in Five Parliaments. 8 vols. London: D.
     Browne et al, 1721.

      Davenant's involvement in the Army Plot is
documented; so too is the ordinance against stage plays
in 1642.

1732

255.   Bellers, Fettiplace. *Injur'd Innocence: A Tragedy.*
     As it is Acted at the Theatre-Royal in Drury-Lane.
     London: J. Brindley, 1732.

      An eighteenth-century play by Bellers, the
plot was taken from Davenant's *Unfortunate Lovers.* See
item 68.

1736

256.   Blackwell, Thomas. *An Enquiry into the Life and*
     Writings of Homer. 2nd ed. London: J. Oswald, 1736.
     Pp. 346.

Blackwell praises Davenant's heroic poem briefly and almost anonymously in a note.

1740

257. Cibber, Colley. *An Apology for the Life of Mr. Colley Cibber, Comedian, and Late Patentee of the Theatre-Royal. With an Historical View of the Stage During His Own Time.* London: J. Watts, 1740. Pp. vi, 346.

In Chapter IV of his *Apology*, Cibber outlines the history of the two patent companies under Killigrew and Davenant and defends the practice of allowing no additional companies because of the limited number of actors and plays. In process, he comments on the introduction of actresses, spectacle, and music to the English public stage.

1741

258. Betterton, Thomas. *The History of the English Stage, From The Restauration to the Present Time. Including the Lives, Characters and Amours, Of the most Eminent Actors and Actresses. With Instructions for Public Speaking; Wherein The Action and Utterance of the Bar, Stage, and Pulpit are Distinctly considered.* London: E. Curll, 1741. Pp. 167.

Although the book has Betterton on the title page as the author, the work is usually attributed to Curll. In any case, the book contains information on Davenant's part in the reopening of the theaters from 1659 to 1662.

1743

259. [Chetwood, W.R.]. *The Case of Our Present Theatrical Disputes.* London: J. Robinson, 1743.

This rare tract, which the Folger Library attributes to Chetwood, praises Davenant and Killigrew for their theatrical abilities and for their low admission prices, made possible through their "living in a Manner suitable to their rank." See *1743*: Ralph.

260. Fitz-crambo, Esq., Patrick [William Rufus Chetwood?]. *Tyranny Triumphant; and Liberty Lost; The Muses Run*

*Mad; Apollo Struck Dumb, and All Covent Garden
Confounded....* London: G. Lyon, 1743.

The author, claiming to be the "Secretary to
Minor Poets," praises Davenant and other past theater
managers who "knew how to use an author well, and
encourage good performance." Attacking the
mid-eighteenth-century theater practices, he applauds
Davenant and others who lived "in a Manner suitable to
their Rank," rather than aspiring "to live with the
Magnificence of Men of Quality from the Profits of a
Playhouse."

261. [Ralph, James]. *The Case of Our Present Theatrical
     Disputes.* London: J. Robinson, 1743.

The Folger Library attributes this work to
W. R. Chetwood. See *1743:* [Chetwood].

1747

262. *Biographia Britannia: or, The Lives of The Most
     Eminent Persons who Have Flourished in Great Britain
     and Ireland, From the Earliest Ages Down to the
     Present Times Collected from the Best Authorities,
     Both Printed and Manuscript, and Digested in the
     Manner of Mr. Bayle's Historical and Critical
     Dictionary.* 6 vols. London: W. Innys, 1747-66.

The volume provides a text, marginalia, and
extensive footnotes that cover Davenant's life and work.
Although copiously documented, the account includes some
significant errors: that Davenant was a convert to
Catholicism and that he wrote *Coelum Britannicum.*

263. Hobbes, Thomas. *"To the Honourable Edward Howard,
     Esq. on his intended impression of his poem of the
     'British Princes'....* Chatsworth, Nov. the 6th,
     1668." In *Biographia Britannia.* London: W. Innys,
     1747-66. III, 1606.

Hobbes writes of Davenant: "his judgement in
poetry hath been once already censured by very good wits
for commending Gondibert. But yet have they not, I
think, ... disabled my testimony. For what authority is
in wit? a jester may have it; a man in drink may have
it, and be fluent over-night, and wise and dry in the

mornings. What is it? .... I will take my liberty to
praise what I like, as well as they do to reprehend what
they do not like.... In the poem there are many remote
and excellent thoughts, with apt and perspicuous
expressions.... there is more in that work to be
praised than pardoned." See *1840*: Hobbes.

1749

264. Chetwood, W.R. *A General History of the Stage, From
     its Origins in Greece down to the present Time*.
     London: W. Owen, 1749. Pp. 256.

          Chetwood's note on Davenant reflects a
     favorable critical attitude. "He was accounted a great
     Poet, in several Branches of that Science: His Poem of
     Gondibert is esteemed a noble Poem." Chetwood mentions
     Law Against Lovers as being "little for the better" than
     Shakespeare's *Measure for Measure*. See *1756*: Chetwood.

1750

265. [Chetwood, W.R.]. *The British Theatre. Containing
     The Lives of the English Dramatic Poets*. Dublin:
     Peter Wilson, 1750. Pp. 200. Rpt. London: R.
     Baldwin, 1752.

          Chetwood presents a brief account of
     Davenant's life and importance, plus an incomplete list
     of his plays. He describes the masques *Luminalia* and
     Salmacida Spolia as anonymously written.

1751

266. [Hurd, Richard.] *Q. Horatii Flacci Epistola ad
     Augustum. With an English Commentary and Notes. To
     which is added, A Discourse concerning Poetical
     Imitation*. London: W. Thurlbourn, 1751. Pp. iv,
     207.

          Hurd faults Davenant who strove too far for
     originality "but for the misconduct [Davenant would
     have] been in the just rank of our poets."

1753

267. Cibber, Theophilus, and Other Hands. *The Lives of the
     Poets of Great Britain and Ireland To the Time of Dean
     Swift*. 5 vols. London: R. Griffiths, 1753.

In a documented and informative chapter
devoted to Davenant, Cibber gives a biographical account
of "a good man and a poet." He tells us that Davenant
"has a right to rank in the first class of poets...."

1756

268. Chetwood, W[illiam]. R[ufus]. *Theatrical Records; or,*
      An Account of English Dramatic Authors and Their
      Works. London: R. and J. Dodsley, 1756. Pp. 135.

Chetwood presents a brief account of
Davenant's life and importance, plus an incomplete list
of his plays. He describes the masques *Luminalia* and
Salmacida Spolia as anonymous. The entry is identical
to that in Chetwood's *British Theatre*. See *1749:*
Chetwood.

1757

269. Thompson, William. *Poems on Several Occasions, To*
      which is added Gondibert and Birtha, A Tragedy.
      Oxford: The Theatre, 1757. Pp. 444.

The play is a five-act dramatization of
Davenant's heroic poem, retaining the characters,
setting, and part of the original plot. Here, however,
the play is in blank verse, and new characters enable
the playwright to pair off couples and conduct marriage
à la *Romeo and Juliet*, and to include an arrest of
Gondibert and Birtha that recalls Lear's arrest with
Cordelia. All is settled justly, with guilt becoming
the punishment and virtuous love the avenue to
happiness.

1762

270. Hurd, Richard. *Letters on Chivalry and Romance.*
      London: A. Millar, W. Thurlbourn, and J. Woodyer,
      1762. Pp. 120.

Hurd sees Davenant's *Preface* to *Gondibert* as
opening the way to a French-dominated English criticism
which continued throughout the seventeenth and first
half of the eighteenth centuries and which weakened
Spenser's reputation among critics of the period. As
Hurd wrote, "What we have gotten, you will say, is a

great deal of good sense. What we have lost is a world
of fine fabling...." See *1811*: Hurd; *1824*: Aikin;
1911: Hurd; and *1963*: Hurd.

1782

271. *Biographia Dramatica; or, A Companion to the
     Playhouse: Containing Historical and Critical
     Memoirs, and Original Anecdotes, of British and Irish
     Dramatic Writers, from the Commencement of Our
     Theatrical Exhibitions: Amongst Whom Are Some of the
     Most Celebrated Actors. Also an Alphabetical Account
     of their Works, the Dates When Printed, and Occasional
     Observations on their Merits. Together with an
     Introductory View of the Rise and Progress of the
     British Stage.* Comp. David Erskine Baker. Continued
     from 1764 to 1782 by Isaac Reed. 2 vols. London:
     Rivington, 1782.

     The material on Davenant's life and works is
flattering. It states, in part: "To this gentleman ...
the English stage perhaps stands more deeply indebted
than to any other writer of this nation...."

1783

272. Davies, Thomas. *Dramatic Miscellanies Consisting of
     Critical Observations on Several Plays of Shakespeare:
     With a Review of His Principal Characters, and Those
     of Various Eminent Writers, as Represented by Mr.
     Garrick, and Other Celebrated Comedians. With
     Anecdotes of Dramatic Poets, Actors, etc.* 3 vols.
     London: Thomas Davies, 1783-84.

     The volumes provide some first- and second-hand
comment on Davenant, his adaptations, directing, and
relationship to Shakespeare.

1787

273. Headley, Henry, ed. *Select Beauties of Ancient
     English Poetry.* 2 vols in one. London: T. Cadell,
     1787.

     Headley includes two of Davenant's poems and
points out Pope's use of Davenant's idea and language:
"Soft as the plumbers of a Saint forgiven."

1790

274.   Malone, Edmond. *An Historical Account of the Rise and
       Progress of the English Stage, and of the Economy and
       Usages of Our Ancient Theatres.* London: Henry
       Baldwin, 1790. Pp. 331.

            Throughout the volume, Malone refers in text
       and note to Davenant, his theater, and his productions.
       He refers to the price of admission; later, he mentions
       the curtain and notes Davenant's use of it at Rutland
       House.

1793

275.   [Anderson, Robert, ed.] *The Poetical Works of Sir
       William Davenant.* Edinburgh: Mundell, 1793.   In
       Select British Poets and Translations. 9 vols.
       London: W. Griffin, [n.d.].

            For the Davenant section, Anderson provides a
       separate title page and a critical introduction, which
       is followed by a selection of the poetry which includes
       Gondibert with the author's "Preface" and Hobbes'
       "Answer," the poem "Madagascar," and twenty-eight
       others. Among these are "The Long Vacation in London,"
       "The Disquisition to the Dying Christian," and "The
       Christian's Reply...," the aubade "The lark now leaves
       his wat'ry nest," "The Souldier going to the Field," and
       "In remembrance of Master William Shakespeare. Ode."
       Anderson included Davenant as the final section of
       volume four in a number of his editions of the British
       poets. Though these editions vary in terms of titles,
       dates, publishers, and contents, they remain constant
       where Davenant is concerned. The editions are listed
       below:

       A Complete Edition of the Poets of Great Britain. 13
            vols. London: J. & A. Arch, 1792-95.

       A Complete Edition of the Poets of Great Britain. 14
            vols. London: J. & A. Arch, 1793-1807.

       The Works of the British Poets. 14 vols. London: John
            & Arthur Arch, 1795.

       The Works of the British Poets. 14 vols. London: J.
            Arch, 1795-[1807?].

1800

276. Dibdin, Charles. *A Complete History of the English Stage. Introduced by a* ...*Review of the Asiatic, the Grecian, the Roman, the Spanish, the Italian, the Portugese, the German, the French, and other Theatres, and*...*Biographical Tracts and Anecdotes*.... 5 vols. London: Charles Dibdin, [1800].

Dibdin comments in the account of the Restoration theater in the fourth volume: "Davenant...introduced what was then and is at this moment the disgrace and reproach of the theatre."

1807

277. Hyde, Edward, First Earl of Clarendon. *The History of the Rebellion and Civil Wars in England.* 3 vols. Oxford: Clarendon, 1807.

Hyde's history is a personal view of an event that involved Davenant with court intrigues. Hyde not only covers portions of the politics but also gives a first-hand account of Davenant himself.

1808

278. Scott, Sir Walter. *The Life of John Dryden.* London: W. Miller, 1808. Pp. ii, 534.

Recognizing that Davenant's purpose in writing went beyond pleasure, politics, or personal interest, Scott applauds the poet for "a mind above those laborious triflers, who called that poetry which was only verse...." Scott also commends Davenant for his stanzaic pattern in *Gondibert* and for his "conciseness," "concentration of thought," and "advance toward true taste."

1810

279. Chalmers, Alexander, ed. "The Poems of Sir William Davenant." In *The Works of the English Poets, From Chaucer to Cowper; including the series Edited with Prefaces, Biographical and Critical, By Dr. Samuel Johnson* ... *the Additional Lives by Alexander Chalmers, F.S.A.* London: J. Johnson, 1810, VI, 339-435.

Chalmer's brief life of the playwright
includes the suggestion, attributed to Wood, that
Shakespeare fathered Davenant but he adds that modern
inquiries find no supporting evidence. The
contributions to stage development are noted and the
poetry is described as of "unequal merit." Included are
selections from *Gondibert*, with the *Preface* and Hobbes'
Answer, "The Long Vacation in London, In Verse
Burlesque, or Mock-Verse," and a good representation of
the shorter poems, including "Song" ("The Lark"), "Song.
The Souldier going to the Field," and "In remembrance of
Master William Shakespeare. Ode."

280. [Scott, Sir Walter, ed.]. Introduction to *The Wits*.
In *The Ancient British Drama*. 3 vols. London:
William Miller, 1810, I, 280-81.

The editor reviews the key points in
Davenant's life but makes no comment on the quality of
the literary or dramatic contribution.

1811

281. Hurd, Richard. "Discourse on Poetical Imitation."
Works. London: T. Cadell & W. Davies, 1811, II,
236-39.

Hurd finds Davenant's ideas on the epic, as
expressed in the *Preface* to *Gondibert*, defective because
the five-act dramatic form eliminates "the opportunity
of digressive ornaments, which contribute so much to the
pomp of epic poetry," and because Davenant's rejection
of "the intervention of *supernatural agency*,
characteristic of Homer, and limiting the epic to the
affairs of men omits a necessary part of the epic plan."
See *1762*: Hurd; *1824*: Aikin; *1911*: Hurd; *1963*:
Hurd.

1818

282. Malone, Edmond, Esq. *A Catalogue of the Greater
Portion of the Library of the Late Edmond Malone,
Editor of Shakespeare... which will be sold by
auction By Mr. Sotheby, November 26, 1818*. London:
Wright and Murphy, 1818.

Among the books, Malone had Davenant's
Gondibert (1651), *Madagascar* (1648), *The Cruell Brother*

(1630), *The Just Italian* (1630), *The Platonic Lovers*
(1636), *The Triumphs of the Prince D'Amour* (1635), *The
Witts* (1636), and the 1673 *Works*. The extensive
collection reflects the taste of one of the leading
critics and scholars of the eighteenth century, and it
places Davenant in a more visible position than might be
supposed.

1819

283. Campbell, Thomas. *Specimens of the British Poets;
with Biographical and Critical Notices, and An Essay
on English Poets by Thomas Campbell.* 7 vols. London:
John Murray, 1819, IV, 96-107.

Writing on *Gondibert*, Campbell praises
Davenant's independence of conception and choice of
subject but criticizes his poetry as being too cold and
abstract--more historical than poetical.

284. Sanford, Ezekiel. "Select Poems of Sir William
Davenant. With a Life of the Author." In *The Works
of the British Poets. With Lives of the Authors.*
Philadelphia: Mitchell, Ames, and White, 1819, V,
125-61.

The volume contains a biographical statement
that perpetuates some of the stories about Davenant and
that judges both Davenant and Malone harshly for
suggesting Shakespeare's fatherhood as part of a "jest."
The volume reprints two cantos from *Gondibert*.

1820

285. [Robinson, G.] "Sir William Davenant's Gondibert."
The Retrospective Review, 2 (1820), 304-24.

Eschewing biographical material on Davenant,
the writer [G. Robinson?] reviews the 1651 edition of
Gondibert, finding it a mixed achievement. About
fourteen of the twenty pages are given to quotations
from the poem.

1824

286. Aikin, Lucy. *Memoir of John Aikin, M.D.*
Philadelphia: A. Small, 1824. Pp. viii, 487.

On pages 197-201, John Aikin takes issue with
Richard Hurd's negative criticisms of Davenant's views
on epic structure and content as found in the *Preface* to
Gondibert. See *1762*: Hurd; see also *1811*: Hurd; and
see *1911*: Hurd; *1963*: Hurd.

1825

287. Dodsley, Robert. *A Select Collection of Old Plays: A
      New Edition with Additional Notes and Corrections, by
      the Late Isaac Reed Octavius Gilchrist and the Editor.*
      London: Septemus Prowett, 1825, VIII, 331-434.

Dodsley's five-page introduction precedes the
text of *The Wits.* The introduction is condescending and
occasionally wrong claiming that Davenant "had embraced
the Roman Catholic religion," and that "It is generally
imagined he owed his life to the interposition of
Milton," an idea that still needs validation.

1828

288. Hunt, Leigh. "Sir William Davenant." *The Companion*,
      9 April 1828, 177-90.

Hunt summarizes and comments on the familiar
information concerning Davenant from John Aubrey and
Anthony a Wood. Hunt also provides several samples of
Davenant's poetry.

1831

289. Collier, J. Payne. *The History of English Dramatic
      Poetry to the Time of Shakespeare; and The Annals of
      the Stage to the Restoration.* 3 vols. London: J.
      Murray, 1831.

Collier uses Davenant's plays to illustrate
points about the theaters, performances, and audiences.
He also discusses the pension Davenant received when he
followed Ben Jonson as poet laureate, the production of
The Siege of Rhodes as a landmark in theater history,
the censorship of *The Wits* by Charles I, and the patent
Davenant received in 1639 to build a playhouse. See
1970: Collier.

290. Southey, Robert, ed. *Select Works of the British
      Poets, From Chaucer to Jonson, with Biographical*

Sketches. London: Longman, Rees, Orme, Brown, and Green, 1831, pp. 912-74.

In the biographical sketch, Southey surveys the major events of Davenant's life, reflecting doubt concerning the Shakespeare paternity and Roman Catholic conversion stories. He treats as fact Milton's aid to Davenant and Davenant's to Milton. He laments that "two men [Davenant and Dryden] of such great and indubitable genius should have combined to debase, and vulgarize, and pollute" *The Tempest*, "which is to this day represented," and further laments that Davenant failed to complete *Gondibert* of which he writes, "there are few poems in our language which exhibit equal proofs of a vigorous mind."

1832

291. Genest, John. *Some Account of the English Stage from the Restoration in 1660 to 1830.* 10 vols. Bath: H.E. Carrington, 1832.

The work provides extensive commentary on the drama and specifically discusses Davenant's *Tempest* and *Macbeth* with brief comments on most of his other plays.

1833

292. Aikin, Lucy. *Memoirs of the Court of King Charles the First.* 2 vols. London: Longman, 1833.

The work includes Davenant's activities as laureate, soldier, and exile, for as Aikin writes: "we shall see him [Davenant], on more than one occasion, freely exposing himself to dangers and sufferings in the royal cause" (p. 40).

1836

293. Hall, S.C., ed. *The Book of Gems: The Poets and Artists of Great Britain.* London: Saunders and Otley, 1836, I, 207-11.

Hall provides a full and sympathetic biography of Davenant whose loss of fame the editor deplores. He concludes by stating that "posterity, in neglecting him, has not done him justice; and it was a silly verdict

that condemned him for having rehearsed [in *Gondibert*]
'A theme ill-chosen in ill-chosen verse.'"

1839

294.   Hallam, Henry. *Introduction to the Literature of
Europe, in the Fifteenth, Sixteenth, and Seventeenth
Centuries.* 4 vols. London: J. Murray, 1839-40, III,
499-500.

Hallam writes of *Gondibert* and finds it
contains both strengths and weaknesses. It is to be
read for its "masculine verse in a good metrical
cadence; for the sake of which we may forgive the
absence of interest in the story ...."

1840

295.   Hobbes, Thomas. "Letter to the Right Honourable Edw.
Howard." In *The English Works of Thomas Hobbes of
Malmesbury.* Ed. Sir William Molesworth. London: John
Bohn, 1840, IV, 458-60.

"My judgment in poetry hath, you know, been
once already censured by very good wits, for commending
Gondibert; but yet they have not I think, disabled my
testimony. For what authority is there in wit? A
jester may have it; a man in drink may have it; be
fluent over night, and wise and dry in the morning.
What is it? Or who can tell whether it be better to
have it or be with out it, especially if it be a pointed
wit? I will take my liberty to praise what I like, as
well as they do reprehend what they do not like." See
1747: Hobbes.

1845

296.   Campbell, Thomas. *Specimens of the British Poets;
with Biographical and Critical Notices, and An Essay
on English Poetry.* 2nd rev. ed. Peter Cunningham.
London: John Murray, 1845.

Campbell describes Davenant as a poet,
dismissing Davenant's personal history as curious.
Focusing on *Gondibert*, Campbell comments on its "high
and independent conception," its "close and compact
symmetry," and its "ingenious and witty images." He

concludes that the poem, however, "wants the charm of
free and forcible narration." Cunningham adds Pope's
comment that "Sir William Davenant's *Gondibert* is not a
good poem, if you take it on the whole; but there are a
good many things in it." In an appendix, Cunningham
corrects an error perpetuated by Johnson. Matthew
Prior, he states, "says that *Davenant* and Waller
improved our versification--not...*Denham* and Waller."

1848

297.　Cunningham, Peter. "Inigo Jones: A Life of the
　　　Architect," *Shakespeare Society Publications*, 17
　　　(1848), 1-51.

　　　　　The biography explains Jones' role in the
court entertainments and his relationship to Davenant,
one of the new poets who replaced Ben Jonson.

298.　Johnson, George W., ed. *The Fairfax Correspondence.
　　　Memoirs of the Reign of Charles the First*. 2 vols.
　　　London: Richard Bentley, 1848.

　　　　　The work includes an account of Goring's Plot
in 1641 initiated to rescue Strafford and implicating
the Royal household. Among those involved were: Henry
Percy, Henry Jermyn, Sir John Suckling, William
Davenant, Captain Palmer, Sir Edward Wardour, and
Captain Billingsley, all of whom immediately absconded.

1851

299.　Haskins, James F. "Play of 'The Spaniards in Peru.'"
　　　Notes & Queries, 4 (1851), 257-58.

　　　　　Haskins asks who wrote the play. The answer
is given, identifying it as Davenant's.

300.　Waring, E. "Cruelty of the Spaniards in Peru." *Notes
　　　& Queries*, 4 (1851), 456.

　　　　　Waring offers the fourth part of Purchas's
Pilgrims, 1569, as the source of Davenant's play.

1853

301.　"Sir William Davenant, *Poet Laureate and Dramatist*."
　　　Retrospective Review, 2 (Nov. 1853), 1-20.

The anonymous critic reviews Davenant's life
and achievements, especially the introduction to the
English stage of painted scenery, Italian style music,
and women. He states that the plays cannot be highly
rated nor can the poetry, except for "The Philosopher to
the Dying Christian," which possesses "singular beauty
and completeness," and *Gondibert*, which achieves its
design "to strip nature naked, and clothe her again in
the perfect shape of virtue."

1854

302.   Corney, Bolton. "Dryden on Shakespere." *Notes &
       Queries*, 9(1854), 95-96.

            Corney attempts to answer the question, "Who
wrote the *Prologue to Julius Caesar*?" which is a poem of
forty lines of rhymed couplets published in 1672 in the
Covent Garden drolery. He suggests that Dryden wrote
the poem and cites as evidence the Davenant-Dryden
alteration of *Julius Caesar* and several poems by Dryden
published in the first twelve pages of the *Covent Garden
drolery*. See *1984*: Hammond.

1856

303.   Charles I. *Letters of King Charles the First to Queen
       Henrietta Maria*. Ed. John Bruce. London: Camden
       Society, 1856. Pp. xxxi, 104.

            Bruce provides a history of the Civil War and
then prints letters in which Davenant is mentioned as a
trusted courier for the monarchs.

1858

304.   *Calendar of State Papers, Domestic Series, of the
       Reign of Charles I, Preserved in the State Paper
       Department of Her Majesty's Public Record Office*. Ed.
       John Bruce, William Douglas Hamilton, and Sophia
       Crawford Lomas. 23 vols. 1858-97.

       a. Vol. 3, 1628-29, pp. 67, 435.
       b. Vol. 7, 1634-35, p. 178.
       c. Vol. 12, 1637-38, pp. 359-60.
       d. Vol. 13, 1638-39, pp. 161, 604.
       e. Vol. 16, 1640, p. 483.

f. Vol. 17, 1640-41, pp. 546, 571, 574.
g. Vol. 18, 1641-43, pp. 29, 566.
h. Vol. 19, 1643-44, p. 159.
i. Vol. 20, 1644-45, pp. 430-31.
j. Vol. 21, 1645-47, p. 23.

The *Calendar of State Papers, Domestic,*
provides a variety of significant material on Davenant
including information on the following:

> military experience (a, e, f, h, j);
> the "Army Plot" (f, g);
> theater experience (d, g);
> the poet laureateship (d);
> royal courier (i);
> relationship with Hyde (a);
> relationship with the Porters (b);
> petition from Mary Davenant to the king (c).

305. Delacourt, Raymond. "The Opera in the Time of the
      Protectorate." *Notes & Queries*, 2nd Ser., 5 (1858),
      231.

      From "a contemporaneous MS," Delacourt notes
that "On Friday, May 14, 1656," Davenant's *The
Entertainment by Musick and Declaratives [qy.
Declamations?] after the Manner of the Ancients* was
performed at the Charterhouse. He adds, "400 persons
were expected, but we learn that there appeared no more
than 150 auditors." See *1912*: Davey; also *1912*:
Nicholson.

1859

306. V. "Davenant's Place of Confinement." *Notes &
      Queries*, 2nd Ser., 8 (1859), 28.

      The query reveals interest in Davenant. It
asks: Was Davenant confined at Cowes Castle or
Carisbrooke Castle? Aubrey says the latter. Where was
Gondibert written?

307. Y.,J. "Sir William D'Avenant (2nd S. viii. 28.)."
      Notes & Queries, 2nd Ser., 8 (1859), 98.

      The entry offers an answer to the questions
above: Davenant was confined in Cowes Castle according

to the postscript after the third book of *Gondibert*.
Half of the third book was written at Cowes.

1860

308. *Calendar of State Papers, Colonial Series, Preserved
      in the State Paper Department of her Majesty's Public
      Record Office.* Vol. I.   Ed. Noel Sainsbury.   1860.

         For Davenant's appointment to the Council of
      the Plantation and Colonies of Virginia in 1650, see
      1574-1660, p. 340.

309. *Calendar of State Papers, Domestic Series, of the
      Reign of Charles II ....*   Ed. Mary Anne Everett Green.
      Vols. I-X.   1860--.

      a. Vol. 1, 1660-61, pp. 114, 124, 188, 423.
      b. Vol. 2, 1661-62, pp. 244, 359, 455, 466, 577.
      c. Vol. 3, 1663-64, pp. 214, 539, 623.
      d. Vol. 4, 1664-65, pp. 218.
      e. Vol. 7, 1667, p. 52.
      f. Vol. 8, 1667-68, p. 341.
      g. Vol. 9, 1668-69, p. 648.
      h. Addenda, 1660-70, p. 655.

         The *Calendar of State Papers, Domestic,*
      provides a variety of significant material on Davenant
      including information on the following:

              family background (c);
              military experience (b);
              theater experience (a, b, c, d, g, h);
              the poet laureateship (f);
              death (f).

310. Halliwell, James O., ed. *Conceits, Clinches, Flashes,
      and Whimzies: A Jest-Book of the Seventeenth Century,
      Hitherto Unknown to Bibliographers, Reprinted from the
      Unique Copy of 1639.* London: Thomas Richards, 1860.
      Pp. vi, 48.

         Only twenty-six copies were printed of the
      1639 book. On page 37, the *Wits* joke is told. See
      1639: Conceits; *1640*: Chamberlain; *1660*: [Armstrong];
      1864: Hazlitt; *1866*: Hazlitt.

311.   Halliwell, James O. *A Dictionary of Old English Plays
       Existing Either in Print or in Manuscript from the
       Earliest Times to the Close of the Seventeenth
       Century*. London: John Russell Smith. 1860. Pp.
       vii, 296.

            Among other information, the volume contains
       material on the 1637 masque *Luminalia; or, The Festival
       of Light*. The masque, however, is ascribed to Thomas
       Lodge and Robert Greene by Winstanley and Wood. See
       1687: Winstanley; *1691*: Wood.

                              1864

312.   Doran, John. *"Their majesties' servants."* *Annals of
       the English Stage, from Thomas Betterton to Edmund
       Kean*. 2 vols. London: Wm. H. Allen, 1864.

            Among other information on Davenant is an
       account of the actresses who boarded with his family in
       1661.

313.   Hazlitt, W. Carey, ed. *Old English Jest Books:
       Conceits, Clinches, Flashes, and Whimzies*. Robert
       Chamberlain. 3 vols. London: Willis and Sotheran,
       1864.

            The collection contains the joke that depends
       on the 1636 quarto edition of *The Wits*. See *1639*:
       Conceits; *1640*: Chamberlain; *1660*: [Armstrong]; *1860*:
       Halliwell; *1866*: Hazlitt.

                              1866

314.   Hazlitt, W. Carey, ed. *Old English Jest Books:
       Conceits, Clinches, Flashes, and Whimzies*. Robert
       Chamberlain. Willis and Sotherne, 1866. Pp. 75.

            The volume contains a joke that depends on the
       1636 quarto edition of *The Wits:*

       *"One, having a play book called the Wits which he much
       valued, by chance lost it: but while he was chafing
       and swearing about the loss of his book, in comes one
       of his friends, who asking the cause of his distemper,
       it was answered that he had lost his wits"* (p. 59,
       item 235). *See 1639*: Conceits; *1640*: Chamberlain;
       1660: [Armstrong]; *1860*: Halliwell; *1864*: Hazlitt.

1867

315.   Corney, Bolton. "William D'Avenant on Shakespere."
       Notes & Queries, 3rd Ser., 12 (1867), 3.

       Corney corrects a series of errors begun by
Moseley and perpetuated by Chalmers. All are in
reference to Davenant's poem on Shakespeare.

1869

316.   Arber, Edward, ed. *The Rehearsal*. George Villers,
       Second Duke of Buckingham. English Reprints. London:
       J. & W. Rider, 1869. Pp. 136.

       The volume, for the most part, carries the
1672 text on the right and explanations on the left
page. The introduction contains Arber's statements on
Davenant, his patent, and heroic drama.

317.   Disraeli, Isaac. "D'Avenant and a Club of Wits." *The
       Quarrels of Authors*. 1814. In *The Calamaties and
       Quarrels of Authors*. A New Edition, ed. by his son.
       London: Frederick Warne, 1869. Pp. vii, 552.

       Disraeli admires Davenant because of his
"dignity and powers of a great dignity." Disraeli
suggests that Davenant fell in among "an age of wits,"
and as a result "he was covered by ridicule." Praising
Gondibert, Disraeli states that it has "impressive
solemnity." He concludes: "D'Avenant is a poetical
Rochefoucault; the sententious force of his maxims on
all human affairs could only have been composed by one
who had lived in a constant intercourse with mankind."

318.   Elze, Karl. "Sir William Davenant." *Jahrbuch der
       Deutschen Shakespeare-Gesehlschaft*, 4 (1869), 125-59.
       Rpt. "Sir William Davenant." In *Essays on
       Shakespeare*. Trans. Dora Schmitz. London:
       Macmillan, 1874, pp. 316-67. Rpt. Port Washington:
       Kennikat, 1970, pp. 316-67.

       The article surveys Davenant's life and works
giving special attention to the evidence for and against
the Shakespeare patrimony theory. The article also
contests Disraeli's praise of *Gondibert*. See *1874:*
Elze.

1870

319. Bates, William. "Elegy on Sir William D'Avenant."
      Notes & Queries, 4th Ser., 5 (1870), 576.

          Bates prints "from the original, written in a
      contemporary hand, with many others, on the blank leaves
      prefixed to a copy of '*Poems and Translations, with the
      Sophy*, written by the Honourable Sir John Denham, Knight
      of the Bath,' 8 vo, London, 1668: 'Though hee is dead,
      th' imortall name...,'" a lovely prayer of praise for
      Davenant.

320. L., S. [Sidney Lee?] "Sir W. Davenant's Wives."
      Notes & Queries, 4th Ser., 5 (1870), 248.

          In response to the query: "Who were
      Davenant's wives?" the note suggests that the answers
      are found in records of their deaths--Anne, buried March
      5, 1654/5, and Lady Mary, February 24, 1690.

1871

321. Dobson, Thomas. "Davenant: Lort: Ellice." *Notes &
      Queries*, 4th Ser., 8 (1871), 304.

          Dobson questions the relationship of Sir
      William Davenant with Bishop Davenant. He asks whether
      there are any descendants of Davenant's family living.

322. Husk, W. H. "London and Paris Contrasted in 1656."
      Notes & Queries, 4th Ser., 8 (1871), 495-99.

          The long note is a description of Davenant's
      Entertainment at Rutland House on May 23, 1656. Husk
      discusses the contrast given by Davenant of London and
      Paris.

1872

323. (*H.M.C*) *Reports Issued By the Royal Commission on
      Historical Manuscripts*, 1872-1911.

          The reports contain information on Davenant,
      especially his activities from 1639 through 1660.
      Pertinent material appears in the following reports:

H.M.C., II, House of Lords MSS., 3rd Rpt. (1872), p.
79.
Jan. 21, 1639/40: The Lord of Northumberland's
lament that unattractive women surround the
queen in *Salmacida Spolia*.

H.M.C., III, House of Lords MSS., 4th Rpt. (1873), p.
35.
May 1639: Davenant, then army paymaster, and the
Earl of Newport bring a case against James
Fawcett for injuring horses belonging to the
military.

H.M.C., IV, House of Lords MSS, 5th Rpt. (1876), p.
413.
May 1649: The General-in-Chief of the Army's order
for Davenant's arrest.
1660: Report of Sir Robert Gaskholl's death in
a tavern brawl by a Scot, Balinden, after a performance of *The Unfortunate Lovers*, p. 200.

H.M.C., VI, Verney MSS, 7th Rpt. (1879), p. 453.
1645: Report of Davenant's trip by sea and then to
Paris by way of Rouen.

H.M.C., XV, MSS of the Marquis of Abergavenny, 10th
Rpt. (1887), Appen. Pt. VI, p. 89.
Nov. 1, 1642: Report of Davenant's departure from
Holland for England prior to November 1st.

H.M.C., XXIX, Portland MSS, 13th Rpt. (1891), I, 17.
1641: Captain Pollard's accusation of Davenant and
others of being involved in the Army Plot.
1645: Identification of Davenant as a pirate and
enemy of Parliament (I, 324).

H.M.C., XXXI, Rye Corporation MSS, 13th Rpt. (1892),
IV, 389.
July 8, 1652: Davenant's unsuccessful appeal to
Colonel Henry Marten to secure freedom from the
Tower.

H.M.C., XLIII, Duke of Somerset MSS, 15th Rpt. (1898),
pp. 73, 78-79.
Aug. 1644: Davenant's successful attempt to secure
a boat to run the Parliamentary Naval blockade

aided by Sir Edward Digby and Colonel Edward
Seymour.

H.M.C., XLV, Duke of Buccleuch MSS, 15th Rpt. (1903),
   II.
   Details on Davenant's children scattered through
      Part II.

H.M.C., LXIII, Earl of Egmont MSS, 16th Rpt. (1905),
   Vol. I, Pt. I, 134.
   May 8, 1641: Davenant cited as conspirator in the
      First Army Plot.

H.M.C., LXX, Pepys MSS, 17th Rpt. (1911), pp. 284,
   302.
   Sept. 1649: Davenant appointed by Charles II as
      Treasurer of Virginia.

H.M.C., XXIII, Coke MSS, 12th Rpt. (1888-89), I, II,
   III.
   Details on Davenant's children scattered through
      Parts I, II, and III.

324. Maidment, James, and W.H. Logan, eds. *The Dramatic*
     Works of Sir William D'Avenant, with Prefatory Memoir
     and Notes. 5 vols. London: Sotheran, 1872-1874.
     Rpt. New York: Russell & Russell, 1964.

       The first volume contains an extended
statement of the life of Davenant and his importance in
the seventeenth and subsequent centuries. Each play
also has an introductory statement by the editors that
explains dramatic, textual, and source problems and
questions. See *1964*: Maidment.

325. Rimbault, Edward F. "Ballad upon Sir William
     Davenant's 'Cruelty of the Spaniards in Peru.'" *Notes*
     & Queries, 4th ser., 9 (1872), 49-50.

       Rimbault notes that on his quarto of *The*
Cruelty of the Spaniards in Peru published in 1658 there
is an advertisement printed: "'Notwithstanding the great
expense necessary to scenes and other ornaments in the
entertainment, there is a good provision made for a
shilling, and it shall begin certainly at three in the
afternoon.'" He comments on Evelyn's guilt pangs when
he attended a performance in light of Cromwell's recent

death, but he went "for the spectacle." The note
concludes with a poem on "The Late New Opera...."

1874

326. D., C. "Sir William Davenant." *Notes & Queries*, 5th
      Ser., 2 (1874), 348.

          After quoting the poem "The lark now leaves
      his wat'ry nest," C.D. questions its source and
      authors.

327. Elze, Karl. "Sir William Davenant." In *Essays on
      Shakespeare*. Trans. Dora Schmitz. London: Macmillan,
      1874, pp. 316-67.

          See *1869*: Elze.

328. Rule, Fredk. John Addis. "Sir William Davenant (5th
      S.ii.348)." *Notes & Queries*, 5th Ser., 2 (1874),
      376.

          Rule affirms Davenant's authorship of a poem
      that Mr. Beller's calls "Song" in his *Poet's Corner*.
      Addis directs C.D. (above) to the 1673 folio of
      Davenant's works, page 320.

1875

329. *Calendar of State Papers, Domestic Series [of the
      Commonwealth]*.... Ed. Mary Anne Everett Green. 13
      vols. 1875-86.

      a. Vol. 2, 1650, pp. 167, 229.
      b. Vol. 3, 1651, p. 251.
      c. Vol. 4, 1651-52, pp. 432, 485.
      d. Vol. 7, 1654, pp. 106, 107, 192, 224, 439.
      e. Vol. 8, 1655, p. 595.
      f. Vol. 9, 1655-56, p. 396.
      g. Vol. 13, 1659-60, pp. 118, 571.

          The *Calendar of State Papers, Domestic*,
      provides a variety of significant material on Davenant
      including information on the following:

              family background (e);
              imprisonment by the Commonwealth (a, b, c, d, g);

theater experience (f);
American experience (c);
pass to France (e, g).

1879

330. Hamilton, Walter. *The Poets Laureate of England;
      Being a History of the Office of Poet Laureate,
      Biographical Notices of its Holders, and a Collection
      of the Satires, Epigrams, and Lampoons Directed
      against them.* London: E. Stock, 1879. Rpt. Detroit:
      Gale Research, 1968. Rpt. NY: B. Franklin, 1970. Pp.
      xxv, 308.

      Davenant is accorded his own chapter (pp.
63-80) and acknowledged to have been poet laureate
during an eventful time. Davenant's work is considered
to be "the boundary which separates the old romantic
poets from the modern school of writers...." The
chapter reviews his life and his achievements concluding
with a list of his dramatic works. See *1968*: Hamilton.

1880

331. Gosse, Edmund W. "Sir William Davenant." In *The
      English Poets: Selections with Critical Introductions
      By Various Writers and a General Introduction by
      Matthew Arnold.* Thomas Humphrey Ward, ed. 4 vols.
      Oxford: Clarendon, 1880.

      Gosse, in a single-page introduction, comments
on Davenant's "hopelessly faded laurel" and on the 1673
folio as "the most deplorable collection of verses
anywhere to be found" except for *Gondibert* although it
too is "incoherent, rambling." See *1883, 1887, 1892*:
Gosse.

1882

332. Fitzgerald, Percy. *A New History of the English
      Stage: From the Restoration to the Liberty of the
      Theatres, In Connection with the Patent Houses.* 2
      vols. London: Tinsley, 1882.

      The work provides a history of the patents and
Davenant's role in the development of Restoration
theater. Some of the earlier background is also

provided; of particular interest is Davenant's letter
under the Great Seal to establish a new theater in 1639,
a plan that was lost in the growing war.

333.   Rosbund, Max. "Dryden als Shakespeare-Bearbeiter."
       Diss. Halle-Wittenberg, 1882. Pp. 72.

         The work is a discussion of Dryden's
Shakespearean drama. Davenant is included, particularly
in relation to *The Tempest*. See *1899*: Witt.

334.   Saintsbury, George, ed. *The Tempest; or, The
       Enchanted Island. A Comedy.* In *The Dramatic Works of
       John Dryden with a Life of the Author by Sir Walter
       Scott, Bart.* Edinburgh: William Paterson, 1882, III,
       99-226.

         Though Saintsbury cites as his source the 1670
edition, he reprints the 1674 edition with the operatic
additions by Shadwell. In his introduction, Saintsbury
reviews Davenant's life and comments on *Gondibert* as
Davenant's "greatest performance, [which] incurred, when
first published, more ridicule, and in latter times more
neglect, than its merit deserves." Saintsbury then
discusses this version of *The Tempest*, carefully
indicating "that very little of this Shakespeare
travesty is Dryden's."

                          1883

335.   Gosse, Edmund W. "Sir William Davenant." In *The
       English Poets: Selections and a General Introduction
       by Matthew Arnold.* Thomas Humphrey Ward, ed. 4 vols.
       Oxford: Clarendon, 1883.

              See *1880*: Gosse.

                          1885

336.   Delius, Von Nicolaus. "Shakespeare's Macbeth and
       Davenant's Macbeth." *Jahrbuch der Deutschen
       Shakespeare-Gesellschaft*, 20 (1885), 69-84. Rpt.
       Vaduz: Kraus Reprint, 1963.

         The article compares the plays, finding that
Davenant's *Macbeth* is a popularization of Shakespeare's
masterpiece, although Davenant's "concoction" held the

English stage for almost eighty years. See *1963:*
Delius.

337. Gillow, Joseph, ed. *A Literary and Biographical
      History, or Biographical Dictionary of the English
      Catholics. From The Breach with Rome in 1504 to the
      Present Time.* 4 vols. London and New York: Burns &
      Oates, 1885.

            Davenant's life and works are given in fulsome
      prose. His Catholicism enters between 1643 and 1646,
      where, according to Gillow, the poet "became a Catholic,
      and it has been asserted that, in 1646, the Queen
      commissioned him to try and persuade Charles to give up
      the Church of England for his security, which so
      displeased the king that he forbade him ever to appear
      before him again." Many other "facts" about Davenant
      are faulty in the essay.

338. Gosse, Sir Edmund. *From Shakespeare to Pope; An
      Inquiry into the Causes and Phenomena of the Rise of
      Classical Poetry in England.* Cambridge, England:
      University Press, 1885. Pp. x, 298. Rpt. New York:
      Kraus, 1968.

            Gosse considers Davenant's early plays as
      "miserable productions, noisy, flashy, insufferably
      dull" (p. 149) and *Gondibert* as evidence of a complete
      transformation in Davenant. He identifies the long poem
      as a "classical manifesto" and he compares Davenant to
      Southey. After identifying the four wits who wrote
      "Certain Verses" against Davenant's poem -- Denham, the
      younger Donne, Sir Allen Broderick, and William Crofts
      (p. 160n)--Gosse prints in full a poem that was designed
      to vindicate *Gondibert.* The only copy extant is in
      Gosse's possession. Finally, Gosse offers his list of
      those qualities of Davenant's poetry that he applauds,
      among them his poetic stanza, his passage on the hunted
      stag, and the dignity of his poetry (pp. 163-66). See
      1968: Gosse.

339. Grimm, Heinrich. "Shakespeare's Sturm en der
      Bearbeitung von Dryden und Davenant." *Funzehn Essays.*
      Berlin: 1885.

1886

340.   Firth, C. H., ed. *The Life of William Cavendish, Duke
        of Newcastle.* London: George Routledge, 1886.   Pp.
        232.

               Firth's introduction offers some information
        on Davenant and his relationship to Newcastle who
        commanded Royalist forces during the early part of the
        Civil War. The text of the biography also provides
        through the Duchess' words Davenant's role in the war.
        See *1667*: Cavendish.

341.   Morgan, Appleton. "William Shakespeare's Literary
        Executor." *Magazine of American History*, 16 (1886)
        516-25.

               Morgan outlines his gratitude to Davenant,
        "neither the worst nor the worthiest," who was
        nonetheless, "the first to bring back from
        oblivion...the dramatic works...of William
        Shakespeare."

342.   Nicholas, Sir Edward. *The Nicholas Papers: The
        Correspondence of Sir Edward Nicholas, Secretary of
        State.* Ed. George F. Warner. 4 vols. Camden
        Society Publication. N.S. vols. 40, 50, 57, 31.
        Westminster: Nichols and Sons, 1886-1920.

               The papers contain scattered but important
        information on Davenant and his relationship with
        members of the court and his activities during the
        Interregnum.

1887

343.   Gosse, Edmund W. "Sir William Davenant."   In *The
        English Poets: Selections with Critical Introductions
        by Various Writers and a General Introduction by
        Matthew Arnold.* Thomas Humphrey Ward, ed. 4 vols.
        Oxford: Clarendon, 1887.

               See *1880*: Gosse.

344.   Halliwell-Phillipps, J. O. *Outlines of the Life of
        Shakespeare.* 7th ed. 2 vols. London: Longmans,
        Green, 1887.

The work presents relevant documents chronologically arranged that cover the years 1629-92. Included is Davenant's father's will.

345. Saintsbury, George. *A History of Elizabethan Literature*. London: Macmillan, 1887. Pp. xiv, 471. Rpt. New York: Russell & Russell, 1970.

The work is of particular interest to Davenant scholarship because it reveals the nineteenth century's approach to the seventeenth century and the Restoration. See pp. 419-20 for an especially negative view. See *1970*: Saintsbury.

1888

346. Elze, Karl. *William Shakespeare, A Literary Biography*. Trans. L. Dora Schmitz. London: G. Bell, 1888. Pp. 587. Rpt. New York: AMS, 1973, pp. 587.

In the book, Elze presents the usual case for Davenant's claim as Shakespeare's illegitimate son. He writes: "Oldys, who was not born till the end of the seventeenth century, is certainly not an authority of the first rank, and it cannot be denied that the anecdote seems to be a well-manufactured joke" (p. 170). See *1973*: Elze.

347. Knight, Joseph. "Davenant, Sir William." *Dictionary of National Biography* [*DNB*]. 64 vols. Ed. Leslie Stephen. London: Smith Elder, 1888, XIV, 101-08.

The essay provides an informative summary of Davenant's life, works, and influence, concluding with a brief but important bibliographical paragraph.

1889

348. T.,H. "Sir William D'Avenant and the Duc de Roquelaure." *Notes & Queries*, 7th Ser., 8 (1889), 285-86.

The story about Davenant's encounter with an old Irishwoman who wished him good eyesight because the poet lacked a nose to rest spectacles on is also told about Gaston Jean-Baptiste, Duc de Roquelaure, who left Rabelais to play the buffoon in Louis XIV's court.

1891

349.   *Alumni Oxonienses: The Members of the University of
       Oxford, 1500-1714: Their Parentage, Birthplace, and
       Year of Birth, with a Record of Their Degree,
       Alphabetically Arranged.* Early Series. Ed. Joseph
       Foster, 4 vols. Oxford: Parker, 1891-1892.

            Davenant is included in volume I.

350.   Fleay, Frederick Gard. *A Biographical Chronicle of
       the English Drama, 1559-1642.* 2 vols. London: [Burt
       Franklin], 1891. Rpt. New York: Lenox Hill, 1973.

            Fleay considers Davenant's career after his
       escape to France "as the principal link between the
       ante- and post-Restoration drama, especially in
       connexion with alterations in Shakespeare's plays." He
       comments also that "Not one of Davenant's plays was left
       unpublished." Other comments focus upon the pre-Civil
       War plays: *Albovine, The Wits, Love and Honor, Temple of
       Love, News from Plymouth,* and *Britannia Triumphans.*
       See *1973*: Fleay.

1892

351.   Gosse, Edmund W. "Sir William Davenant." In *The
       English Poets: Selections with Critical Introductions
       By Various Writers and a General Introduction by
       Matthew Arnold.* Thomas Humphrey Ward, ed. 4 vols.
       Oxford: Clarendon, 1892.

            See *1880*: Gosse.

352.   Howell, James. *Epistolae Ho-Elianae. The Familiar
       Letters.* Joseph Jacobs, ed. 2 vols. London: D.
       Nutt, 1892.

            The letters contain information on the court
       activities with particularly useful references to
       Davenant's plays. Bentley warns, however, that
       "Howell's dates are often faked." See *1941*: Bentley.

353.   Terry, F.C. Birkbeck. "'Davenant on Shakespeare' (8th
       S.i. 274)." *Notes & Queries*, 8th Ser., 1 (1892),
       461.

Responding to two questions, Terry explains the change from *captive* to *captain* and the interpretation of "rifled falls" in Davenant's poem on Shakespeare. See *1892*: Ward.

354.   Ward, C.A. "Davenant on Shakespeare." *Notes & Queries*, 8th Ser., 1 (1892), 274.

Ward asks about Davenant's poem on Shakespeare, specifically the words "rifled falls" of a plume, and "the teares of his last rage." See *1892*: Terry.

1895

355.   Case, R.H. "D'Avenant and Cromwell." *Notes & Queries*, 8th Ser., 7 (1895), 507.

Case asks about Davenant's epithalamium for the marriage of Cromwell's daughter in 1657.

356.   Krusenbaum, A. "Das Verhaeltnis von Davenant's Drama *The Rivals* zu *The Two Noble Kinsmen*." Diss. Halle, 1895.

1896

357.   Davey, H. "Samuel Pepys (8th Ser. ix. 307, 489)." *Notes & Queries*, 8th Ser., 10 (1896), 33-34.

Davey identifies the composers and musicians of Davenant's *Siege of Rhodes*.

358.   Marshall, George. "Replies: Samuel Pepys. (8th S. ix, 307)." *Notes & Queries*, 8th Ser., 9 (1896), 489-90.

In response to a query, Marshall identifies Davenant's lines from *Siege of Rhodes II*. He then discusses the music of the play and the various musicians.

359.   Marshall, George. "Samuel Pepys (8th Ser. ix. 307, 489, x. 33)." *Notes & Queries*, 8th Ser., 10 (1896), 96-97.

Marshall insists that Cooke, not Lawes or Locke, wrote most of the music for the "later productions of 'The Siege of Rhodes.'"

1897

360.   Evans, Herbert Arthur, ed. *English Masques*. London:
       Blackie, 1897. Rpt. Freeport, New York: Books for
       Library Presses, 1971. Pp. lxiii, 245.

              In a lengthy introduction, Evans explains the
       critical problems confronting the editor of a masque.
       He discusses among others Davenant's *Salmacida Spolia*,
       concluding with comments on the antimasque. Of the
       sixteen masques that he prints, Davenant's *Salmacida
       Spolia* is the last. See *1971*: Evans.

361.   Townshend, Dorothea (Baker). *The Life and Letters of
       Mr. Endymion Porter: Sometime Gentleman of the
       Bedchamber to King Charles the First*. London: T.
       Fisher Unwin, 1897. Pp. xii, 260.

              The book includes a discussion of Porter's
       friendship with Davenant. Their relationship is traced
       from 1628 when Lord Brooke died and Davenant lost his
       first patron. Porter became his new patron and, as the
       book shows, "did his best to foreward his friend's
       [Davenant's] interest at Court."

1898

362.   Aubrey, John. *'Brief Lives,' Chiefly of
       Contemporaries, Set Down by John Aubrey, Between the
       Years 1669-1696*. Ed. Andrew Clark. 2 vols. Oxford:
       Clarendon, 1898.

              The work provides the earliest account of
       Davenant's life by someone who knew him. The biography
       became the source for subsequent accounts of Davenant.

363.   Campbell, Killis. "The Sources of Davenant's *The
       Siege of Rhodes*." *Modern Language Notes*, 13 (1898),
       353-63.

              Deploring Maidment and Logan's neglect of the
       sources for Davenant's plays, Campbell cites in addition
       to Knolle's history, Wotton's translation of *Le
       Printemps d'Yver* (1592) and Kyd's *Solyman and Perseda*.
       He also points out Davenant's purposes in changing his
       material: to preserve the unities and to have a comic or
       tragi-comic denouement. So, Davenant used the
       historical account and the Solyman-Perseda episode.

364.   Schmerback, M. *Das Verhaltnis von Davenants "The*
       Man's the Master" zu Scarrons "Jodelet, ou le Maitre
       Valet." Halle, 1899.

365.   Warburton, Eliot. *Memoirs of Prince Rupert and the*
       Cavaliers. 3 vols. London: Richard Bentley, 1899.

              Among the several references to Davenant are
       two that suggest the Duke of Newcastle was behaving
       irresponsibly when he appointed the poet as
       Lieutenant-General of the Ordnance.

366.   Ward, Adolphus William. *A History of English Dramatic*
       Literature To the Death of Queen Anne. New and
       revised ed. 3 vols. London: Macmillan, 1899.

              In the third volume, Ward devotes two segments
       to Davenant. One contains commentaries on Davenant's
       biography, on *Gondibert*, and on his early plays and
       masques; the other discusses the later plays including
       the adaptations. The second segment concludes with a
       summary of "Davenant's position in our dramatic
       literature," as "the chief connecting link between two
       periods of our dramatic literature."

367.   Witt, Otto. "The Tempest, or The Enchanted Island. A
       Comedy by John Dryden. 1670. The Sea Voyage. A
       Comedy by Beaumont and Fletcher. 1647. The Goblins;
       Tragi-Comedy by Sir John Suckling. 1646. in ihrem
       Verhaltnis zu Shakespeares 'Tempest' und den ubrigen
       Quellen." Diss. Rostock 1899. Pp. 183.

              The title reveals some of the problems with
       the work: *The Sea Voyage* is by Massinger and Fletcher,
       not Beaumont and Fletcher, and *The Tempest* is not by
       Dryden alone. The segment on *The Tempest* gives a
       scene-by-scene analysis that concludes with references
       to Rosbund's dissertation (see *1882*) and a five-page
       table in which Witt compares Dryden's with Shakespeare's
       play. Davenant is intermittently mentioned as Dryden's
       collaborator.

D. TWENTIETH-CENTURY STUDIES: 1900-1985

1. 1900-1909

1900

368. Brotanek, R. "Ein Unerkanntes Werk Sir Will
Davenants." *Anglia Beiblatt*, 11 (1900), 177-81.

   The article discusses *Luminalia* and attributes
it to Davenant. Brotanek notes Davenant's relationship
to Lord Brooke, Ben Jonson, and Henrietta Maria and mentions the masque *The Temple of Love* and compares the
structure of *Britannia Triumphans* with that of
Luminalia. Finally, he suggests through the acting
parts of Jeffrey Hudson in both *Luminalia* and *Salmacida
Spolia* that Davenant wrote *Luminalia*. See *1913*:
Hooper.

369. Illies, Georg. "Das Verhaltnis von Davenants 'The
Law against Lovers' zu Shakespeares 'Measure for
Measure' und 'Much Ado about Nothing.'" Diss. Halle
1900. Pp. 90.

   The dissertation examines Davenant's synthesis
of *Measure for Measure* and *Much Ado About Nothing* to
form *The Law against Lovers*.

370. Ker, W. P., ed. *Essays of John Dryden*. 2 vols.
Oxford: Clarendon, 1900. Rpt. New York: Russell &
Russell, 1961.

   Dryden's debts and deference to Davenant are
reprinted in his "Epistle Dedicatory of the Rival
Ladies," "Preface to Annus Mirabilis," "Of Heroic Plays:
An Essay," and "A Parallel of Poetry and Painting." See
1961: Ker.

371. Saintsbury, George Edward Bateman. *A History of
Criticism and Literary Taste in Europe from the
Earliest Texts to the Present Day*. 3 vols. Edinburgh
and London: Blackwood, 1900-1904, II, 367.

   In a brief but incisive account of Davenant,
Saintsbury places *Gondibert* and the *Preface* in an
historical context that brings out the impact of French
literature and philosophy on the poet during his exile.

1902

372. Brotanek, R. Rudolf. *Die englischen Maskenspiele*.
      Wien und Leipzieg: W. Braumuller, 1902. Pp. xiv,
      371.

         Brotanek discusses Davenant's masques in
      detail, particularly *Britannia Triumphans, Luminalia,
      The Prince d'Amour, Salmicida Spolia,* and *The Temple of
      Love*.

373. Campbell, Killis. "The Source of Davenant's
      Albovine." *The Journal of English and Germanic
      Philology*, 4 (1902), 20-24.

         Campbell conjectures that Davenant's immediate
      source of *Albovine* was *De Gestis Longobardorum* of Paulus
      Disconus, and not literary versions of the story.
      Bentley disagrees, offering Belleforest's *Histoires
      Tragiques* as the source. See *1941*: Bentley.

374. Seccombe, Thomas. "The Poet Laureate of England."
      The Bookman, 15 (Aug. 1902), 544-56.

         Seccombe presents a brief but lively account
      of Davenant's laureateship with special emphasis on
      Gondibert.

1903

375. Arber, Edward. *The Term Catalogues, 1668-1709, With a
      Number for Easter Term, 1711*. 3 vols. London:
      Privately Printed, 1903-06.

         The volumes contain lists of works by
      contemporary authors identified in their booksellers'
      quarterly registers. Begun the year of Davenant's
      death, the volumes contain references to some work by
      Davenant himself and others by his imitators.

376. *A Calendar of the Middle Temple Records*. Ed. Charles
      Henry Hopwood. London: Butterworth, 1903.

         According to Edward Bagsheur, Treasurer from
      1660-62, Davenant was permitted by Richard Baddeley to
      use and reserve the Middle Temple Hall for the acting of
      a play "on last All Hallows' Eve."

377.   Campbell, Killis.   "Notes on D'Avenant's Life."
       Modern Language Notes, 18 (1903), 236-39.

              The article establishes some of Davenant's
       biographical background through a genealogical chart, an
       account of his early military experience, and his
       aborted trip to Maryland that concluded with his
       imprisonment by the Puritans.

378.   Chase, Lewis Nathaniel.   *The English Heroic Play: A
       Critical Description of the Rhymed Tragedy of the
       Restoration.*   Columbia University Studies in
       Comparative Literature.   New York: Columbia Univ.
       Press, 1903.   Pp. xii, 250.

              Chase uses Davenant's dramas, especially *The
       Siege of Rhodes*, for his definition of the English
       heroic play, and he discusses its form, poetry, theme,
       and development.   See *1965*: Chase.

379.   Firth, C. H.   "Sir William Davenant and the Revival of
       Drama during the Protectorate."   *English Historical
       Review*, 18 (1903), 319-20.

              Firth presents a document entitled "Some
       observations concerning the people of this nation" that
       he dates about 1656.   In the work, Davenant persuasively
       argues the moral value of public recreation, preparing
       London for his *First Day's Entertainment*.

380.   Fletcher, Jefferson Butler.   "Precieuses at the Court
       of Charles I."   *Journal of Comparative Literature*, 1
       (1903), 120-53.

              The article is an early and significant study
       of the court fad that prevailed during Davenant's early
       tenure as court poet and dramatist.   See *1911*:
       Fletcher.

381.   Lawrence, William J.   "A Forgotten Stage
       Conventionality."   *Anglia*, 26 (1903), 447-60.

              Lawrence traces the development of the
       proscenium doors and balconies from 1661-1822.   He
       begins with the Duke's Theatre in Lincoln's Inn Fields,
       citing in his discussion Davenant's *Siege of Rhodes* for
       stage directions to support his interpretation of the

location and uses of the proscenium doors. He uses also
Davenant's *The Man's the Master* and its epilogue for
references to balconies.

382. "Little Boyes." *Academy and Literature*, 64 (1903),
     34-36.

         The article suggests that *The Rehearsal* was
originally intended as an attack on Davenant.

383. Weber, Gustav. *Davenants "Macbeth" im Verhaltnis zu
     Shakespeares Gleichnamiger Tragodie.* Rostock: Carl
     Boldt, 1903. Pp. 76.

         Davenant's "modernized" production of *Macbeth*
at the Duke's Theater in 1674 with its alterations is
found to be unfortunate.

                           1904

384. Child, C.G. "The Rise of the Heroic Play." *Modern
     Language Notes*, 19 (1904), 166-73.

         Noting that Davenant predates Dryden in the
use and development of the heroic play, Child studies
The Siege of Rhodes as a contribution to the genre, and
argues that *Love and Honour* may be read as a
pre-Restoration heroic play.

385. Godfrey, Elizabeth [Jessie Bedford]. *Social Life
     Under the Stuarts.* London: Grant Richards, 1904. Pp.
     xxiv, 273.

         The book is a survey of all the elements that
comprise the social order under the Stuarts. It
includes Davenant as a Caroline playwright.

386. Kilbourne, Frederick W. "Stage Versions of
     Shakespeare before 1800." *Poet-Lore*, 15 (1904),
     111-22.

         The article lists those Restoration and
eighteenth-century plays that are alterations of
Shakespeare's plays. Kilbourne considers the plays as
"manifestations of dramatic notions forever and
rightfully rejected." He includes Davenant's
alterations along with the 1719 *Julius Caesar*. He does
not mention the 1676 *Hamlet*.

387. Lawrence, William. "Did Shadwell Write an Opera on
      'The Tempest'?" *Anglia*, 27 (1904), 205-17. Rpt.
      Anglia, 29 (1906), 539-41; *The Elizabethan Playhouse
      and Other Studies.* Stratford-on-Avon: Shakespeare
      Head, 1912, pp. 193-206; New York: Russell & Russell,
      1963.

           Lawrence argues that Shadwell was commissioned
      by the Duke's Company for the 1674 quarto of *The
      Tempest*. Lawrence arrives at his conclusion after
      tracing the stage history of the play covering the
      "brutally augmented revision of Shakespeare's play, the
      work of Dryden and Davenant." He also traces the
      publication history of the play. See *1947*: Milton;
      1946: Ward; *1963*: Lawrence.

388. Lawrence, William. "Purcell's Music for 'The
      Tempest.'" *Notes & Queries*, 10th Ser., 2 (August 27,
      1904), 164-65.

           Dating Shadwell's *Tempest* as April 1674,
      Lawrence argues that Purcell worked with Matthew Locke
      on the score, although Purcell was sixteen years old at
      the time.

389. Lawrence, W.J. "Locke's Music for 'Macbeth.'" *Notes
      & Queries*, 10th Ser., 2 (August 20, 1904), 142.

           Lawrence states that the first performance of
      Davenant's *Macbeth* predated 1672, citing instead
      1666-67 because of the date of Matthew Locke's music for
      the production and Pepy's entries for January 7, and
      April 19, 1667. He calls Downes "that arch-blunderer."

390. Squire, William B. "Purcell's Dramatic Music." *SIMG*,
      5 (1904), 489-564.

           Squire discusses Purcell's participation in
      the 1674 *Tempest*, the adaptation by Shadwell of the
      Davenant-Dryden version.

1905

391. Johnson, Samuel. *Lives of the English Poets.* Ed.
      George Birkbeck Hill. 3 vols. Oxford: Clarendon,
      1905. Rpt. New York: Octagon, 1967.

In his accounts of Milton and Dryden, Johnson
refers often to Davenant, occasionally in flattering
terms. For example, Davenant is considered Milton's
savior after the Restoration and the model for Dryden
and his use of rhyme in the drama. See *1967*: Johnson.

392. Lawrence, W.J. "A Forgotten Restoration Playhouse."
Englische Studien, 35 (1905), 279-89.

The essay deals with the Cockpit Theatre in
Drury Lane. On the basis of Chappuzeau's *Europe Vivante*
(1666), Lawrence identifies "another fully equipped
playhouse in Drury Lane in 1665 as well as the Theatre
Royal" as "the historic old Phoenix or Cockpit" that
George Jolly may have been using and continued to use
through 1667 despite Davenant and Killigrew's objections
and the king's edicts.

393. *Report on the Manuscripts of the Earl of Egmont.*
London: His Majesty's Stationers Office, 1905.

The Historical Manuscript Commission (LXIII)
includes a letter dated May 8, 1641, that cites Davenant
as a conspirator in the First Army Plot (Vol. I, Part I,
p. 134). See *1872*: (*H.M.C.*).

394. Williams, John David Ellis. "Sir William Davenant's
Relation to Shakespeare: With an Analysis of the Chief
Characters of Davenant's Plays." Diss. Strassburg
1905. Pp. 120.

Williams discusses Shakespeare's influence on
Davenant's original plays and his creation of
characters, citing many examples.

1906

395. Clarke, Ernest. "'The Tempest' as an 'Opera.'" *The
Athenaeum*, 4113 (25 Aug. 1906), 222-23.

Clarke opens his article with the comment, "No
play of Shakespeare has suffered more at the hands of
adapters than 'The Tempest.'" He documents Davenant's
adaptation with dates of performance and publication and
he reviews Davenant's changes. Attributing the opera to
Shadwell, Clarke concludes, "the version of 'The
Tempest' which is known amongst commentators as the

'Davenant' or the 'Dryden' or the 'Davenant-Dryden' must
not be credited wholly to these authors, unless
quotation be made exclusively from the very rare 1670
edition, a copy of which is in the British Museum but
which is not reprinted either by Maidment or Logan in
their edition of Davenant or by Professor Saintsbury in
his edition of Dryden."

396. Kilbourne, Frederick W. *Alterations and Adaptations
      of Shakespeare.* Boston: Poet Lore, 1906.

            The book covers Davenant's alterations in
      which "changes were made to suit certain hastily
      conceived and bad theories of dramatic art" (p. 19).
      Kilbourne describes and discusses Davenant's *Tempest*--an
      "eternal disgrace"--*Law against Lovers, Julius Caesar,*
      and *Macbeth.* The book's basic thesis is that
      Shakespeare was the supreme playwright, and alteration
      and adaptation of his plays weakened them.

397. Lawrence, William. "Did Shadwell Write an Opera on
      'The Tempest'?" *Anglia,* 29 (1906), 539-41.

            See *1904*: Lawrence.

398. Lee, Sidney. *Pepys and Shakespeare: A Paper read at
      the Sixth Meeting of the Samuel Pepys Club, on
      Thursday, November 30, 1905.* London: Bedford, 1906.
      Pp. 40. Rpt. Folcroft, Pa.: Folcroft Library, 1974.
      Pp. 40.

            First printed in the *Fortnightly Review*
      (January 1906), the work focuses on Pepys' theatergoing
      (351 times in 9 years and 5 months) much of it at
      Davenant's theater. See *1974*: Lee.

399. Meyers, C. "Opera in England from 1656-1728."
      Western Reserve Bulletin, 9 (1906).

                        1908

400. Schelling, Felix E. *Elizabethan Drama 1558-1642. A
      History of the Drama in England from the Accession of
      Queen Elizabeth to the Closing of the Theatres, to
      which is prefixed a Resume of the Earlier Drama from
      its Beginnings.* 2 vols. Boston and New York:
      Houghton Mifflin, 1908.

Davenant is cited for his masques, romances, and heroic and platonic dramas. In the chapter "Decadent Romance" Schelling summarizes *The Siege*, *Love and Honour*, *The Platonic Lovers*, and *The Fair Favorite* because they are the "forebears of the heroic play." He sees *The Just Italian*, *The Wits*, and *News from Plymouth* also as precursors of the later drama.

401.   Spingarn, Joel Elias, ed. *Critical Essays of the Seventeenth Century*. 3 vols. Oxford: Clarendon, 1908-09.

The third volume contains Davenant's discourse on *Gondibert* and Hobbes' *Answer*. See *1963*: Spingarn.

402.   Upham, Alfred Horatio. *The French Influence in English Literature from the Accession of Elizabeth to the Restoration*. Columbia University Studies in Comparative Literature. New York: Columbia Univ. Press, 1908. Pp. ix, 560.

Upham examines at length the precieuses and Platonists in relationship to Davenant, his poems, plays, and masques.

1909

403.   Bradford, Gamaliel, Jr. "The Second Poet Laureate." *The Nation*, 89 (August 1909), 135-38.

Valuable as a source of information on Davenant's reputation early in the twentieth century, the essay both praises and damns the poet. According to Bradford, Davenant "is chiefly known as the initiator of the corrupt Restoration stage and the debaser of Shakespeare." Yet, by the end of the essay, Bradford reaffirms the fine quality of Davenant's *Gondibert* when he says, "love and death and almost all things human are clarified and glorified by the divine magic of beauty."

404.   "Commission to Governor Berkeley and Council [from Charles II at Breda]. June 3, 1650." *The Virginia Magazine of History and Biography*, 17 (Jan. 1909), 134-41.

The "Commission" names Davenant to the Council of the Colonies and Plantation of Virginia. The

original document is among the McDonald Papers in the
Virginia State Library.

405.   Reyher, Paul. *Les Masques Anglais. Etude sur les
        ballets et la vie de cour en Angleterre
        (1512-1640)*.... Paris: Hachette, 1909. Pp. x, 563.

        The book is a lengthy study of the masques
including important segments about *Britannia Triumphans,
Luminalia, Salmacida Spolia,* and *The Temple of Love.*
See *1964*: Reyher.

406.   Tupper, James W., ed. *Love and Honour*; and *The Seige
        of Rhodes.* Belles-Lettres Series. New York: Heath,
        1909. Pp. xxxviii, 410.

        Tupper provides a brief biography and a useful
introduction to the 1649 quarto edition of the first
play and the 1663 edition of the second play. He has
also compiled a brief bibliography and glossary.

1910

407.   Aicard, Jean. *William Davenant*. In *Theatre*. Paris:
       Ernest Flammarion, 1910, I, 17-76.

              A one-act play, *William Davenant* is set in
       Oxford in 1623 and represents Davenant as a youth of
       sixteen. The play was written for the 1879 visit of the
       Comedie Francaise to London's Gaiety Theater, where the
       company performed from July 1st to 12th.

408.   Bayne, Ronald. "Lesser Jacobean and Caroline
       Dramatists." In *The Drama to 1642, Part Two*.
       Vol. VI of *The Cambridge History of English
       Literature*. 14 vols. Ed. Sir A.W. Ward and A.R.
       Waller. Cambridge: University Press, 1910, pp.
       210-40.

              The last dramatist in the chapter is Davenant
       who is presented as a transitional figure because his
       work begins in the style of Fletcher and ends with the
       heroic style later employed by Dryden.

409.   Bolland, William Craddock. "The Morocco Ambassador of
       1682." *The Antiquary*, 6 (1910), 124-34, 179-84.

              During his visit to London, the Moroccan
       Ambassador saw *The Tempest*, probably Shadwell's
       adaptation of the Davenant-Dryden, at the Duke's Theatre
       in Dorset Garden, which pleased him, though he could not
       understand English.

410.   Hall, Clayton Colman, ed. *Narratives of Early
       Maryland, 1633-1684*. New York: Scribner's, 1910. Pp.
       ix, 460.

              The work contains an introduction that places
       Davenant's aborted trip and commission to Maryland in
       perspective, and it reprints in pamphlet form the
       announcement of Davenant's appointment as
       lieutenant-governor by Charles II. See *1653*: Calvert.

411.   Miles, Dudley Howe. *The Influence of Moliere on
       Restoration Comedy*. Columbia University Studies in
       Comparative Literature. New York: Columbia Univ.
       Press, 1910. Pp. xi, 272. Rpt. New York: Octagon,
       1971. Pp. xi, 272.

Miles examines Moliere's impact on comedy from 1660 to 1700. He notes Davenant's use of Moliere's comedy for *The Play-house to be Let*. Generally, he sees the French drama as superior to the English. See *1971*: Miles.

412. Ristine, Frank Humphrey. *English Tragicomedy: Its Origin and History*. New York: Columbia Univ. Press, 1910. Pp. xv, 247.

The work's fifth chapter, "The Heyday of English Tragicomedy (1610 to 1642)" and sixth, "The Decline of Tragicomedy (1642-1700)," contain frequent references to Davenant's Fletcherian drama as chief contributions to the genre with plays such as *The Distresses*, *The Platonic Lovers*, and *The Just Italian*. The hint of heroic drama is noted in *The Siege*, *The Fair Favorite*, and *Love and Honor*. Ristine notes Davenant's revivals after 1660 of his own plays and adaptations of others with *Law against Lovers* and *The Rivals*.

1911

413. Fletcher, Jefferson Butler. *The Religion of Beauty in Women, and other Essays on Platonic Love in Poetry and Society*. New York: Haskell House, 1911. Pp. xi, 205.

The final chapter is a restatement of his earlier article on the court practice of the precieuses influenced by Henrietta Maria. He notes the practice of the court that was to be counterbalanced by the code and its expression in the writings of Davenant and others. See *1903*: Fletcher.

414. Greg, W. W. "The Bakings of Betsy." *The Library*, 3rd Ser., 2 (1911), 225-59.

Greg writes of invented figures, i.e., Betsy Baker, as an analogy to Warburton and his conclusions about the circumstances behind the publication of Davenant's *Love and Honour* in 1649. Greg finds that Warburton, on the basis of evidence offered, can not be proved right or wrong.

415. Gronauer, Georg. "Sir William Davenant's Gondibert." Diss. Munchen, 1911.

The work is an early twentieth-century
dissertation from Germany that examines Davenant's
Gondibert. It offers the idea that the last four books
of the *Aeneid* were a source.

416.   Hurd, Richard. *Hurd's Letters on Chivalry and
        Romance, with the Third Elizabethan Dialogue.* Ed.
        Edith J. Morley. London: Henry Frowde, 1911.

               See *1762*: Hurd; *1811*: Hurd; *1824*: Aikin; and
        1963: Hurd.

417.   Jaggard, William. *Shakespeare Bibliography. A
        Dictionary of Every Known Issue of the Writings of Our
        National Poet and of Recorded Opinion Thereon in the
        English Language.* Stratford-on-Avon: Shakespeare
        Head, 1911. Pp. xxi, 729.

               The volume contains information on the
        Restoration and eighteenth-century theaters, actors,
        adaptations, and editors, all of which are incorporated
        into a history of Shakespeare studies and performances.
        In the section labelled "Davenant," Jaggard lists
        Davenant's Shakespeare adaptations and he comments on a
        letter from the king to Shakespeare, that Davenant
        owned.

418.   Morgenroth, Hugo. *Quellenstudien zu William Davenants
        Albovine.* Borna-Leipzig: R. Noske, 1911. Pp. 29.

               The work is a source study of *Albovine*.

419.   *The Pepys Manuscripts at Magdalene College, Cambridge.*
        London: His Majesty's Stationers Office, 1911.

               The Historical Manuscript Commission (LXX),
        Seventeenth Report, publishes the Pepys Manuscripts,
        which include copies of several documents dated
        September 1649 concerning Davenant's appointment as
        Treasurer of Virginia, an office that he never held
        because of his imprisonment by Parliamentary forces.
        Also included is information on his arms and ammunition
        accounts. See *1872*: (*H.M.C.*).

420.   Spingarn, J. E. "Jacobean and Caroline Criticism."
        In *Cavalier and Puritan.* Vol. VII of *The Cambridge
        History of English Literature.* 14 vols. Eds. Sir A.

W. Ward and A. R. Waller. Cambridge: University
Press, 1911, pp. 259-75.

       Spingarn discusses Davenant's "Preface" to
Gondibert as both a dilution of Hobbes' philosophy and a
precursor to Dryden. Davenant is again a transitional
figure.

421. Thompson, A. Hamilton. "Writers of the Couplet."
     In *Cavalier and Puritan*. Vol. VII of *The Cambridge
     History of English Literature*. 14 vols. Eds. Sir A.
     W. Ward and A. R. Waller. Cambridge: University
     Press, 1911, pp. 48-71.

       The chapter concludes with Davenant and a
discussion of *Gondibert*.

422. Winter, William. *Shakespeare on the Stage*. New York:
     Moffat, Yard, 1911. Pp. 564.

       See *1911*: Winter, "Shakespere."

423. Winter, William. "Shakespere on the Stage: *Hamlet*."
     The Century Magazine, 81 (1911), 485-500. Rpt.
     Shakespeare on the Stage. New York: Moffat, Yard,
     1911. Pp. 564.

       The article discusses productions and
performances from Shakespeare's time to 1911. Included
is commentary on Betterton and Davenant. See *1911*:
Winter, *Shakespeare*.

424. Winter, William. "Shakespere on the Stage Second
     Paper: Macbeth." *The Century Magazine*, 81 (1911)
     923-938.

       Opening with a description of Davenant's
Macbeth as acted by Betterton, Winter argues that
Matthew Locke composed the music for the songs and
indicates that the alteration held the stage until 1774,
when Garrick returned to Shakespeare's text. See *1911*:
Winter, *Shakespeare*.

1912

425. Davey, H. "Sir William Davenant's 'Entertainment at
     Rutland House' (2nd Ser.v.8)." *Notes & Queries*, 11
     Ser., 5 (1912), 77.

Davey identifies the *Calendar of State Papers, Domestic*, 128, for information on the performance on 23 May 1656. See *1858*: Delacourt. See also *1912*: Nicholson.

426. Lawrence, W.J. "Did Thomas Shadwell Write an Opera on 'The Tempest'?" *The Elizabethan Playhouse and Other Studies*. First Series. Stratford-on-Avon: Shakespeare Head, 1912, pp. 193-206.

Lawrence argues that the play issued by Herringman as the Dryden-Davenant *Tempest* with Dryden's preface, prologue, and epilogue, is by Shadwell. According to Lawrence, Shadwell's *Tempest* prevailed from the time of its first performance. See *1904*: Lawrence; *1947*: Milton; *1946*: Ward.

427. Lawrence, W.J. "Proscenium Doors: An Elizabethan Heritage." *The Elizabethan Playhouse and Other Studies*. First Series. Stratford-on-Avon: Shakespeare Head, 1912, pp. 159-89. Rpt. with some revisions in *The Elizabethan Playhouse and Other Studies*. 2nd Ser. Stratford-upon-Avon: Shakespeare Head, 1912, pp. 121-47.

Lawrence examines the proscenium doors and their use. He also examines the use of curtains, musicians, audience, and the conventions of London and Dublin theaters, citing the patents, their complex history, *The Siege of Rhodes*, *The Cruelty of the Spaniards in Peru*, and *The History of Sir Francis Drake*.

428. Lawrence, W.J. "The Seventeenth Century Theatre: Systems of Admission." *Anglia*, 35 (1912), 526-38. Rpt. with some additions as "Early Systems of Admission." *The Elizabethan Playhouse and Other Studies*. 2nd Ser. Stratford-on-Avon: Shakespeare Head, 1912, pp. 96-118.

Lawrence describes various modes of collecting tickets during the seventeenth century. He notes the abuses by the public, the door keepers, and bookkeepers. He cites Davenant's theater and the ballad-epilogue to *The Man's the Master* for some of the problems, particularly one that permitted people to see an act before they paid for admission. In 1670 Charles II

issued a proclamation that no one could enter "rudely"
or "by force." All had to pay.

429.   Lawrence, W.J. "Who Wrote the Famous 'Macbeth'
       Music?" *The Elizabethan Playhouse and Other Studies.*
       1st Ser. Stratford-on-Avon: Shakespeare Head, 1912,
       pp. 209-24.

          The article identifies Purcell as the composer
       and points out that Downes wrongly stated that Locke
       wrote it.

430.   Nicholson, Watson. "Sir William Davenant's
       'Entertainment at Rutland House.'" *Notes & Queries,*
       11 Ser., 5 (1912), 8.

          Responding to Delacourt's question in 1858,
       Nicholson asks for information about Davenant's
       manuscript. See *1858*: Delacourt; see *1912*: Davey.

431.   Schelling, Felix. "The Restoration Drama, I." In *The
       Age of Dryden.* Vol. VIII of *The Cambridge History of
       English Literature.* 14 vols. Ed. Sir A. W. Ward and
       A. R. Waller. Cambridge: Cambridge Univ. Press, 1912,
       pp. 115-45.

          The chapter offers information from the period
       after the theaters closed, discusses influences on the
       English stage, and concludes with a commentary on one
       play. Davenant dominates a third of the chapter, and
       Schelling places him in perspective over the period
       beginning just before the Restoration to 1700.

432.   Ward, A. W. "Dryden." *The Age of Dryden.* Vol. VIII
       of *The Cambridge History of English Literature.* Ed.
       A. W. Ward and A. R. Waller. Cambridge: Cambridge
       Univ. Press, 1912, pp. 1-57.

          The first chapter contains numerous references
       to Davenant because of his influence on the Restoration
       generally and Dryden specifically.

1913

433.   Acheson, Arthur. *Mistress Davenant: The Dark Lady of
       Shakespeare's Sonnets.* London: Bernard Quaritch,
       1913. Pp. 332.

Acheson argues from evidence and conjecture that Mistress Davenant is the Dark Lady of the sonnets.

434. Acheson, Arthur. *Woman Coloured Ill.* London: Bernard Quaritch, 1913. Pp. 16.

First published in another form, the pamphlet claims to establish "beyond the possibility of doubt the identity of Mistress Davenant, wife of John Davenant, the Oxford vintner, as the Dark Lady of Shakespeare's Sonnets...."

435. Fowell, Frank, and Frank Palmer. *Censorship in England.* London: Frank Palmer, 1913. Pp. 390.

In Chapter IV "Suppression and Reaction," Fowell and Palmer discuss ordinances by Parliament in 1644 and 1647 against "Acts of Stage-Players, Interludes, and Common Players" and Davenant's defiance of these ordinances in 1658, with the production of *The Cruelty of the Spaniards in Peru* "at Drury Lane." They also describe the patents granted to Killigrew and Davenant, which enjoined them "not anytime hereafter cause to be acted or represented any play, enterlude, opera, containing any matter of prophanation scurrility or obscenity" (p. 89). In effect, Killigrew and Davenant had become Royal censors, a fact that brought a vigorous response from Sir Henry Herbert, the Master of the Revels. The jurisdictional argument that ensued is outlined as well.

436. Gillet, J.E. *Moliere en Angleterre, 1660-1700.* Paris: Champion, 1913. Pp. 240.

Upon examining nineteen adaptations of Moliere's plays, Gillet notes major schools of development in England. One of the playwrights examined is Davenant.

437. Hooper, Edith S. "The Authorship of 'Luminalia' and Notes on Some Other Poems of Sir William D'Avenant." *Modern Language Review*, 8 (1913), 540-43.

Hooper establishes Brotanek's conjecture that Davenant wrote both *Luminalia* and *Britannia Triumphans.* Brotanek cited stylistic similarities; Hooper cites information from the Stationers' Hall Register. She

also notes an entry on December 7, 1657, for the
publication of Davenant's poetry, suggesting that this
too might be an instance of a notice of publication
without actual publication occurring. See *1900*:
Brotanek.

438. Lawrence, W.J. *The Elizabethan Playhouse and Other
      Studies.* 2nd ser. Stratford-upon-Avon: Shakespeare
      Head, 1913. Pp. xvi, 261.

              In an essay on theater programs, Lawrence
      refers to Davenant's opera; in one on admissions to
      plays, he refers to lines from *Man's the Master*; in
      another on the "picture-stage," he refers to the
      patents, their complex history, and *The Siege of Rhodes,
      The Cruelty of the Spaniards in Peru*, and *The History of
      Sir Francis Drake.* In the extended discussion, Lawrence
      includes Davenant's post-1660 theater productions as
      well. See *1912*: Lawrence.

439. Wheatley, Henry B. "Post-Restoration Quartos of
      Shakespeare's Plays." *The Library*, 3rd Ser., 4
      (1913), 237-69.

              Wheatley gives the quarto editions of each
      play from 1660-1771 along with adaptations. He notes,
      "With the exception of Davenant and Dryden, the names of
      the original 'improvers' do not impress us with
      confidence as to their capability for the task which
      they light-heartedly undertook." He deplores, however,
      Davenant's "vulgarization" and "supposed improvement" of
      Shakespeare's plays. He gives notice of Shakespeare's
      plays after 1660.

                              1914

440. Keith, William Grant. "The Designs for the First
      Movable Scenery on the English Public Stage."
      Burlington Magazine, 25 (1914), 29-33, 85-98.

              Upon examining some plans of scenes and stages
      for *The Siege of Rhodes* at Rutland House, Keith declares
      that Webb transposed Inigo Jones' type of staging for
      the court theaters into the public theater. The article
      refutes the claim of foreign influence on the public
      stage design.

441. Lawrence, W.J. "Restoration Stage Nurseries." *Archiv fur das Studium der neuren Sprachen und Literaturen*, 132 (1914), 301-25.

The nurseries began under the managements of Killigrew and Davenant. Lawrence suggests that actresses were introduced because of the vacuum for "boy-apprentices to play female parts" during the Interregnum. Lawrence traces the development of "a Nursery for the training of players for both theatres under the supervision" of Davenant and Killigrew from a warrant dated July 23, 1663. The involvement of George Jolly and Colonel William Legg is clarified by the patent issued on March 30, 1664. Lawrence concludes that two nurseries existed at first and that, after the deaths of Davenant and Legg, only one remained. The graduates of the nurseries were undistinguished actors.

442. Winter, William. "Twelfth Night: Shakespeare on the Stage." *The Century Magazine*, 88 (1914), 683-94.

Winter presents a summary of the Davenant acting company of 1661 with special attention to Betterton.

1916

443. Bartlett, Henrietta Collins, and Alfred W. Pollard. *A Census of Shakespeare's Plays in Quarto, 1594-1709*. New Haven: Yale Univ. Press, 1916. Pp. xli, 153.

The work contains an annotated, alphabetical list of the plays and a chronological list of the editions according to their titles.

444. Brett-Smith, H.F.B. "Vaughan and D'avenant." *Modern Language Review*, 11 (1916), 66-78.

The article identifies the "aged Sire" in Vaughan's poem "TO Sir *William D'avenant*, upon his *Gondibert*" as Homer. See *1948*: Marilla.

445. McAfee, Helen. *Pepys on the Restoration Stage*. New Haven: Yale Univ. Press, 1916. Pp. 353. Rpt. New York: Benjamin Blom, 1963. Pp. 353.

The book collects those passages from Pepys' diary that relate to the theater and to the drama. It

also provides an introduction on Pepys' life and his
relationship to the theater, a bibliography, notes, and
illustrations. Many of the references relate to
Davenant, his life, plays, and theater. See *1963*:
McAfee.

446.   Stonex, Arthur B. "The Usurer in Elizabethan Drama."
       Publications of the Modern Language Association, 31
       (1916), 190-210.

       The article examines the impact of the
character of the usurer on plots in Renaissance
literature. Among a number of plays, Stonex examines
Davenant's *The Wits*.

447.   Winter, William. *Shakespeare on the Stage*. 3rd Ser.
       New York: Moffat, Yard, 1916. Pp. 538.

       Winter continues his account of Shakespeare on
the stage with *Cymbeline* by Davenant, as well as the
better known production of *Macbeth* and the introduction
of scenery. See *1969*: Winter.

1917

448.   Adams, Joseph Quincy, ed. *The Dramatic Records of Sir
       Henry Herbert, Master of the Revels, 1623-1673*.
       Cornell Studies in English, Vol. III. New Haven: Yale
       Univ. Press, 1917. Pp. xiii, 155. Rpt. New York:
       Benjamin Blom, [1964?]. Pp. xiii, 155.

       The work contains Sir Henry Herbert's Office
Book (1622-1642), documents relating to that period,
and, of importance here, several documents and records
that relate to Davenant's theater and playwriting before
the Civil War and after the Restoration. Significant
accounts include the August 21, 1660, patent, quoted in
full, and subsequent items relating to the separate and
united companies of Davenant and Killigrew. See *1964*:
Adams.

449.   Adams, Joseph Quincy. *Shakespearean Playhouses: A
       History of English Theatres from the Beginnings to the
       Restoration*. Boston: Houghton Mifflin, 1917. Pp.
       473. Rpt. Gloucester, Mass.: P. Smith, 1960. Pp.
       473.

The work provides information on the royal
patents given to Davenant and others and the theater
managerial positions. See *1960*: Adams.

450.   Ibershoff, C.H. "Dryden's *Tempest* as a Source of
       Bodmer's *Noah*." *Modern Philology*, 15 (1917), 247-53.

Ibershoff alludes to Davenant as Dryden's
collaborator and then gives parallel items from one play
to the other to support his title.

451.   Lawrence, W.J. "The English Theatre Orchestra: Its
       Rise and Early Characteristics." *Musical Quarterly*, 3
       (1917), 9-27.

After suggesting that the first placement of
the orchestra outside of the stage area occurred in 1627
with the opening of the Teatro di San Cassiano in
Venice, Lawrence examines Inigo Jones' masques and
Davenant's Commonwealth entertainments in an unsuccessful search for a similar handling of music in the
English theater. Shadwell's lavish musical adaptation
of the Davenant-Dryden *Tempest* provides the first
example of musicians placed between the stage and the
spectators. Yet the Duke's Theatre in Dorset Garden
provided an Elizabethan style musicians loft, as well.

1918

452.   Perry, Henry Ten Eyck. *The First Duchess of Newcastle
       and Her Husband as Figures in Literary History*.
       Harvard Studies in English, Vol. IV. Boston and
       London: Ginn, 1918. Pp. 335.

The book is a study of two figures whose
activities as Royalist exiles and writers clarify
Davenant's life. Davenant was an officer under
Newcastle's command; he was also in exile during the
Interregnum while the Newcastles were in exile; and he
was read by both Newcastles. Of particular interest is
the Duchess' literary critique of *Gondibert* that Perry
notes.

3. 1920-1929

1920

453. Lawrence, W.J. "Doors and Curtains in Restoration Theatres." *Modern Language Review*, 15 (1920), 414-20.

      He offers a date when two doors were placed behind the curtain; he states that the curtain was dropped before the end of the play only six times in the forty years and that happened after the epilogue. In the course of his argument, Lawrence refers to Davenant's Commonwealth operas.

454. Nicoll, Allardyce. "The Origin and Types of the Heroic Tragedy." *Anglia*, 44 (1920), 325-36.

      Nicoll suggests that Davenant "was the chief channel" through which influence of the past and of the continental drama came to England to form the heroic drama. He traces the language, theme, characterization, and staging of the rhymed drama that survived in a way in eighteenth-century melodrama.

455. Nicoll, Allardyce. "Scenery in the Restoration Theatre." *Anglia*, 44 (1920), 217-25.

      The article provides a history of scenery and machinery as it was used in Restoration theaters, correlating some uses with particular plays. Nicoll focuses on the actual scenery used in seventeenth-century productions, many of them Davenant's.

456. Odell, George C.D. *Shakespeare from Betterton to Irving*. 2 vols. New York: Charles Scribner's, 1920. Rpt. New York: Benjamin Blom, 1963; rpt. With a New Introduction by Robert Hamilton Ball. New York: Dover, 1966.

      Odell traces in the first volume the treatment of Shakespeare during the Restoration and eighteenth century. He begins by discussing Davenant, his theater, and his adaptations. The work offers details and illustrations. See *1963*: Odell; *1966*: Odell.

457. Thaler, Alwin. "The Elizabethan Dramatic Companies." *Publications of the Modern Language Association*, 35 (1920), 123-59.

Thaler provides a history of the companies
that includes Davenant's activities.

458. Thaler, Alwin. "The Players at Court, 1564-1642."
      Journal of English and Germanic Philology, 19 (1920),
      19-46.

The article provides background, writers, and
costs of the court masques. Davenant is part of the
account.

1921

459. "An Elegy Upon the Death of S^{r}· William Davenant." *A
      Little Ark Containing Sundry Pieces of
      Seventeenth-Century Verse*. G. Thorn-Drury, ed.
      London: P.J. and A.E. Dobell, 1921, pp. 35-37.

Thorn-Drury's small volume of fifty-seven
pages contains sixteen poems, one an elegy to Davenant
with a concluding comic couplet. In the poem Davenant
is surrounded by Jonson, Shakespeare, Beaumont, and
Fletcher, all great seventeenth-century dramatists.

460. Broadus, Edmund Kemper. *The Laureateship: A Study of
      the Office of Poet Laureate in England with Some
      Account of the Poets*. Oxford: Clarendon, 1921. Pp.
      vi, 239.

The book places Davenant's claim to the
laureateship in perspective, citing that he was stated
to be the successor to Ben Jonson according to the
monarch's patent. See *1969*: Broadus.

461. Nettleton, George Henry. *English Drama of the
      Restoration and Eighteenth Century (1642-1780)*. New
      York: Macmillan, 1921. Pp. xv, 366.

In his commentary of the drama, Nettleton
devotes an early segment to Davenant. Beginning with
Davenant as the major link between the Elizabethan and
Restoration drama, Nettleton traces the
playwright-manager's career through the Interregnum to
his operas and his patents after 1660. The playwright
continues to appear throughout the book.

462. Poston, Mervyn L. "The Origin of the English Heroic
      Play." *Modern Language Review*, 16 (1921), 18-22.

Poston emphasizes the importance of the French
drama as an influence on post-Restoration English
theater. Admitting the purely English features of the
shape of the stage, the introduction of scenery and
actresses, and the new opera, Poston notes that the main
elements of the heroic play came from the French. He
begins with *The Siege of Rhodes* and moves to Orrery and
Philips and their use of French sources for their
rhymed heroic dramas.

463. Rollins, Hyder E. "A Contribution to the History of
English Commonwealth Drama." *Studies in Philology*, 18
(1921), 267-333.

The article provides a history of the
Interregnum drama that depends upon the British Museum's
Thomason Collection's newsbooks, bills, and pamphlets.
See *1923*: Rollins.

464. Squire, William B. "The Music of Shadwell's *Tempest*."
Music Quarterly, 7 (1921), 565-78.

Squire continues the discussion of Purcell's
role in the music for *The Tempest* adaptation by Shadwell
of the Davenant-Dryden version.

1922

465. Acheson, Arthur. *Shakespeare's Sonnet Story,
1592-1598: Restoring the Sonnets written to the Earl
of Southampton to their original books and correlating
them with personal phases of the Plays of the Sonnet
period; with documentary evidence identifying Mistress
Davenant as the Dark Lady*. London: Bernard Quaritch,
1922. Pp. xxxi, 676.

The book includes Acheson's familiar story of
Davenant's mother and Shakespeare. Of the four
appendices, the second traces the Davenant's of London,
and the fourth traces John Davenant of Oxford and the
Houghs.

466. Bartlett, Henrietta Collins. *Mr. William Shakespeare,
Original and Early Editions of His Quartos and Folios;
His Source Book and those Containing Contemporary
Notices*. New Haven: Yale Univ. Press, 1922. Pp.
xxviii, 217.

Bartlett provides a checklist of Davenant's
published Shakespeare adaptations.

467.   Ehrle, Karl. "Studien zu Sir William Davenant's
       Tragodien und Tragikomodien." Diss. Munich 1922.

The dissertation examines Davenant's tragedies
and tragicomedies.

468.   Nicoll, Allardyce. "Charles II at the Theatre."
       Times Literary Supplement, September 14, 1922, p.
       584; September 21, 1922, pp. 600-01; October 5, 1922,
       pp. 631-32.

Nicoll, after mentioning that most Restoration
plays are dated through evidence from Pepys, Evelyn,
Herbert, and Downes, offers additional documentation
from the Lord Chamberlain's Warrant Books that include
negotiations involving Davenant's widow and his plays
*The Siege of Rhodes, The Man's the Master, The Tempest,
Macbeth,* and *Hamlet.* The information is also available
in Nicoll's *Restoration Drama.* See *1923:* Nicoll.

469.   Nicoll, Allardyce. *Dryden as an Adapter of
       Shakespeare.* London: Oxford Univ. Press, 1922. Pp.
       34. Also Milford: Shakespeare Society, 1922. Pp.
       31.

The work is a printing of Nicoll's lecture to
the Shakespeare Society in 1921. Nicoll considers in
some detail the Davenant-Dryden *Tempest, or, The
Enchanted Island,* and the changes the adapters made.
The work has a brief bibliography of Shakespeare
adaptations, 1660-1700.

470.   Summers, Montague. *Shakespeare Adaptations. The
       Tempest, The Mock Tempest, and King Lear.* With an
       Introduction and Notes. London: Jonathan Cape, 1922.
       Pp. cviii, 282. Rpt. New York: Benjamin Blom, 1966.
       Pp. cviii, 282. Rpt. New York: Haskell House, 1966.
       Pp. 282.

The volume contains the 1670 version of *The
Tempest* by Davenant. The introduction discusses each
play and the background of the adaptation, bringing the
reader to the nineteenth century. See *1966:* Summers.

471.   Thaler, Alwin. *Shakespere to Sheridan, A Book About
       the Theatre of Yesterday and Today.* Cambridge:
       Harvard Univ. Press, 1922. Pp. xviii, 339. Rpt. New
       York: Benjamin Blom, 1963. Pp. 339.

              Thaler discusses in detail the playwrights,
       players, managers, playhouses, and the court. Davenant
       as playwright-manager appears throughout the book.
       Longer commentaries that include Davenant concern the
       patents, Pepys' reactions to the plays, and the Duke's
       men. See *1963*: Thaler.

                              1923

472.   Boas, Frederick Samuel. *Shakespeare and the
       Universities, and Other Studies in Elizabethan Drama.*
       Oxford: B. Blackwell, 1923. Pp. vii, 272.

              Boas gives an account of the two different
       kinds of influence exerted on productions of Shakespeare
       in the sixteenth and seventeenth centuries by the
       universities and the Office of the Revels. Davenant is
       cited at first because of his family's residence,
       Oxford, where his father was mayor. He becomes, Boas
       notes, a link between the town/gown association. Boas
       then mentions Davenant as manager and playwright, noting
       The Siege of Rhodes, The Witts, and *The Tempest* in the
       course of the book.

473.   Campbell, Lily B. *Scenes and Machines on the English
       Stage During the Renaissance.* Cambridge: Cambridge
       Univ. Press, 1923. Pp. x, 302.

              The book examines the development of
       stagecraft from classical times and the classical
       influence on England through the Restoration. The
       writer argues that prior to the Restoration most of the
       classical influence came through Italy but after the
       Restoration the classical influence came both through
       France and Italy. The fourth section considers
       stagecraft as it developed in England after the
       Restoration, a useful study for anyone working on
       Davenant. See *1960*: Campbell.

474.   Eich, Louis M. "Alterations of Shakespeare 1660-1710:
       And an Investigation of the Critical and Dramatic
       Principles and Theatrical Conventions which Prompted
       These Revisions." Diss. Michigan 1923. Pp. 211.

Eich discusses the changes in society and the theaters of the Restoration that enabled playwrights and managers to alter and adapt Shakespeare's plays. Some were altered so that poetic justice would prevail, women's parts would be larger, and plays could be more elaborately produced. Particular attention is given to Davenant.

475. Hotson, J. Leslie. "George Jolly, Actor-Manager: New Light on the Restoration Stage." *Studies in Philology*, 20 (1923), 422-43.

Hotson describes Jolly as "a dangerous rival of Davenant and Killigrew" and he offers new evidence of Jolly's activities on the Continent during the Commonwealth and he introduces documents important to a study of the English stage. Hotson's chronology depends upon Davenant's parallel activities. The article also examines the complex history of the licenses and theater companies.

476. Hotson, Leslie. "Sir William Davenant and the Commonwealth Stage." Diss. Harvard, 1923.

The dissertation opens with a biography of Davenant that contains material not offered in other works. The remainder is an account of the Commonwealth stage from the view that Davenant and Killigrew were active in that period and sought to cheat George Jolly.

477. Nicoll, Allardyce. *A History of Restoration Drama, 1660-1700*. Cambridge: Cambridge Univ. Press, 1923. Pp. 403. Rpt. with revisions Cambridge: Cambridge Univ. Press, 1928. Pp. ix, 410.

The volume contains accounts of plays, theaters, and stage conditions. It has three appendices: "History of the Playhouses, 1660-1700"; "Documents Illustrating the History of the Stage"; and "A Hand-List of Restoration Plays." Of Davenant, Nicoll provides comment on all his plays, his career as playwright-manager, and his importance to Restoration drama. In the second revised edition, Nicoll corrects several errors and offers new evidence. See *1922*: Nicoll; *1928*: Nicoll; *1952*: Nicoll.

478. Pendlebury, Bevin John. *Dryden's Heroic Plays: A Study of the Origins*. London: Selwyn, 1923. Pp. 141. Rpt. New York: Russell & Russell, 1967. Pp. 138.

Pendlebury discusses the heroic tradition before Dryden's plays and he evaluates Dryden's achievement. In process, he discusses Davenant's heroic plays and theory. See *1967*: Pendlebury.

479.   Rollins, Hyder E. "The Commonwealth Drama: Miscellaneous Notes." *Studies in Philology*, 20 (1923), 52-69.

Rollins provides a collection of notes on the Interregnum drama labelled "The London Theatres." Among them are: a reference to a play that bitterly denounces Cromwell and contains in the "Prologue" references to Davenant; a reference to a Turk later used by Davenant in *Play-House*; a reference from a calendar of the Inner-Temple to the impact of Davenant's ventures in 1657; another from the *Memoirs of the Verney* family, this time to one who attended *The Siege of Rhodes* in 1657; a reference to a ballad by Davenant, and so on. The notes include reference to the birth of his son in 1664 as well as news of his opera. See *1921*: Rollins.

480.   Spencer, Hazelton. "*Hamlet* under the Restoration." *Publications of the Modern Language Association*, 38 (1923), 770-91.

Spencer tries to show that the source of Davenant's *Hamlet* (1661) is Quarto 6, printed in 1637, that the Restoration text was probably the work of Davenant, and that it should be numbered among the Shakespearean alterations.

481.   Welsford, Enid. "Italian Influence on the English Court Masque." *Modern Language Review*, 18 (1923), 394-409.

Cited among other works is Davenant's collaborative effort with Inigo Jones, *Britannia Triumphans*, as evidence of the influence of Italian events and methods upon the masque's design and libretto. *The Temple of Love* and especially *Luminalia* are described in detail, primarily in conjunction with illustrations from the Chatsworth Collection. Welsford concludes that Jonson only borrowed from the Italian when it suited his scheme and his poetry. "The Philistines at the Stuart court," she states, "sided with Inigo Jones, but posterity has justified Ben Jonson."

1924

482. *Calendar of State Papers and Manuscripts Relating to
      English Affairs in the Archives and Collections of
      Venice, and in Other Libraries in Northern Italy.*
      Vol. 25. Ed. Allen B. Hinds. 1924.

> The *Calendar of State Papers Venetian* contains
two letters from the Venetian ambassador to the Doge and
the Senate about Davenant's part in the Army Plot. See
Vol. 25, *1640-42*, pp. 149, 153.

483. Courthope, William John. "Cavalier and Roundhead."
      *The Intellectual Conflict of the Seventeenth Century:
      Decadent Influence of the Feudal Monarchy.* Vol. III
      of *A History of English Poetry.* London: Macmillan,
      1924, 300-05.

> "[N]either in morals nor art did he ever
attain to a knowledge of principle." This quotation
sets the tone for Courthope's article which concentrates
on *Gondibert.* However, he does praise "The lark now
leaves his wat'ry nest."

484. Dobree, Bonamy. *Restoration Comedy 1660-1720.*
      Oxford: Clarendon, 1924. Pp. 182.

> Dobree sees the Restoration period as
unstable, thus more receptive to comic perspectives. He
uses Davenant's *The Wits* as a drama that presents an
antagonism between love and marriage and as one that
anticipates dramas by Etherege and Wycherley, among
others. Dobree sees Restoration comedy as "a brilliant
picture of its time."

485. Lynch, Kathleen M. "English Sources of Restoration
      Comedy of Manners." Diss. Michigan 1924. Pp. 127.

> See *1926*: Lynch.

486. Simpson, Percy, and C.F. Bell. *Designs by Inigo Jones
      for Masques and Plays at Court.* Oxford: Walpole and
      Malone Societies, 1924. Pp. viii, 158.

> After an introduction to the masque, which
includes comment on scenery, lights, and costumes in
Part I, the authors present in Part II a catalogue of

drawings including those by Inigo Jones for Davenant's masques, which are part of the Chatsworth Collection and the Library of the Royal Institute of British Architects. The volume has 401 plates.

487.   Thaler, Alwin. "Thomas Heywood, D'Avenant, and *The Siege of Rhodes.*" *Publications of the Modern Language Association*, 39 (1924), 624-41.

        Thaler discusses Heywood's *Fair Maid of the West* as a source of Davenant's play. Citing *The Siege of Rhodes* as "one of the most influential of the pioneer works of Restoration drama," Thaler notes the debt of the play to Knolles' *History of the Turks* and suggests Heywood's play as another possibility.

1925

488.   Andrews, Matthew Page. *Tercentenary History of Maryland.* 4 vols. Chicago: Clarke, 1925.

        The first volume contains historical background on the young king's disenchantment with Lord Baltimore and his commission of Davenant as lieutenant governor of Maryland.

489.   Eich, Louis M. "Alterations of Shakespeare in the Theatre of the Restoration." *The Quarterly Journal of Speech Education*, 11 (1925), 229-36.

        Eich provides the bases of Shakespeare adaptations during the Restoration, the major one being that theater structure and dramatic teachings had been affected in particular by the pre-war productions of the masques. Davenant's role is central to that discussion.

490.   Graves, Thornton Shirley. "Women on the Pre-Restoration Stage." *Studies in Philology*, 22 (1925), 184-97.

        Taking issue with scholars before him, Graves suggests that there "was nothing particularly novel in Elizabethan England" of having women on stage. He denies Nicoll's claim that Davenant introduced women to the British stage. See *1923*: Nicoll, *History of Restoration Drama.*

491. Keith, William Grant. "John Webb and the Court
      Theatre of Charles II." *The Architectural Review*, 57
      (1925), 51-55.

            Keith suggests that the sketch by Inigo Jones
      for a play in the Cockpit, 1639, was for Davenant's *The
      Siege*. He uses as the basis for his suggestion the
      proscenium which is unlike those in other sketches for
      Habington's *Queen of Aragon*, a play usually cited as the
      object of Jones' sketch.

492. Nicoll, Allardyce. *British Drama: An Historical
      Survey from the Beginnings to the Present Time.*
      London: Harrap, 1925. Pp. 498. Rev. ed. New York:
      Barnes and Noble, 1963. Pp. 365.

            Through a general overview, Nicoll suggests
      that the English drama has developed continuously and he
      attributes to Davenant much of the development of early
      Restoration drama. Davenant is cited also as having
      influenced the masque, the opera, and theater
      management. The work places Davenant in perspective.
      See *1963*: Nicoll.

493. Nicoll, Allardyce. *A History of Early Eighteenth
      Century Drama, 1700-1750.* Cambridge: The Univ. Press,
      1925. Pp. xii, 431.

            The history continues the author's history of
      Restoration drama, 1600-1700. The overview offers the
      thesis that the first half of the eighteenth century saw
      critics' views of the drama rejected, active
      experimentation, the impact of heroic drama, the growing
      popularity of masques, pantomimes, and burlesques, and
      the limited appeal of sentimental drama. The appendix
      has a valuable list of theaters, 1700-1750; select
      documents; and a handlist of plays and operas. See
      1952: Nicoll.

494. Nicoll, Allardyce. "The Rights of Beeston and
      D'Avenant in Elizabethan Plays." *Review of English
      Studies*, 1 (January 1925), 84-91.

            Davenant's actors were descendants of William
      Beeston's company and believed they were the inheritors
      of those prompt copies of Shakespeare's plays that had
      been Beeston's. See *1965*: Sorelius.

495. Spencer, Hazelton. "D'Avenant's *Macbeth* and
      Shakespeare's." *Publications of the Modern Language
      Association*, 40 (1925), 619-44.

           Spencer notes Davenant's changes that appeared
      in the 1672-73 revival of the play which introduced
      flying witches and several new songs. He clarifies some
      passages. See *1965*: Sorelius.

496. Thorn-Drury, George. "Some Notes on Dryden." *Review
      of English Studies*, 1 (1925), 324-30.

           In an article that is part of a series he
      wrote on Dryden, Thorn-Drury takes issue with Lawrence's
      use of the word "write" in his article on Shadwell.
      Agreeing that Shadwell may have contributed a song or
      so, Thorn-Drury says: "That Shadwell may between the
      date of Davenant's death and the issue of the 1674 4to
      to have had a hand in *The Tempest* as it proceeded on its
      successful career is, I should think, quite possible"
      (p. 209), but he cannot consider that it is Shadwell's
      Tempest. See *1904*: Lawrence, "Shadwell"; *1947*: Milton.

                              1926

497. Corvesor, D. "Shakespeare Adaptations from Dryden to
      Garrick." Diss. London (Birkbeck) 1926.

498. "[Davenant's Birth]." *Notes & Queries*, 150 (1926),
      163.

           The note gives March 3, 1606, as the date of
      Sir William Davenant's baptism.

499. Greene, Herbert W. "Sources of Quotation Wanted."
      Notes & Queries, 150 (1926), 269.

           Greene notes that the song "Awake" was first
      set to music by J. L. Hatton and then by H. G.
      Pellissier.

500. H., J.H. "[Answer to Query]." *Notes & Queries*, 150
      (1926), 161.

           Davenant's "The lark now" is identified with
      the information that the first verse is repeated at the
      end.

501.   Lynch, Kathleen M. *The Social Mode of Restoration
       Comedy.* Univ. of Michigan Publications in Language
       and Literature, 3. New York: Macmillan, 1926. Pp.
       xi, 242.

             Lynch examines late Elizabethan comedy, the
       comedy of Charles I's court, and the comedy of the
       Commonwealth to explain the social attitudes that
       characterize Restoration comedy. She provides a
       comprehensive discussion of the *precieuse* doctrine and
       its impact on the drama. She examines *The Temple of
       Love, Love and Honour, The Platonic Lovers, The Fair
       Favorite, The Distresses,* and *The Unfortunate Lovers.*
       Part of Lynch's thesis is that Davenant was constrained
       by Queen Henrietta Maria to assume leadership in the
       presentation of the notion. Lynch also discusses the
       Interregnum plays: *The First Day's Entertainment, The
       Siege of Rhodes, I, The Cruelty of the Spaniards in
       Peru,* and *The History of Sir Francis Drake.* See *1924:*
       Lynch.

502.   Spencer, Hazelton. "The Blackfriars Mystery." *Modern
       Philology,* 24 (1926), 173-80.

             Spencer points out that Pepys' entry on
       January 29, 1661, is wrong. Instead of Blackfriars, he
       should have written Whitefriars or Salisbury Court where
       Davenant's men were performing. For evidence, Spencer
       reviews the 1660 patents, the existing theaters, the
       play lists, the two companies, and other scholars.

503.   Spencer, Hazelton. "Improving Shakespeare: Some
       Bibliographical Notes on the Restoration Adaptations."
       Publications of the Modern Language Association, 42
       (1926), 727-46.

             Spencer gives bibliographies of Restoration
       alterations and first editions of altered versions. He
       organizes the bibliography in three parts:
       "Bibliographies of Restoration Alterations," "First
       Editions of Altered Stage Versions of Shakespeare's
       Plays (1660-1710)," "Plays Sometimes Mistaken for
       Altered Versions of Shakespeare." In the second
       section, he quotes the full title pages of each edition
       and adds notes identifying those plays with misleading
       titles while in the third section he presents full
       essays justifying his dismissal of five plays from his
       list of adaptations.

504. Sprague, Arthur Colby. *Beaumont and Fletcher on the
      Restoration Stage.* Cambridge: Harvard Univ. Press,
      1926. Pp. xx, 299. Rpt. New York: Benjamin Blom,
      1965. Pp. 299.

            The work includes a discussion of *The Rivals*,
      Davenant's adaptation of *The Two Noble Kinsmen*, in its
      survey of influence on the Restoration drama. See *1965*:
      Sprague.

505. Steele, Mary Susan. *Plays & Masques at Court During
      the Reigns of Elizabeth, James and Charles.* New
      Haven: Yale Univ. Press, 1926. Pp. xiii, 300.

            Steele records the court performances of
      Davenant's plays and masques during the reign of Charles
      I. For each entry, she presents the authority for the
      date and location of the performance.

506. Walmsley, D.M. "Shadwell and the Operatic *Tempest*."
      Review of English Studies, 2 (1926), 463-66.

            The writer identifies the 1674 *Tempest*, the
      operatic version of the Dryden and Davenant play, as
      Shadwell's, attributing Shadwell's "reticence" to lack
      of pride in the "'authorship'of something which was
      really no more than an elaborated version of another
      man's play." Wamsley also draws parallels between *The
      Tempest* and Shadwell's *Timon*. See *1927*: Thorn-Drury;
      1947: Milton.

                              1927

507. DeBeer, Esmond S.   "A Statement of Sir William
      D'Avenant." *Notes & Queries*, 153 (1927), 327.

            DeBeer provides a statement on the complaints
      against the Dutch who in 1643 and 1644 inspired the
      English to fight the Second Dutch War. He points out
      that piracy and the confiscation of goods involved
      Davenant who on April 25, 1664, bought and sold a
      frigate, and that he captured two ships which were then
      confiscated by the Dutch.

508. Gilder, Rosamond. "Enter Ianthe, Veil'd." *Theatre
      Arts Monthly*, 11 (1927), 49-58.

The article studies the first actresses on the English stage, put there by Davenant in *The Siege of Rhodes*. Ianthe enters in Act II, veiled, thereby delaying revelation of the actress, an example of Davenant's showmanship.

509.   Nicoll, Allardyce. *The Development of the Theatre; A Study of Theatrical Art from Beginnings to the Present Day*. London: Harrap, 1927. Pp. 246. Rev. and enlarged ed. London: Harrap, 1948. Pp. 318.

See *1937*: Nicoll; *1948*: Nicoll.

510.   Nicoll, Allardyce. *A History of Late Eighteenth Century Drama, 1750-1800*. Cambridge: Cambridge Univ. Press, 1927. Pp. x, 387. Rpt. Cambridge: Univ. Press, 1961. Pp. 423.

The volume contains extensive hand-lists of plays as well as commentary. Included are references to Davenant, particularly in relationship to Aaron Hill's *The Insolvent* (6/3/1758) and Henry Woodward's *The Man's the Master* (3/11/1775), since both depended upon Davenant's earlier work. See *1952*: Nicoll; *1961*: Nicoll.

511.   Shadwell, Thomas. "A Session of the Poets." In *The Complete Works*. Ed. Montague Summers. London: Fortune, 1927, V, 449.

Two stanzas of the poem refer to Davenant's nose:

> Will. Davenant, ashamed of a foolish mischance,
> That he had got lately travelling in France,
> Modestly hoped the handsomeness of's muse
> Might any deformity about him excuse.

And

> Surely the company would have been content,
> If they could have found any precedent;
> But in all their records either in verse or in
>   prose,
> There was not one laureate without a nose.

512.   Shadwell, Thomas. *The Tory Poets: A Satyr*. In *The Complete Works*. Ed. Montague Summers. London Fortune, V, 1927, 283.

Shadwell may have written the work that contains lines about Davenant's nose:

'Tis wit in him, if he all Sense oppose,
'Twas wit in Davenant too to lose his Nose,
If so, then Bays is D'avenant wisest Son,
After so many claps to keep his on.   (1682)

513.   Spencer, Hazelton. *Shakespeare Improved*. Cambridge: Harvard Univ. Press, 1927. Pp. xii, 406. New ed. New York: Ungar, 1963.

Spencer states that most of the changes came from Davenant's and others' desires to use scenery. He offers details of productions to prove his point. The work studies the plays produced from 1660 to 1710, the year of Betterton's death. See *1963*: Spencer.

514.   Thorn-Drury, George. "Shadwell and the Operatic *Tempest*." *Review of English Studies*, 3 (1927), 204-08.

Objecting to Walmsley's refutation, Thorn-Drury finds that the key to authorship of the operatic *Tempest* is "whether [Shadwell] had any conceivable motive for concealing and inducing others to assist in concealing the fact that he had, with conspicious financial success, made their comedy into an opera...." He concludes that Shadwell did write it. See *1926*: Walmsley; *1947*: Milton.

515.   Welsford, Enid. *The Court Masque: A Study in the Relationship Between Poetry and the Revels*. Cambridge: Cambridge Univ. Press, 1927. Pp. 434.

The work is a perceptive, thorough study of the masque in two parts. Welsford discusses in the first part the Platonic influences, the roles of Inigo Jones and Prynne, and some of the Caroline masques, particularly Davenant's. She also traces in the second part the elements that influenced the masque and the influence of the masque itself. See *1962*: Welsford.

1928

516.   Clark, William S. "The Sources of the Restoration Heroic Play." *Review of English Studies*, 4 (1928), 49-63.

The article adds to the English influence on
the heroic play by citing *Gondibert*, its theory as
stated in the *Preface* and Davenant's *Siege of Rhodes*.
After examining French influences through their
romances, Clark concludes that despite all the exotic
influences the Restoration heroic play is a unique
English genre. See *1930*: Clark; *1930*: Lynch.

517. Denham, John. *The Poetical Works of Sir John Denham*.
      Ed. with notes and introd. by Theodore Howard Banks.
      New Haven: Yale Univ. Press, 1928. Pp. xi, 362.

          The volume contains on p. 323 Denham's elegy
on Davenant. See *1969*: Denham.

518. Dent, Edward Joseph. *Foundations of English Opera: A*
      Study of Musical Drama in England During the
      Seventeenth Century. Cambridge: Cambridge Univ.
      Press, 1928. Pp. xi, 242.

          The author discusses *The Triumph of the Prince*
D'Amour, The Siege of Rhodes, The Cruelty of the
Spaniards in Peru, and *The History of Sir Francis Drake*.
He also traces the English opera from Davenant's first
patent from Charles I before the Civil War. See *1965*:
Dent.

519. Elwin, Malcolm. *Handbook to Restoration Drama*.
      London: Jonathan Cope, 1928. Pp. 260.

          Elwin covers the period 1660 through 1710, the
year of Betterton's death. Viewing the period with
greater sympathy than most critics of his time, Elwin
devotes "Chapter Two" to the 1660s, giving a
biographical sketch of Davenant, his theatrical pieces,
innovations, alterations, and collaborations. See *1966*:
Elwin.

520. Hotson, Leslie J. *The Commonwealth and Restoration*
      Stage. Cambridge: Harvard Univ. Press, 1928. Pp. ix,
      424.

          The work is an invaluable study for those
interested in Davenant. Hotson writes of Davenant's
opera, young actors' nurseries, the patent companies,
and law suits. He provides in an extensive index lists
of relevant Chancery Bills and Answers, some of the more

significant documents in full, and other important
documents from the Public Records Office. See *1962*:
Hotson.

521.   Nicoll, Allardyce. *A History of Restoration Drama,*
       1660-1700. Revised ed. Cambridge: Cambridge Univ.
       Press, 1928. Pp. ix, 410.

              See *1923*: Nicoll; *1952*: Nicoll.

522.   Walmsley, D.M. "The Development of Dramatic Opera in
       England." Diss. London 1928.

523.   Walmsley, D.M. "The Influence of Foreign Opera on
       English Operatic Plays of the Restoration Period."
       Anglia, 52 (1928), 37-50.

              Walmsley believes that *The Siege of Rhodes*
       "shews clearly the influence of foreign Opera in the use
       of recitative music for the dialogue." He notes also
       Davenant's second opera, *The Cruelty of the Spaniards in*
       Peru, is more a masque with six parts. He brings in
       also *The History of Sir Francis Drake* and considers its
       use of dialogue rather than song. He then turns to
       Davenant's scenic decoration.

524.   Wilson, John Harold. *The Influence of Beaumont and*
       Fletcher on Restoration Drama. Ohio State University
       Studies. Graduate School Series: Contributions in
       Languages and Literature, Number 4. Columbus: Ohio
       State Univ. Press, 1928. Pp. vii, 156. Rpt. New
       York: Benjamin Blom, 1967.

              Wilson surveys stage history between 1660 and
       1710 and notes that Restoration playwrights used much of
       Beaumont and Fletcher's material. To Wilson, Davenant's
       use of *The Two Noble Kinsmen* in 1664 for *The Rivals* and
       his unique adaptation of *Much Ado* and *Measure for*
       Measure become prototypes for some of the playwrights
       who adapted Beaumont and Fletcher's plays. See *1967*:
       Wilson.

                          1929

525.   Baskervill, Charles Read. *The Elizabethan Jig and*
       Related Song Drama. Chicago: Univ. of Chicago Press,
       1929. Pp. x, 642.

The book is in two parts. The first contains the history of the jig and the second the texts used in the drama. The volume has an index that refers to the Caroline dramatists, particularly Davenant and Shirley.

526. Deane, Cecil Victor. "Dramatic Theory and the Rhymed Heroic Play." Diss. Cambridge (Emmanuel) 1929.

> See *1931*: Deane; *1967*: Deane.

527. Dobree, Bonamy. *Restoration Tragedy 1660-1720.* Oxford: Clarendon, 1929. Pp. 189.

In the first chapter, Dobree discusses "The Necessity for Heroism," and he quotes Davenant who wrote that "'to make great actions credible is the principal art of poets'" (p. 17). Dobree fits Davenant into his interpretation of the serious drama of the period, frequently citing Davenant's stagecraft, his plays and operas, and his use of rhymed poetry for dialogue.

528. Downes, John. *Roscius Anglicanus.* Ed. Montague Summers. London: Fortune, 1929. Pp. xiii, 286. Rpt. New York: Benjamin Blom, 1968.

Providing a facsimile of the original 1708 edition, the book is a valuable source of the data on the theaters, casts, and performances kept by Downes, the bookkeeper and prompter in Davenant's company at Lincoln's Inn Fields from the time it opened in 1661 until 1706. It outlines more fully the activities of Davenant, not just as playhouse manager but also as adaptor of Shakespeare's plays and innovator of texts with new characters, scenes, and songs. See *1968*: Downes.

529. Durham, W. H. "'Measure for Measure' as Measure for Critics." *Essays in Criticism by Members of the Department of English.* University of California Publications in English, Vol. I. Ed. Willard H. Durham et al. Berkeley: Univ. of California Press, 1929, pp. 111-32.

Durham focuses on *Law Against Lovers*, Davenant's alteration of *Measure for Measure*, which includes the Beatrice and Benedick episodes from *Much Ado About Nothing*. Durham believes the new play reveals theories of drama, "which give the name of comedy not only to a play which was witty and obviously amusing, but which also decreed that a comedy must serve the interests of morality."

530. Lynch, Kathleen M. "Conventions of Platonic Drama in the Heroic Plays of Orrery and Dryden." *Publications of the Modern Language Association*, 44 (1929), 456-71.

         The Platonic elements apparent in early Davenant plays as well as in some by Suckling, Killigrew, and Cartwright, were altered by Orrery and Dryden when the theaters reopened in 1660. See *1928*: Clark; *1930*: Clark.

531. Nicoll, Allardyce. *Readings from British Drama: Extracts from British and Irish Plays*. New York: Thomas Y. Crowell, 1929. Pp. 446.

         Nicoll illustrates the growth of drama through passages from plays of the Restoration and eighteenth century. He uses a few pages from Davenant's masque *The Temple of Love* and a couple from *The Siege of Rhodes* to highlight developments in the drama.

532. Thorndike, Ashley H. *English Comedy*. New York: Macmillan, 1929. Pp. vi, 635.

         In a volume that contains much information, helpful condensation, characterizations, and summaries, Thorndike includes Davenant as part of the late Renaissance. In his discussion of the Restoration, Thorndike focuses on Davenant as patentee, theater-manager, and adaptor of Shakespeare.

4.   1930-1939

533.   Clark, William S.   "The Platonic Elements in the
       Restoration Heroic Play."   *Publications of the Modern
       Language Association*, 45 (1930), 623-24.

         Clark argues with Kathleen M. Lynch about the
   need to discuss Platonic elements in heroic plays of the
   Restoration.   He does not see them as important legacies
   of Caroline drama.   See *1928*: Clark; and *1929*: Lynch;
   and *1930*: Lynch.

534.   Harbage, Alfred.   *Thomas Killigrew, Cavalier
       Dramatist, 1612-1683*.   Philadelphia: Univ. of
       Pennsylvania Press, 1930.   Pp. ix, 247.   Rpt. New
       York: Benjamin Blom, 1967.   Pp. 256.

         The work is a biography of Killigrew covering
   his career in the theater as a dramatist and a manager.
   The work is of interest because of its necessary
   reference to Davenant who, with Killigrew, held the
   patents for the theaters in London during the early
   years of the Restoration.   See *1967*: Harbage.

535.   Lynch, Kathleen M.   [Rebuttal to Clark].   "Comment and
       Criticism."   *Publications of the Modern Language
       Association*, 45 (1930), 625-26.

         Lynch defends her position concerning the
   importance and source of Platonic elements in
   Restoration drama.   See *1928*: Clark; *1929*: Lynch; *1930*:
   Clark.

536.   Murrie, Eleanor (Boswell).   "The Court Stage.
       1660-1702." Diss.   London 1930.

         See *1932*: Murrie; *1965*: Murrie; *1966*:
   Murrie.

537.   Wagner, Bernard M.   "George Jolly at Norwich."   *Review
       of English Studies*, 6 (1930), 449-52.

         The article provides more facts about "this
   opportunist," George Jolly, who, in December of 1662,
   rented his patent to Davenant and Killigrew.   He left
   London after receiving a patent from Herbert for a
   traveling company (January 1, 1663).   Early in 1663

Jolly appeared at Norwich. The article reprints pertinent information on Jolly's activities.

538.   Walley, Harold Reinoehl and John Harold Wilson, eds. "Introduction" and "Love and Honour." *Early Seventeenth-Century Plays, 1600-1642*. New York: Harcourt, Brace, 1930, pp. 3-28, 917-81.

        The volume contains the 1649 quarto text of *Love and Honour*, along with a two-page introduction to the play and a long, informed introduction to the entire volume that places Davenant in perspective.

1931

539.   [*Albovine* by Sir William Davenant.] "A D'Avenant Play is at Oxford." *The Times*, 19 Feb. 1931, p. 10, col. 2.

        The article announces the following: The play is to be produced by the D'Avenant Society in the Hall of Lincoln College, Oxford, Friday, February 27. It is to be produced by Montague Summers. The text is to be unexpurgated, and it is to include contemporary music arranged by Bernard Naylor of the Oxford University Opera Club. The poet laureate is to be present; a ceremony will follow in memory of Davenant. See *1931*: "The Tragedy of Albovine."

540.   Boswell, Eleanor. "Chaucer, Dryden and the Laureateship: A Seventeenth-Century Tradition." *Review of English Studies*, 7 (1931), 337-39.

        The article reviews the tradition of the laureateship and Davenant's place in it.

541.   Deane, Cecil V. *Dramatic Theory and the Rhymed Heroic Play*. London: Oxford Univ. Press, 1931. Pp. vi, 235.

        In the first chapter, Section 5, "The Elizabethan Legacy," Deane discusses Davenant as progenitor of the heroic play, giving special attention to Davenant's "attempts to secure official tolerance for his 'Representations' and operatic entertainments" after 1656. Later in chapter five, "The Conflict between Rhyme and Blank Verse," Deane discusses Davenant's

position in relationship with others, especially Dryden.
Finally, chapter six contains analyses of seven plays,
the first of which is *The Siege of Rhodes.* See *1929*:
Deane; *1967*: Deane.

542.   Green, Adwin Wigfall. *The Inns of Court and Early
        English Drama.* With a Preface by Roscoe Pound. New
        Haven: Yale Univ. Press, 1931. Pp. xii, 199. Rpt.
        New York: Benjamin Blom, 1965, 1968.

        The author discusses Davenant's *The Triumphs
of the Prince D'amour* and provides a bibliography. See
1965: Green; *1968*: Green.

543.   MacMillan, Dougald, and Howard Mumford Jones, eds.
        The Siege of Rhodes, Part I. In *Plays of the
        Restoration and Eighteenth Century as they were acted
        at the Theatres-Royal by their Majesties' Servants.*
        New York: Henry Holt, 1931, pp. 3-26.

        The introduction to the play provides a brief
biographical sketch of Davenant, a list of his works
giving the date and place of their first performances,
and background to the history of the play and its
dramatic qualities and success.

544.   Souers, Philip Webster. *The Matchless Orinda.*
        Cambridge, Mass.: Harvard Univ. Press, 1931. Pp.
        viii, 326.

        The work is a biography of Katherine Philips,
the woman who translated Corneille's *Pompee* and who also
produced it in Dublin in an elaborate production that
was subsequently burlesqued by Davenant.

545.   "The Tragedy of 'Albovine.'" Rev. of *Albovine*, by
        William Davenant. *The Times*, 28 Feb. 1931, p. 8, col.
        1.

        The reviewer describes the Montague Summers
production of *Albovine*, which was presented by the
D'Avenant Society in the Hall of Lincoln College,
Oxford. This first known performance, "rich in humour,
although much of it unconscious, was excellently staged
and performed." John Masefield, Poet Laureate, joined
in this celebration of the playwright's birth. See
1931: *Albovine*.

1932

546.   Bayne, Ronald. "Lesser Jacobean and Caroline
       Dramatists." *The Drama to 1642*. Part II. VI. *The
       Cambridge History of English Literature*. Ed. A.W.
       Ward and A.R. Waller. New York: Macmillan, 1932, pp.
       236-70.

            Citing Davenant as a transitional playwright,
       Bayne reviews his pre-Civil War work along with that of
       other minor writers.

547.   Bond, Richmond P. *English Burlesque Poetry:
       1700-1750*. Cambridge: Harvard Univ. Press, 1932.

            Citing Davenant's *Playhouse to Be Let* and
       Gondibert, Bond discusses the definition and method of
       burlesque as it developed in the seventeenth century.

548.   Clark, William S. "The Definition of the 'Heroic
       Play' in the Restoration Period." *Review of English
       Studies*, 8 (1932), 437-44.

            Clark places *The Siege of Rhodes* at the
       beginning of the development of the heroic play and
       suggests that Davenant may have coined the term.

549.   Darbishire, Helen, ed. *The Early Lives of Milton*.
       London: Constable, 1932.

            The volume helps to remove some of the
       uncertainties from the events associating Davenant and
       Milton. Using *Whitelock's Memorials*, for example, the
       editor notes on p. 338, Davenant's debt to Whitelock in
       1652: "Davenant wrote a letter from the Tower, October
       9, 1652, thanking Bulstrode Whitelock for his release:
       the letter only implies that he had made a request for
       his liberty, and now that he was free he thanked him
       'for the success of it' (*Whitelock's Memorials*, 1853,
       vol. III, p. 462)."

550.   Greg, Walter Wilson, et al, eds. *English Literary
       Autographs, 1550-1650: Selected for Reproduction and
       Edited*. 3 vols. London: Oxford Univ. Press, 1932.

            The work contains the autograph of Sir William
       Davenant, among others.

551. Hart, Alfred. "The Time Allotted for Representation
      of Elizabethan and Jacobean Plays." *Review of English
      Studies*, 8 (1932), 395-413.

            The article bases its conclusions on plays of
      the period, including the plays of Davenant that reflect
      the duration of time. Hart concludes that they lasted
      about 2 1/4 hours.

552. Murrie, Eleanor (Boswell). *The Restoration Court
      Stage (1660-1702) With a Particular Account of the
      Production of Calisto*. Cambridge: Harvard Univ.
      Press, 1932. Pp. xviii, 370. Rpt. New York: Benjamin
      Blom, 1965; rpt. London: George Allen and Unwin.
      1966.

            The book is divided into three parts: Part I
      is about court theaters; Part II is about problems of
      theatrical maintenance and production; and Part III
      gives an account of the masque *Calisto* (1675). See
      1930: Murrie; *1965*: Murrie; *1966*: Murrie.

553. Routledge, F.J., ed. *State Papers Collected by
      Edward, Earl of Clarendon*. 5 vols. Oxford:
      Clarendon, 1932.

            Important documents offer information on
      Davenant's activities, particularly during the years
      1659 and 1660. See volume 4.

554. Stroup, Thomas Bradley. "*Promos and Cassandra* and *The
      Law Against Lovers*." *Review of English Studies*, 8
      (1932), 309-10.

            Stroup draws parallels between Whetstone's
      version of the story and Davenant's.

                        1933

555. Griswold, B. Howell. "A Maryland Governor Who Never
      Governed." *Maryland Historical Magazine*, 28 (1933),
      101-18.

            The article concerns Davenant who was
      appointed by Charles II to govern Maryland but never
      reached his destination in the New World.

556.   Stroup, Thomas Bradley.   "Type-Characters in the
        Serious Drama of the Restoration with Special
        Attention to the Plays of Davenant, Dryden, Lee, and
        Otway." Diss. North Carolina 1933. Pp. 534.

            The work is a long, methodical account of the
        appearance of twenty-nine type-characters in many plays
        including Davenant's.

1934

557.   Dowlin, Cornell March.   "Sir William Davenant's
        Gondibert." Diss. Pennsylvania 1934.   Pp. 127.

            The study gives an introduction to the text of
        Gondibert, which is based on the quarto and octavo and
        1673 folio, followed by a chapter of critical
        commentary.

558.   Dowlin, Cornell March.   *Sir William Davenant's
        'Gondibert.' Its Preface and Hobbes's Answer: A Study
        in English Neo-Classicism*. Philadelphia: Univ. of
        Pennsylvania Press, 1934.   Pp. 127.

            After an introduction that describes the
        quarto (1650), octavo (1651), and folio (1673) editions
        of *Gondibert*, Dowlin discusses in a series of five
        chapters the "Preface" and "Answer," the continental
        influences on the work, the English influences, heroic
        virtue and the heroic play, and, finally, the poem
        itself, its relationship to the "Preface" and its
        position as literature.

559.   Laig, Friedrich.   *Englische und franzosische Elemente
        in Sir William Davenants dramatischer Kunst*.
        Emsdetten: Anstalt Heine und J. Lechte, 1934.   Pp.
        133.

            The first half of the work covers the French
        elements in Davenant's plays. The work discusses *The
        Cruel Brother, The Just Italian, Love and Honor, News
        from Plymouth, The Unfortunate Lovers, The Fair
        Favorite, The Distresses*, and *The Siege*. A bibliography
        follows.

560.   Paul, Henry N.   "Players' Quartos and Duodecimos of
        Hamlet." *Modern Language Notes*, 49(1934), 369-75.

The article affirms Davenant's participation in Betterton's *Hamlet*.

561. Richardson, W.R. "Sir William Davenant as American Colonizer." *English Literary History, 1 (1934), 61-62.*

The brief article provides documented material on Davenant's activities during the two years, 1649 and 1650. It includes a discussion of Jean Chevalier's account of Davenant's capture in 1650.

562. Summers, Montague. *A Bibliography of the Restoration Drama.* London: Fortune, [1934]. Pp. 143.

Summers offers an alphabetical list of "plays, acted and unacted, printed and unprinted, belonging to the Restoration Theatre (1600-1700)." Davenant's plays are included.

563. Summers, Montague. *The Restoration Theatre.* London: Kegan Paul, 1934. Pp. xxi, 352.

In a readable, informative history, Summers touches on many aspects of the topic. Davenant's role during the Interregnum, his admissions charges, his actresses, his introduction of the jig in 1661 are part of Summers' text. He discusses Davenant's machines, his Shakespeare adaptations, and costuming of the plays in relationship to an emerging realism on the Restoration stage.

564. Wright, Louis B. "The Reading of Plays during the Puritan Revolution." *Huntington Library Bulletin,* 6 (1934), 73-108.

In the list of plays that Wright discusses, he includes the plays of Davenant. He notes the circulation and reading of old and new plays between 1642 and 1660 and the political implications of the plays read, "particularly those newly written or revised for publication during this period" (p. 74). Of Davenant's plays, Wright notes that *The Wits, The Platonic Lovers,* and *The Triumphs of the Prince D'Amour* were to be reprinted along with other popular plays in 1656. Pre-Civil War playwrights who had enjoyed large audiences continued to be read because of enterprising

publishers like Moseley who printed *Love and Honor* and
The Unfortunate Lovers.

1935

565.   Berry, E.G. "Sir William Davenant and the Seventeenth
Century Theatre." Thesis. McGill 1935.

566.   Harbage, Alfred. *Sir William Davenant, Poet Venturer,
1606-1668*. Philadelphia: Univ. of Pennsylvania Press,
1935. Pp. viii, 317. Rpt. New York: Octagon, 1971.

"Designed as a companion study to the life and
critical estimate of Thomas Killigrew published five
years" earlier, the book provides a researched biography
and a critical evaluation of Davenant. Impressed by
"Davenant's key position as chief link between the
common and courtly schools of play-writing, and between
the old seventeenth-century drama and the new," Harbage
nonetheless keeps to his original intention: "to present
as an individual a neglected or misunderstood figure--an
engaging old writer whose life was always picturesque
and whose poetry was sometimes inspired" (p. vi). The
book outlines Davenant's eventful life and times and
provides valuable commentary on the works. It is all
carefully indexed and has a bibliography. See *1971*:
Harbage.

567.   Lawrence, William J. *Those Nut-Cracking Elizabethans:
Studies in the Early Theatre and Drama*. London:
Argonaut, 1935. Pp. viii, 212.

Lawrence offers a series of essays on a
variety of topics: animals in dramatic presentations,
stage furniture, songs. The index enables the reader to
find references to Davenant's directing of Betterton as
Hamlet, of lawyers in *News from Plymouth*, and of the
monarchs acting in his masques.

568.   Mosher, Mary T. "The Life of Sir William Davenant."
Thesis. Columbia 1935.

569.   Summers, Montague. *The Playhouse of Pepys*. London:
Routledge and Kegan Paul, 1935. Pp. xv, 485. Rpt.
New York: Humanities Press, 1964. Pp. xv, 485.

Summers gives a history of the drama from
1660-82 and, in process, a biography of the dramatists

and the stage histories of their plays. His treatment
of Davenant is perceptive and illuminating.

70. Walker, William D., Jr., ed. *"Madagascar with Other
     Poems* by Sir William Davenant." Thesis. Columbia
     1935. Pp. xviii, 172.

          In his introduction, Walker analyzes the
differences between the 1638 and 1648 editions. Using
the 1638 edition as his basic text, he then provides a
172-page edition. There are also comments on the title
pages, the type, and the variants.

                              1936

71. Bradford, Gamaliel. *Elizabethan Women.* Ed. Harold
     Ogden White. Cambridge: Houghton Mifflin, 1936. Pp.
     [x], 243.

          In an examination of the treatment of women,
Bradford, who wrote his essays between 1890 and 1910,
comments on literary and dramatic representations. His
overview of seventeenth-century treatments includes
Davenant and his plays, which he views with favor. He
reserves special praise for the poetry, especially
Gondibert.

72. Colby, Elbridge. *English Catholic Poets: Chaucer to
     Dryden.* Milwaukee: Bruce, 1936. Pp. xix, 208.

          Colby records "the noteworthy Catholic
elements found in a reading of those early authors whose
writings are universally accepted as part of the canon
of classic English letters." Davenant is among his
subjects. Colby writes in the "Preface," that Davenant
"in the full splendor of his reputation far outshone his
stern Puritan contemporary, Milton.... Davenant has
widely been regarded as a Catholic.... His continued
presence in the entourage of a Catholic queen certainly
rendered him suspect...but his poetry is less
convincing" (p. xi). Pages 167-75 are devoted to
Davenant. See *1967*: Colby.

73. Harbage, Alfred. *Cavalier Drama.* New York: Modern
     Language Association, 1936. Pp. ix, 302. Rpt. New
     York: Russell & Russell, 1964.

The book is an historical and critical study
of the seventeenth-century stage, and as such it
includes frequent commentary on Davenant. See *1964:*
Harbage.

574.   Iwanicki, Charles P.   "Mid-Seventeenth Century Epic
       Theory as Illustrated by Davenant's *Gondibert* and
       Cowley's *Davideis*." Thesis. George Washington Univ.
       1936. Pp. 73.

575.   Marchant, Edgar Cardew. *Sir William Davenant: An
       Informal Address...on occasion of the 330th Birthday
       of the Society's Patron.* Oxford: Printed for the
       Davenant Society, Lincoln College, at the Univ. Press,
       1936. Pp. 28.

            The small volume is a tribute to Davenant and
       to the group that met in 1936 on the occasion of
       Davenant's birthday to celebrate his life and his
       achievements. Most of the material is an acknowledged
       paraphrase of Harbage's book.

576.   Pickel, Margaret Barnard. *Charles I as Patron of
       Poetry and Drama.* London: Frederick Muller, 1936.
       Pp. [v], 192.

            The book examines the monarch's impact on
       poetry and drama. In the chapter "Court Influence and
       Platonic Love," Davenant's leading role is examined in
       the masque *The Temple of Love* and in the plays *Love and
       Honour, The Fair Favourite,* and *The Platonic Lovers.* In
       the chapter "The Court Poets," Davenant's succession to
       the poet laureateship is examined, perpetuating the
       notion that Davenant converted to Catholicism.
       Davenant's influence as dramatist is placed in
       perspective in the chapter "Court Drama" where he runs
       fourth in frequency of performance behind Beaumont and
       Fletcher, Shakespeare, and Carlell. Davenant's masques
       are discussed as well.

577.   Smith, Dane Farnsworth. *Plays About the Theatre in
       England, from The Rehearsal in 1671 to the Licensing
       Act in 1737; or, The Self-Conscious State and Its
       Burlesque and Satirical Reflections in the Age of
       Criticism.* London: Oxford Univ. Press, 1936. Pp.
       xxii, 287.

The first chapter is devoted to a discussion
of Davenant's play *The Play-house To Be Let* and contains
frequent quotations from the 1673 folio *Works*. Smith
summarizes by noting that the play is a new type of
burlesque that contains mock-heroics and that will
"drain sources of creation which might otherwise have
strengthened currents more purely dramatic and more
geniunely profound."

578. Spriggs, Charles O. "*Hamlet* on the Eighteenth Century
Stage." *Quarterly Journal of Speech*, 22 (1936),
78-85.

Spriggs attributes to Betterton, rather than
Davenant, the alterations in the 1676 quarto.

579. Stockwell, La Tourette. "The Dublin Theatre,
1637-1820." Diss. Radcliff 1936.

This dissertation provided the background for
the book *Dublin Theatres and Theatre Customs* which was
published two years later. See *1938*: Stockwell; *1968*:
Stockwell.

1937

580. Frohmann, Daniel. "O Rare Sir William D'Avenant."
Encore. New York: Furman, 1937, pp. 181-96.

In Chapter 14, Frohmann presents a lively,
though sometimes inaccurate account of Davenant's life
and adventures in and out of the theater.

581. Nicoll, Allardyce. *The Development of the Theatre; A
Study of Theatrical Art from the Beginnings to the
Present Day*. Rev. ed. New York: Harcourt, Brace,
1937. Pp. 246.

See *1927*: Nicoll; *1948*: Nicoll.

582. Nicoll, Allardyce. *Stuart Masques and the Renaissance
Stage*. London: Harrap, 1937. Pp. 223.

The volume includes illustrations and
commentary on *The Triumphs of the Prince d'Amour,
Britannia Triumphans, Luminalia*, and *Salmacida Spolia* by
Davenant and a chapter on the Banquet House. See *1963*:
Nicoll, *Stuart*.

583.   Shaver, Chester Lynn. "The Life and Works of Henry
       Glapthorne, M.S." Diss. Harvard 1937.

            The dissertation includes a reference to the
       anti-Dutch comments in the fourth act of *News from
       Plymouth* and their similarity to other speeches in *The
       Wits* and *The Hollander*.

584.   Stroup, Thomas B. "Supernatural Beings in Restorati
       Drama." *Anglia*, 61 (1937), 186-92.

            Noting the excessive use of supernatural
       beings in Restoration drama, Stroup attributes
       Davenant's reluctance to use them in his original play
       to Hobbes' influence. He concludes that "the
       Restoration dramatists in general made a distinction
       between their use of 'spirits' who are native to
       unearthly regions and the ghosts of departed mortals."

                            1938

585.   Nethercot, Arthur H. *Sir William D'Avenant: Poet
       Laureate and Playwright-Manager*. Chicago: Univ. of
       Chicago Press, 1938. Pp. vii, 488. Rpt. New York:
       Russell & Russell, 1967. Pp. 488, [7].

            Nethercot's is a thoroughly researched life
       Davenant. Included in the five appendices are
       transcripts of key contemporary documents. The work h
       an extensive index. See *1967*: Nethercot.

586.   Ormsbee, Helen. "Ways of Betterton and Others."
       *Backstage with the Actors, From the Time of
       Shakespeare to the Present Day*. New York: Crowell,
       1938, pp. 47-67.

            Chapter 3, which is devoted to Betterton and
       his times, contains an account of Davenant's life and
       contributions to the English theatre.

587.   Parsons, A.E. "The English Heroic Play." *Modern
       Language Review*, 33 (Jan. 1938), 1-14.

            Parsons attributes the development of the
       heroic play to rules formulated during the Renaissanc
       for the heroic poem and heroic prose romances. He cit
       the epic tradition as it was set forth by Scaliger.

Gondibert, he notes, is the "true link" between the
heroic poem and the heroic play with the epic's five-act
scheme. Parsons also discusses *The Siege of Rhodes* and
its possible impact on Dryden.

588. Sensabaugh, George F. "Love Ethics in Platonic Court
      Drama, 1625-1642." *Huntington Library Quarterly*, 1
      (April 1938), 277-304.

            The article provides a useful summary of the
      cult of Platonic love. Davenant's *The Temple of Love,
      The Platonic Lovers, The Unfortunate Lovers*, and *The
      Fair Favourite* are among the plays included.

589. Stockwell, LaTourette. *Dublin Theatres and Theatre
      Customs (1637-1820)*. Kingsport, Tennessee: Kingsport,
      1938. Pp. xviii, 406. Rpt. New York: Benjamin Blom,
      1968. Pp. xviii, 406.

            The work provides a history of the Dublin
      theaters that includes plays performed, conditions for
      performance, and information about the actors and
      actresses. Davenant is discussed as John Ogilby's rival
      for Master of the Revels in Ireland (1661), later as
      Katherine Philips' competition in scenes and machines
      (1662), and as one who complained that he was raided by
      Ogilby for players. See *1936*: Stockwell; *1968*:
      Stockwell.

590. Swedenberg, H.T., Jr. "Rules and English Critics of
      the Epic, 1650-1800." *Studies in Philology*, 35
      (1938), 566-87.

            Swedenberg surveys the criticism of the
      English epic in order to clarify the relationship of the
      rules to the general theory from the late seventeenth
      century to 1800. The article is divided into three
      parts; the first encompasses the years 1650-1700 and
      includes a discussion of Davenant, his theories, and his
      poem *Gondibert*. That period established the neoclassic
      notion that rules are founded on nature and reasonable
      men accept them. Those rules were questioned throughout
      the eighteenth century.

591. Wilcox, John. *The Relation of Moliere to Restoration
      Comedy*. New York: Columbia Univ. Press, 1938. Pp.
      ix, 240. Rpt. New York: Benjamin Blom, 1964. Pp.
      240.

The book is a documented study of the use of
Moliere's plays by Restoration playwrights. Of
particular interest is the citation of Davenant as the
first to use Moliere in his 1663 play, *Playhouse to Be
Let*. Chapter VII, "The Minor Borrowers," devotes one
segment entitled "Sir William D'Avenant" to that
citation. See *1964*: Wilcox.

1939

592. Dowlin, Cornell March. "The First Edition of
      Gondibert: Quarto or Octavo?" *Library*, 4th Ser., 20
      (1939), 167-79.

            According to Dowlin, there is no altogether
      satisfying solution to the question of which is the
      first edition of *Gondibert*, the 1651 quarto or 1651
      octavo. Dowlin reviews the evidence and the views of
      Nethercot and Harbage, and then he gives some evidence
      to support the view that it is the quarto edition. He
      uses as evidence Davenant's renumbering of some
      stanzas.

593. Steible, Daniel Joseph. "A Critical Edition of Sir
      William Davenant's *The Temple of Love* and *The Platonic
      Lovers*." Diss. Cincinnati 1939. Pp. cliv, 162.

            The dissertation contains in the introduction
      a biographical sketch of Davenant, an explanation of
      Platonic love, and a note on the texts. The rest of the
      dissertation contains critical editions of the masque
      using three texts and of the play using four.

594. Swedenberg, H.T., Jr. "Fable, Action, Unity, and
      Supernatural Machinery in English Epic Theory,
      1650-1800." *Englische Studien*, 73 (1939), 39-48.

            Swedenberg defines the terms *fable, action,
      unity*, and *supernatural*, and he notes how they were
      implemented. Machines, as Davenant used them, caused
      adverse criticism for years.

595. Bowers, Fredson Thayer. *Elizabethan Revenge Tragedy,*
      1587-1642. Princeton: Princeton Univ. Press, 1940.
      Pp. viii, 288.

         The work is a specialized study of revenge
      tragedy, occasionally mentioning Davenant's use of the
      revenge motif in his dramas. In particular, Bowers
      discusses *Albovine* and *The Cruel Brother.* See *1959*:
      Bowers.

596. Cawley, Robert Ralston. "Characteristic Uses of the
      Voyagers: Davenant." *Unpathed Waters. Studies in*
      the Influence of the Voyagers on Elizabethan
      Literature. Princeton: Princeton Univ. Press, 1940,
      pp. 249-53.

         Cawley discusses Davenant's plays after 1640,
      emphasizing the playwright's use of voyages and his
      knowledge of geography in *The Cruelty of the Spaniards*
      in Peru and *The History of Sir Francis Drake.* Cawley
      also refers to Davenant's Restoration plays.

597. Day, Cyrus Lawrence, and Eleanore Boswell Murrie.
      English Songbooks, 1651-1702: A Bibliography, With a
      First-Line Index of Songs. London: Bibliographical
      Society at the Univ. Press, Oxford, 1940 (for 1937).
      Pp. xii, 439.

         The book lists, describes, and indexes almost
      all the secular songbooks published in England and
      Scotland between 1651 and 1702. The bibliography of
      books runs about 160 pages and is followed by indexes of
      first lines, composers, authors, singers and actors,
      tunes and airs, sources, song-books, and printers,
      publishers, and booksellers. Easily accessible, then,
      are references to Davenant, his songs, and the books
      where they appeared. See *1975*: Day.

598. Evans, G. Blakemore. "The Source of Shadwell's
      Character of Sir Formal Trifle in *The Virtuoso*."
      Modern Language Review, 35 (1940), 211-14.

         Evans cites Davenant's play *News from Plymouth*
      as a source of Shadwell's play, specifically Sir Solemn
      Trifle as the original for Shadwell's Sir Formal Trifle

in *The Virtuoso*. The characters have the same last
name, they are boringly loquacious, and they are tricked
into leaving the scene, much to the relief of the other
characters. He argues further that Davenant's influence
extends to Sir Positive At-All in *The Sullen Lovers*.
See *1944*: Scott.

599. Fulford, G.L. "The History and the Development of
Scenery and Lighting of the English Stage from
Medieval Times to the Year 1700." Thesis. McGill
1940.

600. Harbage, Alfred. *Annals of English Drama, 975-1700.
An Analytical Record of All Plays, Extant or Lost,
Chronologically Arranged and Indexed by Author,
Titles, Dramatic Companies, etc.* Philadelphia: Univ.
of Pennsylvania Press, 1940. Pp. 264.

See *1964*: Harbage.

601. Jonas, Leah. *The Divine Science: The Aesthetic of
Some Representative Seventeenth-Century English Poets.*
Columbia University Studies in English and Comparative
Literature, No. 151. New York: Columbia Univ. Press,
1940. Pp. xii, 292.

Davenant is among the seventeen poets examined
in the volume. Jonas identifies the poet's opinions in
order to show the similarities with the aesthetics of
the other poets.

602. Lewis, Arthur O., Jr. "Sir William Davenant's *Macbeth*
in Relation to Shakespeare's *Macbeth*." Thesis.
Harvard 1940.

603. McManaway, James G. "The 'Lost' Canto of *Gondibert*."
Modern Language Quarterly, 2 (1940), 63-78.

The article reprints and discusses the
fragment of Book III, Canto vii, originally published in
1685. McManaway demonstrates Davenant's authorship of
the canto with considerable documentation. See *1961*:
Dust; *1969*: McManaway.

604. Osborn, James M. *John Dryden: Some Biographical Facts
and Problems.* New York: Columbia Univ. Press, 1940.
Pp. 295. Rev. ed. Gainesville: Univ. of Florida
Press, 1965. Pp. 316.

The portion of the work important to Davenant
scholars deals with the relationship between Dryden and
Davenant and the nature of their collaborations.
Chapter seven surveys Dryden scholarship for the
previous twenty-five years. See *1965*: Osborn.

605. Sharp, Robert Lathrop. "Return to Nature." In *From
Donne to Dryden: The Revolt Against Metaphysical
Poetry*. Chapel Hill: Univ. of North Carolina Press,
1940, pp. 121-49.

The work discusses critical theories that
involve the protest of poets such as Waller and Cowley,
the return to nature by such writers as Davenant and
Hobbes, the evolution of new standards and the theories
of Dryden.

606. Spencer, Hazelton. "Mr. Pepys Is Not Amused."
English Literary History, 7 (1940), 163-76.

Spencer shows how the diarist's judgments of
plays were affected by other events. Spencer reviews
Pepys' reactions to Davenant's *Macbeth, Hamlet, Henry
VIII, Law Against Lovers, The Rivals, The Tempest*, and
Twelfth Night. Spencer suggests that Pepys dislike of
Davenant's production of *Twelfth Night* "may indicate
superior taste."

607. Thorpe, Clarence DeWitt. *The Aesthetic Theory of
Thomas Hobbes. With Special Reference to His
Contribution to the Psychological Approach in English
Literary Criticism*. University of Michigan
Publications, Language and Literature, 18. Ann Arbor:
Univ. of Michigan Press, 1940. Pp. ix, 339.

The book is a lengthy discussion of Davenant's
and Hobbes' critical theories.

1941

608. Bald, R.G. "Shakespeare on the Stage in Restoration
Dublin." *Publications of the Modern Language
Association*, 56 (1941), 369-78.

Upon examining some annotated plays at the
Folger Shakespeare Library, Bald discovered three
imperfect plays from Shakespeare's third folio that had

annotations from six different hands. One of the plays,
Macbeth, seems to have been Davenant's adaptation that
was printed in 1674. See *1942*: Spencer.

609. Bentley, Gerald Eades. *The Jacobean and Caroline
      Stage*. 7 vols. Oxford: Clarendon, 1941-68.

           The multivolume work is a basic and valuable
source for information on all aspects of the stage
during the Jacobean and Caroline periods. Volume III
contains useful guides to Davenant, from the ten other
ways his name is spelled to the basic biographies and
Bentley's own biographical commentary, the collected
editions, and an inclusive list of all the plays with an
accompanying list of the important commentaries on each
play, and finally a brief summary for each play that
includes relevant documentation. The work is an
important source of dates, places of performances,
publication information, and production of Davenant's
pre-Restoration plays. See *1902*: Campbell.

610. Evans, Willa McClung. *Henry Lawes: Musician and
      Friend of the Poets*. New York: Modern Language
      Association of America, 1941. Pp. xvi, 250.

           Evans traces the relationship of Lawes and
Davenant. She notes Lawes' part in the masques *The
Temple of Love* and *The Triumphs of the Prince d'Amour*.
She suggests that *Gondibert* was to have been set to
music and chanted "after the Greek fashion" and that "It
represented what most of the seventeenth-century poets,
from Berkenhead to D'Avenant, were attempting: imitation
of the Greeks, in their union of music and verse" (pp.
118, 164-65).

611. Mead, Herman Ralph. [Variant issues of D'Avenant's
      Gondibert (1651).] *Papers of the Bibliographical
      Society of America*, 35 (1941), 68-69.

           The note describes the 1651 octavo editions of
Gondibert printed by John Holden: the "Hoe copy, old
English black morocco, gilt"; "The Halsey copy (red
morocco), by Bedford"; and "The Grolier Club."

612. Stone, George Winchester, Jr. "Garrick's Handling of
      Macbeth." *Studies in Philology*, 38 (1941), 609-28.

        Stone compares the 1744 prompt book that
Garrick used with the Davenant version of *Macbeth*.

                        1942

613.   Southern, Richard. "Curtain Drops for Scene-Change:
        How a One-Time Spectacle Became Hidden." *Life and
        Letters To-day*, 33 (1942), 32-41.

            Citing Davenant's innovative theater, Southern
        points out that audience-observed scene changes are as
        old as the seventeenth century. He explains the
        development of scene changes in the Stuart masques and
        Davenant's use of scenery in 1661.

614.   Southern, Richard. "Davenant, Father of English
        Scenery." *Life and Letters To-day*, 32 (1942),
        114-26.

            The article begins with the idea that "the
        setting of shows is almost synonymous with the very art
        of the theatre." The sudden change in 1661 from the
        bare Renaissance stage to the modern stage in form and
        scenery is owed to "a surprising deal to one
        man"--Davenant. The article reviews Davenant's career
        in the court masques, in Rutland House with *The Siege of
        Rhodes*, and in the Duke's Theatre with the same play
        with full scenery. The article is a tribute to Davenant
        as "a great showman."

615.   Spencer, Hazelton. "Shakespearean Cuts in Restoration
        Dublin." *Publications of the Modern Language
        Association*, 57 (1942), 575-76.

            Spencer responds to R. G. Bald's article. See
        1941: Bald.

616.   Stamm, Rudolf. "Sir William Davenant and
        Shakespeare's Imagery." *English Studies*, 24 (1942),
        65-79, 97-116.

            The article discusses Davenant's imagery in
        his own plays--*Albovine, The Unfortunate Lovers, The
        Siege of Rhodes*--and in his adaptations of
        Shakespeare's plays--*The Law Against Lovers*, from
        Measure for Measure, and *Macbeth*.

1943

617.   Bush, Douglas. *Selected Poems of Sir William
        Davenant*. Cambridge: Willow, 1943. Pp. 43.

            Privately printed by Bush's son, the small
        volume contains a few of Davenant's poems that the
        editor found especially fine. He writes in the brief
        introduction of the poet's "massive dignity" and his
        "thoughtful sobriety."

618.   Hooker, Helene Maxwell. "Dryden's and Shadwell's
        Tempest." *Huntington Library Quarterly*, 6 (1943),
        224-28.

            She focuses on the concluding couplet:

        That as a fire the former house o'erthrew
        Machines and tempests will destroy the new.

        She suggests that Dryden was not attacking Davenant but
        rather the rival's version of *The Tempest*.

619.   Parrott, Thomas Marc, and Robert Hamilton Ball. *A
        Short View of Elizabethan Drama, Together with Some
        Account of Its Principal Playwrights and the
        Conditions Under Which It Was Produced*. Rev. ed. New
        York: Scribner's, 1943. Pp. vii, 311. Rpt. New
        York: Scribner's, 1958.

            The work is a general history that includes
        major divisions on court masques and Davenant. The work
        contains a bibliography and an index. See *1958*:
        Parrott.

1944

620.   Scott, Florence R. "*News from Plymouth* and Sir
        Positive At-All." *Modern Language Review*, 39 (April
        1944), 183-85.

            Scott is responding to G. Blakemore Evan's
        argument (See *1940*: Evans) that Davenant's Sir Solemn
        Trifle in *News from Plymouth* was the original for
        Shadwell's Sir Formal Trifle in *The Virtuoso* because of
        their last names and their boring loquacity. Evans
        argues further that the influence extends to Sir

Positive At-all in *The Sullen Lovers*. Scott accepts
Evans' point concerning *The Virtuoso*, but she rejects
that concerning *The Sullen Lovers* because Sir Positive
is based on Sir Robert Howard. See *1940*: Evans.

621.   Sensabaugh, George Frank. *The Tragic Muse of John*
       Ford. Stanford: Stanford Univ. Press, 1944. Pp. ix,
       196.

            In his attempt to re-evaluate Ford, Sensabaugh
       also examines contemporary playwrights, including
       Davenant, in relationship to the fashions of the court
       and the pressures placed upon them.

622.   Sprague, Arthur Colby. *Shakespeare and the Actors:*
       The Stage Business in His Plays (1660-1905).
       Cambridge: Harvard Univ. Press, 1944. Pp. xxxiii,
       442.

            In his discussion of stage business, Sprague
       refers to Davenant, his productions, and his actors.

623.   Swedenberg, Hugh Thomas., Jr. *The Theory of the Epic*
       in England, 1650-1800. Univ. of California
       Publications in English, 15. Berkeley and Los
       Angeles: Univ. of California Press, 1944. Pp. xi,
       396.

            Swedenberg summarizes Richard Hurd's
       unfavorable and John Aikin's favorable views on the
       merits of Davenant's ideas on epic structure and
       content, as expressed in the *Preface* to *Gondibert*. See
       1762: Hurd; *1811*: Hurd; *1824*: Aikin.

                             1945

624.   Mandach, Andre De. *Moliere et la comedie de moeurs en*
       Angleterre (1660-68). Diss. Neuchatel 1945.
       Neuchatel: Seiler, 1945. Pp. [7], 128.

            In his dissertation, Mandach argues that *The*
       Playhouse to be Let was staged in the autumn of 1662.
       He also gives a quick history of the Royalists before
       and during the Civil War, their exile, and their
       theatrical activities in the late 1660s. Davenant's
       career is examined including every Restoration
       production.

625. McDowell, J.H. "Tudor Court Staging." *Journal of
      English and Germanic Philology*, 44 (1945), 194-207.

           This has a good explanation of Serlian staging
      which through Inigo Jones and Davenant influenced the
      later development of the English stage.

                              1946

626. Boas, Frederick S. *An Introduction to Stuart Drama*.
      London: Oxford Univ. Press, 1946. Pp. viii, 443.

           Boas devotes the final seventeen pages of his
      book to a chapter labelled "The Drolls -- Sir William
      Davenant." Boas describes Davenant as "a remarkable
      link between the Elizabethan and the Restoration stage."
      In addition to surveying Davenant's life and
      achievement, Boas provides useful commentaries on the
      comedies and on the historically important Commonwealth
      plays.

627. Mandach, Andre De. "The First Translator of Moliere:
      Sir William Davenant or Colonel Henry Howard."
      Comparative Literature Studies (Cardiff), 21-22
      (1946), 2-9.

           Mandach argues that Colonel Henry Howard, not
      Davenant, was the first translator of Moliere.   See
      1951: Mandach.

628. Perkinson, Richard H. "The Epic in Five Acts."
      Studies in Philology, 43 (1946), 465-81.

           Perkinson identifies three English Renaissance
      epics, Sidney's *Old Arcadia* (c. 1580), Davenant's
      Gondibert (1651), and Chamberlayne's *Pharonnida* (1659),
      all divided into five parts. He uses Davenant's *Preface*
      and other classical and theoretical commentaries to
      analyze the structural relationship of the three epics
      to the drama. He concludes that the form is "not an
      affectation": its "character is Senecan, and its
      beginnings are...in the Middle Ages...."

629. Smith, John H. "Heroes and Heroines in English
      Comedy. 1660-1750." Diss. Harvard 1946. Pp. 250.

           This is the basic study that led to Smith's
      key work *The Gay Couple in Restoration Comedy*. See
      1948: Smith; *1971*: Smith.

630.   Van Lennep, William. "The Smock Alley Players of
       Dublin." *English Literary History*, 13 (1946), 216-22.

            Van Lennep, the Curator of the Harvard Theater
       Collection, provides from the Harvard Manuscript
       Collection prologues and epilogues that illustrate the
       history of the players in Dublin. He rejects the claim
       that Davenant adapted Shakespeare's *Julius Caesar*.

631.   Ward, Charles E.   "*The Tempest*: A Restoration Opera
       Problem." *English Literary History*, 13 (1946),
       119-30.

            Shadwell is not the author of the operatic
       Tempest (1674), according to Ward. After discounting
       Downes' evidence, Lawrence's theses, and Dryden's
       participation, Ward suggests that it was probably
       revised by Betterton. He examines the 1670 and 1674
       quartos for the number and nature of the changes, and he
       decides Betterton is a more likely author than Shadwell.
       See *1904*: Lawrence ("Did Shadwell"); *1912*: Lawrence
       ("Did Thomas Shadwell"); *1947*: Milton.

                              1947

632.   Grout, Donald Jay. *A Short History of Opera*. 2 vols.
       New York: Columbia Univ. Press, 1947.

            The work cites the five-act *The Siege of
       Rhodes* with its music, recitatives, and arias, as "the
       first English opera."

633.   Milton, William M. "Tempest in a Teapot." *English
       Literary History*, 14 (1947), 207-18.

            The article summarizes an extended
       forty-three-year debate involving a number of articles
       and scholars and states that Shadwell, not Dryden, was
       responsible for the revisions of *The Tempest*. See
       1904: Lawrence; 1925: Thorn-Drury; *1926*: Walmsley;
       1927: Thorn-Drury; and *1946*: Ward.

634.   Young, C.B. "The Stage History of *Macbeth*."   In
       Macbeth. John Dover Wilson, ed. Cambridge: Univ.
       Press, 1947. Pp. lxix-lxxxii.

            Young notes that the play was performed often
       and cites in particular Betterton, as an early and

popular Macbeth. He also deplores the Davenant version
noting some of the changes in poetry.

1948

635. Brooke, Tucker. *The Renaissance (1500-1660).* Book II
     of *A Literary History of England.* Ed. Albert C.
     Baugh. New York: Appleton-Century-Crofts, 1948. Pp.
     315-696.

          Although Brooke cites Davenant as an important
     court dramatist, Davenant receives little attention in
     the account of Renaissance literary figures and their
     work. Two plays are noted: *Love and Honour* and *The
     Platonic Lovers.* In the section on poetry, Davenant is
     mentioned and cross-referenced to the next book, *The
     Restoration and Eighteenth Century.* See *1967*: Brooke.

636. Gilbert, Allan H. *The Symbolic Persons in the Masques
     of Ben Jonson.* Durham: Duke Univ. Press, 1948. Pp.
     xi, 297.

          The work suggests meanings to some of
     Davenant's masques, especially *Luminalia.*

637. Greg, W.W. "Paper-Saving in 1639." *The Library*, 5th
     Ser., 2 (1948), 61.

          Greg notes a problem in printing that he found
     in Davenant's *Salmacida Spolia* (B.M., 162,c.42).

638. Marilla, E.L. "Henry Vaughan to Sir William
     Davenant." *Philological Quarterly*, 27 (1948), 181-84.

          Marilla accepts H.F.B. Brett-Smith's
     identification of "aged Sire" as Homer and then
     discusses Vaughan's comparison of Homer and Davenant:
     both overcame severe obstacles in life, the former
     blindness, the latter imprisonment. As a result, they
     gained artistic maturity and wrote great poetry. See
     1916: Brett-Smith.

639. Nicoll, Allardyce. *The Development of the Theatre; A
     Study of Theatrical Art from the Beginnings to the
     Present Day.* London: Harrap, 1948. Pp. 318.

          This is a revised and enlarged edition of the
     1927 and 1937 editions. In his chapter on Restoration

theater, Nicoll surveys briefly the stage history, mentioning specifically the crucial importance of Davenant's *The First Day's Entertainment at Rutland House* and *The Siege of Rhodes*. He notes that they represent the earliest use in Commonwealth and Restoration productions of techniques developed by Inigo Jones for the Caroline masque. See *1927*: Nicoll; *1937*, Nicoll.

640.   Russell, Trusten W. "Dryden, Inspirateur de Voltaire." *Revue de Litterature Comparee*, 22 (1948), 321-28.

In his statements about Dryden's poetry and drama, Voltaire refers to Davenant, *Gondibert*, and the philosophical climate of the seventeenth century.

641.   Sherburn, George. *The Restoration and Eighteenth Century*. Book III of *A Literary History of England*. Ed. Albert C. Baugh. New York: Appleton-Century-Crofts, 1948. Pp. 699-1108.

Davenant is cited in many sections of the work as a playwright, theater-manager, philosopher, and creator of the opera. He is described and discussed within the framework of his time as well as of all British literature. See *1967*: Sherburn.

642.   Smith, John Harrington. *The Gay Couple in Restoration Comedy*. Cambridge: Harvard Univ. Press, 1948. Pp. xi, 252.

The work offers a detailed study of the witty lovers in seventeenth-century comedy. Smith refers to Davenant's antiplatonic "spirit" in the masque and drama as part of the development toward the witty, gay couple. Davenant is noted here as a link between the late Elizabethan and Restoration drama. See *1946*: Smith; *1971*: Smith.

643.   Stead, Philip John, ed. *Songs of the Restoration Theatre, Edited from the Printed Books of the Time*. London: Methuen, 1948. Pp. xvii, 91.

Suggesting in his introduction that the excellent literary content of songs was assured by poets such as Davenant who wrote for the stage, Stead explains

that Davenant in addition "reminds us that the
Elizabethans are not far away. He bridges the gap of
the Commonwealth." The Restoration songs differ, he
says, because they have "an unholy joy," and "one finds
oneself in the presence of realistic art."

644. Turner, W. Arthur. "Milton's Aid to Davenant."
      Modern Language Notes, 63 (1948), 538-39.

          This is a good source for the poets' contacts
      1653-54, examining "not whether Milton saved Davenant's
      life, but how he might have helped him."

645. Wilson, John Harold. *The Court Wits of the
      Restoration: An Introduction*. Princeton: Princeton
      Univ. Press, 1948. Pp. vi, 264. Rpt. New York:
      Octagon, 1962. Pp. vi, 264.

          A study that traces the group of wits, *The
      Court Wits* provides both the ambience and the social
      milieu that surrounded and often derided Davenant. See
      1962: Wilson.

                              1949

646. Arthos, John. *The Language of Natural Description in
      Eighteenth-Century Poetry*. Univ. of Michigan
      Publications, Language and Literature, 24. Ann Arbor:
      Univ. of Michigan Press, 1949. Pp. xiv, 463.

          Davenant's language is cited in the catalogue
      of "stock diction."

647. Dick, Oliver Lawson, ed. *Aubrey's Brief Lives*.
      London: Secker and Warburg, 1949. Pp. cxiv, 408.

          Not only does Aubrey give an account of
      Davenant under his name but also in a number of other
      places, so that many of the poet's activities and
      relationships are given with some authority. See *1949*:
      Powell.

648. Gordon, D.J. "Poet and Architect: The Intellectual
      Setting of the Quarrel Between Ben Jonson and Inigo
      Jones." *Journal of the Warburg and Courtauld
      Institution*, 12 (1949), 152-78.

In a lengthy, illustrated article that is divided into four parts ("The Course of the Quarrel," "The Poet," "The Architect," and "The True Harmony"), Gordon outlines his main purpose to show the doctrines underlying the positions of architect and poet, their intellectual context, and the individuals' personal expressions of their positions in terms acceptable to the age. Gordon moves the conflict from gossip to history, and Davenant's relationship is given both artistically and personally in Appendix I.

649. Lamborn, E. A. Greening. "Great Tew and the Chandos Portrait." *Notes & Queries*, 194 (1949), 71-72.

In his discussion of the Kecks of Great Tew, Lamborn refers to the portrait of Shakespeare once at Tew and now in the National Gallery, known as the Chandos Portrait. Lamborn states that the portrait "was certainly the property of Sir William Davenant, Shakespeare's godson, to whom it is supposed to have been left as a legacy by John Taylor." Davenant died in debt; the portrait was bought by Betterton; on Betterton's death it was bought by Elizabeth Barry and son.

650. Olive, W.J. "Davenant and Davenport." *Notes & Queries*, 194 (1949), 320.

The item corrects an error noted by Swinburne that Washington Irving introduced Robert Davenport to his readers as "Thomas Davenport." Even earlier, Olive points out, the title page of his tragedy *King John and Matilda* has "'Written by W. Daven. Gent.'" "The error should not pass uncorrected."

651. Powell, Anthony, ed. *Aubrey's Brief Lives*. Cressett Library Edition. New York: Scribner's, 1949. Pp. cxiv 419.

See *1949*: Dick.

1950

652. Francis, F.C. "The Shakespeare Collection in the
British Museum." *Shakespeare Survey*, 3 (1950),
43-57.

The Ashby library, bought in 1937, greatly
enriched the British Museum collection of
seventeenth-century drama, including Davenant's.

653. Leech, Clifford. *Shakespeare's Tragedies and Other
Studies in Seventeenth-Century Drama*. London: Chatto
and Windus, 1950. Pp. vii, 232.

Leech contends that *The Platonic Lovers*
deserves better reception because it contains "some of
the best topical satire of Caroline years." Leech finds
that the play is an effort to expose the Platonic
lovers' snobbery.

654. MacMillan, Dougald. "The Sources of Dryden's *The
Indian Emperour*." *Huntington Library Quarterly*, 13
(1950), 355-70.

The writer suggests that Dryden derived some
of the ideas for his play from Davenant's *The Cruelty of
the Spaniards in Peru*.

655. Rundle, James U. "D'Avenant's *The Man's the Master*
and the Spanish Source." *Modern Language Notes*, 65
(1950), 194-96.

Rundle points out that Davenant depended upon
Scarron's Spanish source *Donde hay agravios no hay
celos*.

656. Wedgwood, C[icely] V[eronca]. *Seventeenth-century
English Literature*. Home Univ. Library. London:
Oxford Univ. Press and Cumberledge, 1950. Pp. 186.
Rev. 2nd ed. London: Oxford Univ. Press, 1970.

Wedgwood provides a harsh treatment of
Davenant as she reviews the century. She labels him
"the ambitious Davenant, self-styled laureate, most of
whose mature pomposities are now generally forgotten,
while his early and exquisite lyric, 'The lark now
leaves her watery nest,' is rightly remembered" (p.
99). See *1970*: Wedgwood.

1951

657. Atkins, J. W. H. *English Literary Criticism 17th and
      18th Centuries*. London: Methuen, 1951; New York:
      Barnes and Noble, 1952. Pp. xi, 383.

            In his chapter "The Transitional Stage:
      Davenant, Hobbes, Cowley, Sprat, and Dryden," Atkins
      sees Davenant's *Preface* to *Gondibert* as the first
      significant criticism of this transitional period
      (1650-1674), linking the Renaissance with the late
      seventeenth century (1674-1700) when English
      translations of French critics produced a decisive
      French influence on English criticism. The French
      influence of the earlier period was generated chiefly by
      Davenant, Hobbes, and Cowley, who brought the ideas back
      from their French exile. The chief interest in
      Davenant's *Preface* "lies in its reflexion of new
      influences from France and in its attempts to establish
      in England a modified form of the ancient epic."

658. Johnston, Albert S., Jr. *"The Wits and The Platonic
      Lovers* by William D'Avenant." Thesis. Florida
      1951.

659. Mandach, Andre De. "The First Translator of Moliere:
      Sir William Davenant or Colonel Henry Howard." *Modern
      Language Notes*, 66 (1951), 513-18.

            The article is a reprint of an earlier work.
      See *1946*: Mandach.

660. Thomas, Wesley W. "A Study of *Gondibert*, a Heroic
      Poem by Sir William D'Avenant." Thesis. Columbia
      1951.

1952

661. Adams, H.M. "The Shakespeare Collection in the
      Library of Trinity College, Cambridge." *Shakespeare
      Survey*, 5 (1952), 50-54.

            Adams states that for *The Tempest* there is
      the edition of 1670 published by H. Herringman, adapted
      by Dryden, and an edition "since altered by Sir William
      Davenant and Mr. J. Dryden, 1710" which was in the
      library of Sir Isaac Newton and which came with the gift

to the college of his books by the Pilgrim Trust in
1943.

662. Berry, Herbert. "Three New Poems by Davenant."
Philological Quarterly, 31 (1952), 70-74.

Berry identifies three unpublished poems among
the manuscripts at the British Museum which seem to be
by Davenant: "To A Gentleman at his uprising," "Upon A
moale in his mistris face," and "On his mistris
Singing." All three are in the Harleian MS. 6917 and
one is also in Additional MS. 11,811. Berry gives his
evidence and then prints all three.

663. Fujimura, Thomas H. *The Restoration Comedy of Wit.*
Princeton: Princeton Univ. Press, 1952. Rpt. New
York: Barnes and Noble, 1968. Pp. vii, 232.

Fujimura provides a history and criticism of
Restoration comedy that interprets the plays on the
basis of wit. Davenant appears both as
dramatist-manager and as one of the definers of terms,
particularly through his relationship with Hobbes. See
1968: Fujimura.

664. Hardacre, Paul H. "The Royalists in Exile During the
Puritan Revolution, 1642-1660." *Huntington Library
Quarterly*, 16 (1952-53), 353-70.

The article examines the impact of exile on
the writers. Davenant, Hardacre suggests, picked up
"the practice of writing critical prefaces to poems and
plays in France."

665. Hogan, Charles Beecher. *Shakespeare in the Theatre,
1701-1800.* 2 vols. Oxford: Clarendon, 1952, 1957.

The two volumes provide information concerning
the performances of Shakespeare's plays and their
adaptations, including the Davenant-Dryden *Tempest*, the
Davenant *Macbeth*, and the other Davenant alterations.
See *1957*: Hogan.

666. Jack, Ian. *Augustan Satire: Intention and Idiom in
English Poetry 1660-1750.* Oxford: Clarendon, 1952.
Pp. x, 163.

Jack's discussion frequently cites the poetry, theory, and influence of Davenant, although his main headings are of *Hudibras, MacFlecknoe*, and *Absalom and Achitophel*.

667. Nicoll, Allardyce. *A History of English Drama, 1660-1900*. 6 vols. Cambridge: Cambridge Univ. Press, 1952-59.

The set contains books printed earlier, revised, and corrected by Nicoll. Those most important to Davenant research are:

Vol. I: *Restoration Drama, 1660-1700*. 4th ed. 1955. See *1923, 1928*: Nicoll.
Vol. II: *Early Eighteenth-Century Drama*. 3rd ed. 1955. See *1925*: Nicoll.
Vol. III: *Late Eighteenth-Century Drama: 1750-1800*. 2nd ed. 1955. See *1927, 1937, 1961*: Nicoll.
Vol. VI: *A Short Title Alphabetical Catalogue of Plays Produced or Printed in England from 1660 to 1900*. 1959.

668. Southern, Richard. *Changeable Scenery: Its Origin and Development in the British Theatre*. London: Faber and Faber, 1952.

Much of the volume demonstrates the uses of theatrical scenery during the Restoration and eighteenth century. Of particular import is Southern's analysis of Davenant's *Salmacida Spolia*.

669. Van Lennep, William. "Henry Harris, Actor, Friend of Pepys." *Studies in English Theatre History in Honor of Gabrielle Enthoven*, O.B.E. Ed. M. St. C. Byrne. London: Society for Theatre Research, 1952, pp. 9-23.

In tracing the acting career of Harris and his friendship with Pepys, Van Lennep also provides information on Davenant's activities that involved the actor.

1953

670. Flecknoe, Richard. *Sr. William D'avenant's Voyage to the Other World*. Ed. A. K. Croston. In *Theatre Miscellany: Six Pieces Connected with the*

Seventeenth-Century Stage. Oxford: Basil Blackwell, 1953, pp. 49-67.

In the introduction, Croston finds the work worth reprinting and discussing because Flecknoe gives "a useful epitome of contemporary comment on D'avenant." He also suggests that Flecknoe's satirical attack arose from anger generated by an inadequate production of Flecknoe's *Love's Kingdom* (c. 1664) at Davenant's theater in Lincoln's-Inn-Fields. See *1668*: Flecknoe.

671. Higgins, Alison I.T. *Secular Heroic Epic Poetry of the Caroline Period*. Swiss Studies in English, 31. Switzerland: R. Francke, 1953. Pp. 136.

The volume contains two parts, one on background, the other on the poets. The last portion of the book is devoted to *Gondibert*, including a description of the poem, its justification, and its relationship to other Caroline poems.

672. Hook, Lucyle. "Shakespeare Improv'd, or A Case for the Affirmative." *Shakespeare Quarterly*, 4 (1953), 289-99.

The article offers an interpretation of Restoration adaptations of Shakespeare's plays from the women's view. Hook begins with Davenant, summarizing his activities in relationship to Killigrew and Betterton. She then stresses Davenant's changes in women's roles which resulted from women being permitted on stage.

673. McManaway, James, ed. "Songs and Masques in *The Tempest*." *Theatre Miscellany*. Luttrell Society Reprints, No. 14. Oxford: Oxford, 1953. Pp. 75-87.

In the passage, McManaway supports the position that *The Tempest* was a joint venture that included contributions by Shadwell.

674. Smith, Dane Farnsworth. *The Critics in the Audience of the London Theatres from Buckingham to Sheridan: A Study of Neoclassicism in the Playhouse, 1671-1779*. Univ. of New Mexico Publications in Language and Literature, No. 12. Albuquerque: Univ. of New Mexico Press, 1953. Pp. 192.

The second chapter "Sir William D'avenant and the Duke of Buckingham" opens with *The Play-House to Be Let* because it contains "perhaps the first reference to the critic in the drama of the Restoration." The book's thesis incorporates Davenant's use of the play to create support in the audience, "a claque," and to satirize the poets.

675. Sprague, Arthur Colby. *Shakesperian Players and Performances.* Cambridge: Harvard Univ. Press, 1953. Pp. viii, 222.

Among others, Sprague discusses Betterton as Hamlet, a role he first played in 1663 under the tutelage of Davenant.

1954

676. Duncan-Jones, Elsie. "Milton's 'Late Court-Poet.'" *Notes & Queries*, 199 (1954), 473.

In the pamphlet, *The Ready and Easy Way to Establish a Commonwealth*, Milton wrote in 1660 of Charles II's return, "For what can be more than another man? who, even in the expression of a late court-poet sets only like a great cypher set to no purpose before a long row of other significant figures." Duncan-Jones suggests the figure is Davenant, and the reference is to a passage in *Gondibert*:

> Nature too oft by birth-right does prefer
>   Less perfect Monarchs to a busie Throne;
> Yet more than her, Courts by weak Counc'lers err
>   In adding Cyphers where she made but one.
>
> (*Gondibert*, II. ii. v. 14)

Milton may have known Davenant and his great poem.

677. Grivelet, Michel. "Note sur Thomas Heywood et le Theatre sous Charles 1er." *Etudes Anglaises*, 7 (1954), 101-06.

Grivelet discusses, among other items, the relationship of Thomas Carew and Thomas Heywood as it is revealed in Carew's poetry published in the 1630 edition of Davenant's *The Just Italian*.

578. Haun, Eugene. "The Libretti of the Restoration Opera
      in English: A Study in Theatrical Genres." Diss.
      Pennsylvania 1954. Pp. 330.

           Haun presents in his dissertation an account
      of the masque that became the dramatic opera. In doing
      so, he discusses, among others, Davenant and Dryden.
      See *1971*: Haun.

579. Holden, William P. *Anti-Puritan Satire*. Yale Studies
      in English, Vol. 126. Ed. Benjamin Christie Nangle.
      New Haven: Yale Univ. Press, 1954. Pp. xii, 165.

           Drawing examples from Davenant's *The Wits,
      News from Plymouth, The Temple of Love*, and *The Cruel
      Brother*, Holden provides additional material to support
      a thesis more fully applied to dramatists such as
      Jonson.

1955

680. Berkeley, David S. "The Art of 'Whining' Love."
      Studies in Philology, 52 (1955), 478-96.

           "Whining" love is identified as "romantic,"
      "*preciosite*," and "*precieuse* gallantry" by Berkeley who
      sees it as the core of sentimental comedy. Berkeley
      sees "romance," "romantic," or "whining" love as "the
      Restoration equivalent of medieval courtly love." He
      identifies Davenant's theme of love and honor as basic
      and traces its uses through a number of late
      seventeenth-century plays.

681. Clark, William S. *The Early Irish Stage: The
      Beginnings to 1720*. Oxford: Clarendon, 1955. Pp. xi,
      227.

           The work briefly outlines Davenant's Irish
      interests.

682. Evelyn, John. *The Diary of John Evelyn*. Ed. Esmond
      S. DeBeer. 6 vols. Oxford: Clarendon, 1955.

           While not as much of a theater-goer as Pepys,
      Evelyn gives some accounts of his responses to the
      second part of *The Siege of Rhodes* and *The Law Against
      Lovers* in 1662, either *The History of Sir Francis Drake*

(1659) or *The Cruelty of the Spaniards in Peru* (1658) i‹
1659, and the appearances of women on stage as
actresses.

683.   *Groves' Dictionary of Music and Musicians.* Ed. Eric
       Blom. 7 vols. 5th ed. New York: St. Martin's, 1955.

            The seventh volume of the work not only
       provides biographical data on the various musicians but
       it also offers a commentary on *The Siege of Rhodes*
       identifying Davenant as the writer of the libretto and
       other facts of its original production. See *1980*:
       Laurie.

684.   Haywood, Charles. "*The Songs and Masques in the New
       Tempest*: An Incident in the Battle of the Two
       Theaters, 1674." *Huntington Library Quarterly*, 19
       (1955), 39-56.

            The article prints the text of *The Songs and
       Masques in the New Tempest* and offers the two versions,
       one at the Huntington Library and the other at the
       Folger Library. Haywood tries to define the battle
       between the Duke's and the King's players by noting the
       King's Company used Duffett to burlesque Shadwell's
       published text of the songs. "The Folger librettos
       contain the songs and masques of Shadwell's operatic
       version of the Davenant-Dryden *Tempest*" (1674) and the
       two versions are an acting and a reading-selling copy.
       The Huntington's is also a copy of Shadwell's to be sold
       at the door.

685.   Herrick, Marvin T. *Tragicomedy: Its Origins and
       Development in Italy, France and England.* Urbana:
       Univ. of Illinois Press, 1955. Pp. vii, 329.

            After discussing the background and
       development of tragicomedy through Beaumont and
       Fletcher, Herrick devotes the last two chapters to
       "English Tragicomedy from Fletcher through Davenant" and
       "The Aftermath of Tragicomedy."

686.   Langhans, Edward Allen. "Staging Practices in the
       Restoration Theatres 1660-1682." Diss. Yale 1955.
       Pp. 544.

            The work examines "the equipment and staging
       practices of the five main public theatres in

Restoration London." Davenant is included as manager of
the Duke's theater and discussed in relationship to the
others.

687. Spencer, Christopher. "The Problems of Davenant's
      Text of Shakespeare's 'Macbeth' Together with a Typed
      Facsimile of the Yale Manuscript." Diss. Yale 1955.

         This study provided the background for the
      book on the same subject published by the Yale
      University Press in 1961. See *1961*: Spencer.

688. Walton, Geoffrey. *Metaphysical to Augustan: Studies
      in Tone and Sensibility in the Seventeenth Century*.
      London: Bowes & Bowes, 1955. Pp. viii, 160.

         Walton begins the book with
      seventeenth-century ideas of wit and with Davenant's
      Gondibert and the *Preface*. Included also is his poem
      "To the Lady Olivia Porter."

689. Wise, Matthew Montgomery. "The Minor Poems of Sir
      William D'Avenant." Diss. Columbia 1955. Pp. 727.

         The dissertation indicates that Davenant
      warrants "larger recognition." The work contains an
      introduction that discusses the quality and range of
      Davenant's poetry, the ideas that the poet expresses,
      the textual problems confronting the editor, and the
      canon. The poems are then provided "in chronological
      order with full textual and commentary notes."

                          1956

690. Bonnard, Georges A. "Shakespeare in the Bibliotheca
      Bodmeriana." *Shakespeare Survey*, 9 (1956), 81-85.

         The Bibliotheca Bodmeriana is a private
      collection in Geneva owned by Martin Bodmer. Among its
      many treasures are the first edition of Davenant's and
      Dryden's *Tempest* and the first and second editions of
      Davenant's *Macbeth*.

691. Branam, George Curtis. *Eighteenth-Century Adaptations
      of Shakespearean Tragedy*. Berkeley: Univ. of
      California Press, 1956. Pp. viii, 220.

The book discusses Davenant's treatments of *Macbeth* and *The Tempest*, noting that "before Garrick's production of *Macbeth*, the eighteenth-century audience saw the play in Sir William Davenant's alteration" and that *The Tempest* retained its operatic qualities introduced by Davenant.

692.   Cutts, John P. "The Original Music to Middleton's *The Witch.*" *Shakespeare Quarterly*, 7 (1956), 203-10.

Cutts notes that Davenant used two of Middleton's songs, "Come Away Hecate" and "Black Spirits and White," for the adaptation of *Macbeth*.

693.   Duncan-Jones, Elsie E. "Two Allusions in Lovelace's Poems." *Modern Language Review*, 51 (1956), 407-09.

Duncan-Jones finds references to Davenant in two of Lovelace's satirical poems, which she relates to the phrase "O costly Opera" in Davenant's "Epithalamium. The morning after the Marriage of the Earl of Barrymore with Mrs. Martha Lawrence." She concludes that "Davenant considered [the first performance of] his opera [*The Siege of Rhodes*] a failure; success must have come after an unprosperous beginning."

694.   Hughes, Leo. *A Century of English Farce.* Princeton: Princeton Univ. Press, 1956. Pp. vii, 307.

Hughes' thesis is that the farce of the Restoration and mid-eighteenth century is more directly linked to the theater in which it was performed than any other dramatic form: "it cannot profitably be thought of apart from the theater in which it was produced." Davenant's career as dramatist, poet, and theater manager justify references to his theories and practices. Hughes cites statements by Davenant in a prologue, in *A Play-House to be Let*, and *The Man's the Master*, and he cites also Davenant's use of European conventions.

695.   Riewald, J.G. "Laureates in Elysium: Sir William Davenant and Robert Southey." *English Studies*, 37 (1956), 133-40.

Richard Flecknoe's prose satire of Davenant is compared with Byron's attack on Southey. The

similarities between the two tracts suggest that the
earlier served as a model for the later.

696. Stone, George Winchester, Jr. "Shakespeare's *Tempest*
at Drury Lane during Garrick's Management."
Shakespeare Quarterly, 7 (1956), 1-7.

Stone examines Garrick's return to the
Davenant-Dryden *Tempest* and suggests that was a good
business move in the theater.

697. Waddell, David. "The Writing of Charles Davenant
(1656-1713)." *Library*, 11 (1956), 206-12.

The article distinguishes between Sir William
Davenant and his son, Charles, bibliographically.

1957

698. Arundel, Dennis. *The Critic at the Opera:
Contemporary Comments on Opera in London Over Three
Centuries.* London: E. Benn, 1957. Pp. xiii, 424.

In the first of its three parts, Arundel's
account of the opera focuses on Davenant: Chapter 3,
"Davenant and Opera," traces Davenant's life and the
development of his interest in opera through his
comedies, masques, and his heroic poem; Chapter 4,
"Opera at Rutland House," is a lengthy description of
every facet of "First Day's Entertainment"; Chapter 5,
"Opera at the Cockpit, Drury Lane," covers the operas
*The Siege of Rhodes, The Cruelty of the Spaniards in
Peru, The History of Sir Francis Drake*; Chapter 6, "The
Duke's Theatre and 'The Slighted Maid,'" is an account
of the early competition between Davenant, Killigrew,
and George Jolly, over the play which was finally
produced by Davenant at his theater; Chapter 7,
"Davenant and Killigrew," begins with an account of *The
Playhouse to Be Let* and returns later to Davenant with
an account of *The Tempest*. The volume concludes with a
tribute to Sir William Davenant, opera's "first great
enthusiast." See *1980*: Arundel.

699. Barber, C.L. *The Idea of Honour in the English Drama
1591-1700.* Gothenburg Studies in English, VI. Ed.
Frank Behre. Goteborg: Univ. of Gothenburg, 1957.
Pp. 364.

In trying to determine what "honour" meant to
the seventeenth century, Barber examines many of
Davenant's plays including *The Distresses, The Fair
Favourite, The Law Against Lovers, Love and Honour, the
Man's the Master, News from Plymouth, The Platonic
Lovers, The Tempest, or The Enchanted Island, The
Unfortunate Lovers,* and *The Wits.*

700. Broeker, Harriet Durkee. "The Influence of *Othello* on
      Jacobean and Caroline Drama." Diss. Minnesota 1957.
      Pp. 349.

Among the plays Broeker discusses are
Davenant's *Albovine, The Platonic Lovers,* and *The Cruel
Brother.*

701. Grant, Douglas. *Margaret the First.* Toronto: Toronto
      Univ. Press, 1957. Pp. 252.

A biography of Margaret Lucas Cavendish, the
Duchess of Newcastle, the book includes not only facts
about her life but also gives a considerable amount of
attention to her works and ideas. She wrote some of the
first literary criticism of Shakespeare, and she wrote a
significant comment on *Gondibert* (pp. 113-15).

702. Hogan, Charles Beecher. *Shakespeare in the Theatre,
      1701-1800.* Vol. II: *A Record of Performances in
      London, 1751-1800.* Oxford: Clarendon, 1957.

This is the companion volume to Hogan's
earlier work. See *1952:* Hogan.

703. Mitra, D. "Adaptations of the Plays of Moliere for
      the English Stage, 1660-1700." Thesis Bedford College
      1957.

704. Wilson, John Harold. "Lord Oxford's 'Roxalana.'"
      Theatre Notebook, 12 (1957), 14-16.

Wilson identifies Mrs. Davenport of the Duke's
Company, one of the actresses who not only acted in
Davenant's company but also lived in his home, as
"Hester, called Countess of Oxford."

705. Parrott, Thomas Marc, and Robert Hamilton Ball. *A Short View of Elizabethan Drama, Together with Some Account of Its Principal Playwrights and the Conditions Under Which It Was Produced.* New York: Scribner's, 1958. Pp. vii, 311.

        See *1943*: Parrot.

706. Roberts, Peter. "Theatrical Cavalier." *Plays and Players*, 6 (1958-59), 7.

        Prompted by the forthcoming production of Davenant's pantomime version of *The Tempest*, Peter Roberts tells of the playwright's life and evaluates his theatrical achievement.

707. Wilson, John Harold. *All The King's Ladies: Actresses of the Restoration.* Chicago: Univ. of Chicago Press, 1958. Pp. ix, 205.

        Wilson offers information about actresses and actors of the period, many of whom acted for Davenant.

708. Bowers, Fredson Thayer. *Elizabethan Revenge Tragedy, 1587-1642.* Gloucester, Mass.: Peter Smith, 1959. Pp. viii, 288.

        See *1940*: Bowers.

709. Cope, Jackson. "Rhetorical Genres in Davenant's *First Day's Entertainment at Rutland House.*" *Quarterly Journal of Speech*, 45 (1959), 191-94.

        Going beyond Nethercot's description of *First Day's Entertainment* as consisting "simply of a debate or rather of two monologues...padded out...with an additional debate," Cope illustrates Davenant's use of two "widely familiar," non-dramatic rhetorical devices, the mock encomium, a form that was at its peak in the 1650s, and the character, a genre that was dependent on conceits, antithesis, and satire.

710. Holland, Norman. *The First Modern Comedies: The Significance of Etherege, Wycherley, and Congreve.* Cambridge: Harvard Univ. Press, 1959. Pp. 274.

In examining Davenant's *Tempest*, Holland decides that the adaptation offers a view of man that is of the "natural man" and that the play is a joke between the audience and the players whereby a contrast is set up between the enchanted isle of the play and Restoration London.

711.   Huxley, Gervas. *Endymion Porter: The Life of a Courtier; 1587-1649*. London: Chatto & Windus, 1959. Pp. 344.

The biography of Porter contains many significant references to Davenant. Their friendship and Davenant's debt to Porter are important to an understanding of both men. Huxley reprints and explains some poems that Davenant wrote for the Porters (pp. 170-75) and offers background for Davenant's masques, plays, and other poems. At one point Huxley identifies Davenant and Suckling as "irresponsible poets" and at another he praises Davenant's friendship and loyalty because the poet, after Porter's death, gave Olivia a tenth of his new theatrical company and later gave a son more shares and produced two plays by another son.

712.   Macomber, Philip Alan. "The Iconography of London Theatre Auditorium Architecture." Diss. Ohio State 1959. Pp. 406.

In Chapter II, "The Tennis Court Theatres, 1660-1672," Macomber presents a conjectural reconstruction of such theatres, including Davenant's.

713.   Owens, William Henry, Jr. "The Dramaturgical Treatment of Character Types by the Playwrights of Heroic Drama." Diss. Denver 1959.

714.   Park, Hugh Winston. "Revenge in Restoration Tragedy." Diss. Utah 1959. Pp. 230.

The dissertation examines twenty-seven of the seventy-six Restoration tragedies that were written 1656-92 by Davenant, Dryden, Lee, and Otway in order to determine the impact of Elizabethan revenge tragedy. Park includes heroic drama and sentimental drama in his definition of Restoration tragedy. He finds Davenant's plays to have been "static and simply designed drama" where revenge was not used much because of the hero's adherence to a code of honor.

15. [Rev. of *Tempest* by Sir William Davenant and John
     Dryden.] "Musical 'Tempest' Seen." *The New York
     Times*, 10 June 1959, p. 42, col. 2.

     The article is a review of the London
     production of the seventeenth-century musical version of
     Shakespeare's *Tempest* by Davenant and Dryden at the Old
     Vic Theatre. The play was directed by Douglas Seale as
     part of a celebration of the 300th anniversary of Henry
     Purcell's birth and the 200th anniversary of George
     Handel's death.

7.   1960-1969

716.   Adams, Joseph Quincy. *Shakespearean Playhouses: A
       History of English Theatres from the Beginnings to the
       Restoration.* Gloucester, Mass.: P. Smith, 1960. Pp.
       473.

           See *1917*: Adams.

717.   Avery, Emmett L., et al. *The London Stage, 1660-1800.*
       5 pts. in 11 vols. Carbondale: Southern Illinois
       Univ. Press, 1960-68.

           The multi-volume work is indispensable to a
       study of Davenant, providing information on
       performances, actors and actresses, and contemporary
       commentary.

718.   Brooks, Cleanth, and Robert Penn Warren.
       Understanding Poetry. 3rd ed. New York: Holt,
       Rinehart and Winston, 1960.

           The critics reprint Shakespeare's "Tomorrow,
       and tomorrow, and tomorrow" beside Davenant's revision
       of the passage in the latter's adaptation of *Macbeth* as
       an exercise in detailed explication and comparison.
       They conclude: "The intention of Sir William Davenant (a
       poet of a generation after Shakespeare) was to remove
       what he considered offenses against 'correctness' and
       'reasonableness.'"

719.   Brown, E.M. "The Reviewing of Shakespearean
       Productions in The Times Newspaper, 1788-1860."
       Thesis. Wales (Cardiff) 1960.

720.   Brown, John Russell. "Three Adaptations."
       Shakespeare Survey. Ed. Allardyce Nicoll. Vol. 13.
       Cambridge: Cambridge Univ. Press, 1960, 137-45.

           The chapter discusses the June 1959 Old Vic
       production of *The Tempest* as it was adapted by Dryden
       and Davenant. Brown notes that the Old Vic used the
       1674 edition which, he states, is basically the 1670
       version with some additional aerial flights, dances, and
       songs in a concluding masque.

721.   Campbell, Lily B. *Scenes and Machines on the English
        Stage During the Renaissance.* New York: Barnes and
        Noble, 1960. Pp. x, 302.

                See *1923*: Campbell.

722.   Collins, Howard Stuart. "The Comedy of Sir William
        Davenant." Diss. Brown 1960. Pp. 206.

                The dissertation is designed "to make a
        thorough study of Sir William Davenant's dramaturgic
        treatment of the Comic Spirit." See *1967*: Collins.

723.   Evans, G. Blakemore. *Shakespearean Prompt-Books of
        the Seventeenth-Century.* Vol. 2. *General
        Introduction and the Padua Macbeth.* Bibliographical
        Society of the University of Virginia.
        Charlottesville: Univ. Press of Virginia, 1960. Pp.
        Pt. i, [vi], 39; Pt. ii, 131-51 (facs. of *Macbeth*,
        F1).

                Among the seventeenth-century prompt-books,
        Evans examines one for *Macbeth* from a First Folio at the
        University Library at Padua. He indicates that the
        annotations, which are written in English, can be
        tentatively dated c. 1625-35 and may have been the work
        of Sir Edward Dering. These alterations resemble those
        later found in Davenant's 1674 and the Smock Alley
        versions of *Macbeth.* Evans analyzes the similarities
        fully. The Smock Alley version also contains a
        manuscript line which is later given to Brutus in the
        Davenant-Dryden *Julius Caesar*; the play was printed in
        Dublin in 1719. See item 199; see also *1946*: Van
        Lennep.

724.   Kaufmann, Rolf James. "Suckling and Davenant
        Satirized by Brome." *Modern Language Review*, 55
        (1960), 332-44.

                Kaufmann identifies Davenant as the ridiculous
        court-wit in Brome's *The Court Beggar.* The character
        satirically reflects Davenant's unsuccessful efforts to
        establish an elaborate new theater in 1639 and his
        successful efforts to take over Beeston's company at the
        Cockpit in 1640.

725.   McElroy, D. "The 'Artificiall Sea' in Jonson's
        'Masque of Blacknesse.'" *Notes & Queries*, 205 (1960),
        419-21.

Questioning that Inigo Jones used a device
similar to one recorded by Sabbatini in 1638 to create
the "artificiall sea" in Jonson's masque (1605), McElroy
refers to Davenant's *The Temple of Love* (1634/5) because
of the sea effects that Jones again used. McElroy notes
the effects in the two masques are similar, and he
describes an etching from *The Temple of Love* along with
two other designs for Italian masques. He concludes: "I
can find no evidence to indicate that a mechanical sea
device was used in any of the four." He opts for a "sea
cloth."

726. Morrah, Patrick. *1660: The Year of Restoration*.
     London: Chatto and Windus, 1960. Pp. 237.

The book carefully traces events that have
documentation relating to the year 1660. Davenant
appears both as a political and a theatrical force.

727. Oras, Ants. *Pause Patterns in Elizabethan and
     Jacobean Drama: An Experiment in Prosody*. Univ. of
     Florida Monographs: Humanities, No. 3. Gainesville,
     Fla.: Univ. of Florida Press, 1960. Pp. 90.

The work includes an examination of Davenant's
*The Cruel Brother, Albovine, The Just Italian, The Wits,
News from Plymouth, The Platonic Lovers, The Distresses,
The Fair Favourite, The Playhouse to be Let,* and The
Siege, for pause patterns. The writer concludes that
the style is reminiscent of earlier seventeenth-century
pause patterns.

728. Wedgwood, C[icely] V[eronica]. "The Last Masque."
     Truth and Opinion: Historical Essays. London:
     Macmillan, 1960, pp. 139-56.

The chapter describes the king, the court, and
their part in Davenant's masque *Salmacida Spolia* against
the background of pre-Civil War turbulence.

729. Wedgwood, C[icely] V[eronica]. *Poetry and Politics
     under the Stuarts.* Cambridge: Cambridge Univ. Press,
     1960. Pp. vii, 220.

Originally presented as the Clark Lectures at
Cambridge in 1958, the work provides an historical
perspective to the relationship between Stuart politics

and English poetry. Using quotes from Davenant's
poetry, Wedgwood emphasizes two notions: the poetry
reflected the politics, and Davenant was a lesser poet.
She admires, however, passages from *Salmacida Spolia*,
and uses his poem "The Plots" to explain the court's
position on the Scots in the 1630s and 40s.

1961

730.   Dust, Alvin I. "The Seventh and Last Canto of
        Gondibert and Two Dedicatory Poems." *Journal of
        English and Germanic Philology*, 60 (1961), 282-85.

                Dust clarifies the composition of the canto
        and the poems and he supports McManaway's view that
        Davenant wrote the canto. See *1940*: McManaway.

731.   Henigan, Robert. "English Dramma per Musica: A Study
        of Musical Drama in England from *The Siege of Rhodes*
        to the Opening of the Haymarket Theatre." Diss.
        Missouri 1961. Pp. 417.

                The dissertation traces the unique development
        of "drama through, or by means of, music" from
        conditions peculiar to the English and defined at first
        by Davenant as dramatist and theater-manager.

732.   Ker, W.P., ed. *Essays of John Dryden*. 2 vols. New
        York: Russell & Russell, 1961.

                See *1900*: Ker.

733.   Knight, L. H. "Stage Adaptations of Shakespeare,
        1660-1900." Diss. Wales (Swansea) 1961.

734.   Morillo, Marvin. "Shirley's 'Preferment' and the
        Court of Charles I." *Studies in English Literature,
        1500-1900*, 1 (1961), 107-17.

                The author argues that Shirley's loss of
        preferment at the Court of Charles I, alluded to in the
        dedication of *The Maid's Revenge*, was in part the result
        of Davenant's gain of royal favor.

735.   Nicoll, Allardyce. *A History of Late Eighteenth
        Century Drama, 1750-1800*. Cambridge: Cambridge Univ.
        Press, 1961. Pp. 423.

See *1927*: Nicoll; *1937*: Nicoll; *1952*: Nicoll.

736.   Spencer, Christopher, ed. *Davenant's* Macbeth *from the Yale Manuscript: An Edition, with a Discussion of the Relation of Davenant's Text to Shakespeare's*. Yale Studies in English, Vol. 146. New Haven: Yale Univ. Press, 1961. Pp. x, 226.

Spencer presents a text of Davenant's play (1674) with line numbers, the Yale MS, and an informative commentary. See *1955*: Spencer; *1963*: McManaway.

737.   Williamson, George. *The Proper Wit of Poetry*. Chicago: Univ. of Chicago Press, 1961. Pp. 136.

Williamson traces wit through history and develops in the process the evolution of the definition of the term. The book serves to place in context Davenant's theories and practices as a seventeenth-century poet who is moving from the Jacobean wit most characterized by Donne to a definition of wit and poetry as demonstrated in his *Preface* to *Gondibert* and in the poem itself.

1962

738.   Blackburn, Thomas H. "Edmund Bolton's *London, King Charles His Augusta, or City Royal*." *The Huntington Library Quarterly*, 25 (1962), 315-23.

Blackburn provides evidence that suggests the poem was not written by Davenant as claimed by the printer of the first (1648) edition, but rather by Edmund Bolton, Endymion Porter's brother-in-law.

739.   Bush, Douglas. *English Literature in the Earlier Seventeenth Century: 1600-1660*. 2nd rev. ed. *The Oxford History of English Literature*. Vol. 5. Ed. F.P. Wilson and Bonamy Dobree. New York: Oxford Univ. Press, 1962. Pp. viii, 680.

The volume surveys the non-dramatic literature of the period and thus discusses Davenant as a poet. Commending him for his "large masculine energy of imagination ... and a distinctive vein of thoughtful

sobriety," Bush notes that Davenant's reputation rests
in large part with his dramatic enterprises. Later in
the large volume, Bush discusses *Gondibert* and its
prefaces by both Davenant and Hobbes as "landmarks from
the Renaissance to the Augustan age." See *1967*: Gibbs.

740.   Gladish, David F. "A Critical Edition of Sir William
       Davenant's *Gondibert*." Diss. Illinois 1962. Pp.
       616.

           The dissertation contains an introduction, the
       text, and editorial apparatus for the poem, its
       prefatory essays, the dedicatory poems, and the
       epilogue. See *1971*: Gladish.

741.   Hotson, Leslie. *The Commonwealth and Restoration
       Stage*. 1928. New York: Russell & Russell,
       1962. Pp. ix, 424.

           See *1928*: Hotson.

742.   Knowland, A.S., ed. *Six Caroline Plays*. The World's
       Classics, 583. London: Oxford Univ. Press, 1962. Pp.
       432.

           In his introduction Knowland discusses
       Davenant as a Caroline dramatist along with three other
       writers. The text of the 1636 *The Wits* is included with
       Thomas Killigrew's *The Parson's Wedding* (1663).

743.   Parsons, P. E. "*The Siege of Rhodes* and Restoration
       Tragedy: An Interpretation of Some Formal
       Developments in the Serious Drama of the Restoration."
       ASLIB (Proceedings of the Association of Special
       Libraries and Information Bureaux), 13 (1962-63).

744.   Renner, Dick Arnold. "The Poetic Theory of Sir
       William Davenant in *Gondibert* and Its *Preface*." Diss.
       Missouri 1962. Pp. 146.

           Renner examines Davenant's post-Restoration
       drama, Hobbes' philosophical system, *Gondibert* and its
       Preface, and Dryden's reaction. According to Renner,
       Gondibert contains a theory of poetry that "transcends
       the aesthetic principles traditionally understood to be
       a part of the Age of Reason." He suggests that
       Davenant's failure to reach an audience was the result
       of "the reaction of his age against enthusiasm."

745.   [Rev. of *The Wits* by Sir William Davenant.]
       "D'Avenant Comedy Played Straight." *The Times*, 24
       Feb. 1962, p. 4, col. 8.

           The Wits was performed at the Embassy Theatre
       at the Central School by the third-year students who
       presented it in period costumes but without painted
       scenery, music, song, or dance. It was treated as a new
       play, "that is a play having something to say, not as
       though it were an old play...; an audience could now be
       expected to give it a hearing." The reviewer found the
       play to have "an easy language on the ear."

746.   Sen, Sailendra Kumar. "Adaptations of Shakespeare and
       His Critics, 1660-1790." *Indian Journal of English
       Studies*, 3 (1962), 44-60.

747.   Welsford, Enid. *The Court Masque: A Study in the
       Relationship Between Poetry and the Revels.* New York:
       Russell & Russell, 1962. Pp. 434.

           See *1927*: Welsford.

748.   Wilson, John Harold. *The Court Wits of the
       Restoration: An Introduction.* New York: Octagon,
       1962. Pp. vi, 264.

           See *1948*: Wilson.

                        1963

749.   Banks, Howard Milton. "A Historical Survey of the
       Mise-en-Scene Employed in Shakespearean Productions
       from the Elizabethan Period to the Present." Diss.
       Southern California 1963. Pp. 821.

           The dissertation considers changes in the
       stage between 1660 and 1800, with particular attention
       to Davenant's scenic innovations.

750.   Delius, Von Nicolaus. "Shakespeare's Macbeth and
       Davenant's Macbeth." Vaduz: Kraus Reprint, 1963.

           This is a reprint of the article that just
       appeared in 1885. See *1885*: Delius.

751.   Feil, J.P. "Davenant Exonerated." *Modern Language
       Review*, 58 (1963), 335-42.

Feil clears Davenant of suspicion of murder by
presenting documentary evidence that another William
Davenant, not the poet laureate as Nethercot indicated,
murdered a Thomas Warren. According to Feil's evidence,
it was a distant cousin from Essex who was the guilty
party.

752.   Hall, Vernon, Jr. *A Short History of Literary
       Criticism.* New York: New York Univ. Press, 1963. Pp.
       xii, 184.

Hall sees Milton as the only important critic
of the Commonwealth years and Davenant and Hobbes as the
only others who wrote substantial criticism. Though
Davenant in his *Preface* to *Gondibert* and Hobbes in his
Answer "mark the transition from Renaissance to
neoclassical criticism in English thought," their views
of poetry are superficial ones in which "inspiration is
replaced by reason, imagination by fancy."

753.   Holzknecht, Karl Julius. *Outlines of Tudor and Stuart
       Plays 1497-1642.* London: Methuen, 1963.

First published in the United States by Barnes
& Noble in 1947 as part of their outline series, the
volume contains a bibliography and good act-by-act
outlines of plays by forty-four dramatists. Davenant's
Love and Honor is included.

754.   Honninghausen, Lothar. "Der Stilwandel im
       dramatischen Werk Sir William Davenants." Diss. Bonn
       1963.

See *1965*: Honninghausen.

755.   Hurd, Richard. *Letters on Chivalry and Romance.*
       London: for A. Millar, W. Thurlbourn, and J. Woodyer,
       1762. Pp. 120. Augustan Reprint Society, 101-02.
       Ed. Hoyt Trowbridge. Los Angeles: Clark Memorial
       Library, 1963.

See *1762*: Hurd; *1811*: Hurd; *1824*: Aikin;
       1911: Hurd.

756.   Lawrence, William. "Did Shadwell Write an Opera on
       'The Tempest'?" *The Elizabethan Playhouse and Other
       Studies.* New York: Russell & Russell, 1963.

See *1904*: Lawrence; *1947*: Milton.

757. Loftis, John. *The Politics of Drama in Augustan England*. Oxford: Clarendon, 1963. Pp. [iv], 173.

Seeing politics as the distinctive feature of all Augustan literature, Loftis examines the drama for its influence. Beginning with the patents, political in themselves, the ties with the court, the lack of clear definition with the ordering of the patents, the resulting confusion and rivalries, Loftis clarifies the elements of the drama that depended on political favor and maneuvering. Davenant is one of the early and important elements.

758. Lord, George de F., ed. *Poems on Affairs of State: Augustan Satirical Verse, 1660-1714*. Vol. I: 1660-1678. New Haven: Yale Univ. Press, 1963. Pp. lvi, 506.

Lord reprints satirical poems originally published between 1660 and 1714 often on unlicensed presses and anonymously. Rather than as literature, the poems are of greater importance politically and historically. Davenant appears as a target in the poems that begin on pages 54 and 327. He is alluded to in the poem on p. 380.

759. McAfee, Helen. *Pepys on the Restoration Stage*. New York: Benjamin Blom, 1963. Pp. 353.

See *1916*: McAfee.

760. McManaway, James G. "The Year's Contribution to Shakespearian Studies." *Shakespeare Studies*, 16 (1963), 172-81.

McManaway disagrees with Christopher Spencer's belief that the play *Macbeth* by Davenant is based on a pre-Restoration manuscript independent of the first folio, and that the first ten lines of the witches' song may have been by Shakespeare. See *1961*: Spencer.

761. Moore, Frank H. *The Nobler Pleasure: Dryden's Comedy in Theory and Practice*. Chapel Hill: Univ. of North Carolina Press, 1963. Pp. 264.

The book traces Dryden's career with six
chapters devoted to the years 1663-1700. Davenant is a
part of Moore's coverage of Dryden's early years,
especially the collaboration on *The Tempest.*

762. Nevo, Ruth. *The Dial of Virtue: A Study of Poems on
      Affairs of State in the Seventeenth Century.*
      Princeton: Princeton Univ. Press, 1963. Pp. x, 283.

Nevo covers the bulk of political verse to
reveal "the antithetical quality of the couplet as the
reflection of an acute sense of dialectical opposites,
as that form most fitted to express the alignment of the
nation into irreconcilable camps, at loggerheads to the
point of civil war at first, and irreducible
nonconformism later.... [T]he achieved Augustan couplet
may indeed represent the binding of the antithesis ...."
Nevo not only discusses Davenant's poetry, but she also
uses a line from "Upon his Sacred Majestys Most Happy
Return" (1660) for her title.

763. Nicoll, Allardyce. *British Drama: An Historical
      Survey from the Beginnings to the Present Time.* 5th
      ed. New York: Barnes and Noble, 1963. Pp. 365.

The book is a revision of the earlier volume.
See *1925*: Nicoll.

764. Nicoll, Allardyce. *Stuart Masques and the Renaissance
      Stage.* 1937; rpt. New York: Benjamin Blom, 1963. Pp.
      223.

See *1937*: Nicoll, *Stuart.*

765. Odell, George C.D. *Shakespeare from Betterton to
      Irving.* 2 vols. New York: Benjamin Blom, 1963.

See *1920*: Odell; and *1966*: Odell.

766. Palmer, Paulina. "Carew: An Unnoticed Allusion to
      Davenant's Illegitimacy." *Notes & Queries*, New Ser.
      10 (1963), 61-62.

Palmer finds evidence in the final couplet of
Carew's commendatory poem to *Madagascar* which suggests
that Shakespeare was Davenant's father:

>   So, oft the Bastard nobler fortune meets,
>   Then the dull Issue of the lawfull sheets.

767.   Payne, Rhoda. "Stage Direction during the
       Restoration." *Theatre Annual*, 20 (1963), 41-63.

            Citing the greater importance of the
       director's role today, the article concludes that many
       of the practices began with the manager-director
       Davenant and were continued by Betterton, Dryden, and
       Cibber among others.

768.   Ram, Tulsit. "The Neo-Classical Epic from Davenant's
       Gondibert to Pope's *Iliad* with Special Reference to
       Ethical Interpretations." Diss. Queen Mary's College
       1963.

769.   Singh, Sarup. *The Theory of Drama in the Restoration
       Period.* Calcutta: Orient Longmans, 1963. Pp. xii,
       299.

            Singh's book examines critical theories
       expressed in dedications, prefaces, prologues, and
       epilogues. Among others, he examines Davenant's *Preface
       to Gondibert* and the prefatory remarks to *The Siege of
       Rhodes* for the "nature and function of tragedy."

770.   Spencer, Hazelton. *Shakespeare Improved.* New York:
       Ungar, 1963. Pp. 406.

            See *1927*: Spencer.

771.   Spingarn, Joel Elias, ed. *Critical Essays of the
       Seventeenth Century.* 3 vols. Bloomington, Ind.:
       Indiana Univ. Press, 1963.

            See *1908*: Spingarn.

772.   Squier, Charles Le Barge. "The Comic Spirit of Sir
       William Davenant: A Critical Study of His Caroline
       Comedies." Diss. Michigan 1963. Pp. 174.

            The dissertation is an examination of *The Just
       Italian, News from Plymouth, The Wits,* and *The Platonic
       Lovers* as plays that parody *precieuse* dialogue.
       Squier's view is that Davenant's "real work as a
       dramatist was done in the Caroline period, and all his

best comedies were written in a brief period of
perfected creativity from 1633 through 1635" (p. 14).

773. Thaler, Alwin. *Shakespeare to Sheridan, A Book About
      the Theatre of Yesterday and Today.* New York:
      Benjamin Blom, 1963. Pp. 339.

           See *1922*: Thaler.

774. Wickham, Glynne, and William Gladstone. *Early English
      Stages 1300-1660.* 3 vols. in 4. London: Routledge &
      Kegan Paul, 1963.

           In Volume 2, 1576-1660, there is detailed
      information along with a documented perspective of
      Davenant's plays, his laureateship, patent, military
      activity, actresses, masques, stage furniture, and his
      playhouses.

                              1964

775. Adams, Joseph Quincy, ed. *The Dramatic Records of Sir
      Henry Herbert, Master of the Revels, 1623-1673.* New
      York: Benjamin Blom, [1964?]. Pp. xiii, 155.

           See *1917*: Adams.

776. Dane, Clemence. [Winifred Ashton]. *The Godson: A
      Fantasy.* New York: Norton, 1964. Pp. 48.

           The fantasy devotes 41 pages to the story of
      Davenant's relationship with Shakespeare. Much of the
      prose work is in dialogue.

777. Fiske, Roger. "The 'Macbeth' Music." *Music and
      Letters*, 45 (1964), 114-25.

           Reviewing the history of *Macbeth* as a
      Restoration and eighteenth-century tragic opera, the
      article includes an account of Davenant's opera.

778. Halliday, F.E. "Four Centuries of Shakespearean
      Production." *History Today*, 14 (1964), 98-106.

           The review of various productions includes
      those by Davenant. Halliday cites in particular: *The
      Law against Lovers*, Davenant's adaptation of

Shakespeare's *Measure for Measure* and *Much Ado; Macbeth*
with a "balanced" cast; *The Tempest* as an opera written
with Dryden. According to Halliday, "Davenant died in
1668, but he had shown the way." Halliday notes
Davenant's modern stage and use of actresses and
scenery. He concludes that "one day we shall learn that
it is Shakespeare's words not the producer's whimsies,
that matter...."

779. Harbage, Alfred. *Annals of English Drama, 975-1700;
An Analytical Record of All Plays, Extant or Lost,
Chronologically Arranged and Indexed by Authors,
Titles, Dramatic Companies, etc.* Revised by S.
Schoenbaum. Philadelphia: Univ. of Pennsylvania
Press, 1964. Pp. xvii, 321.

A revised edition of Harbage's 1940 list of
works written for the English stage provides,
adaptations, translations, royal entertainments, and all
plays extant or lost, arranged in chronological order
and indexed by authors, titles, and companies. The
newer edition also contains doctoral dissertation
editions of the plays, locations of play manuscripts,
and the theaters operating during the period. The
Davenant canon is included. See *1940*: Harbage.

780. Harbage, Alfred. *Cavalier Drama.* New York: Russell &
Russell, 1964. Pp. 302.

See *1936*: Harbage.

781. Langhans, Edward A. "Theatrical References in the
Greenwich Hospital Newsletters." *Notes & Queries,* 209
(1964), 338.

The note offers evidence of performances of
Davenant's *Circe,* among others, in 1682. The Davenant
here is Sir William Davenant's son.

782. Maidment, James, and W. H. Logan, eds. *The Dramatic
Works of Sir William D'Avenant, with Prefatory Memoir
and Notes.* 5 vols. New York: Russell & Russell,
1964.

See *1872*: Maidment.

783. Parsons, Philip E. "*The Siege of Rhodes* and
Restoration Tragedy: An Interpretation of Some Formal

Developments in the Serious Drama of the Restoration."
Diss. Cambridge (King's and Christ's) 1964.   Pp. x,
418.

The dissertation contains six chapters that
discuss Restoration melodrama, the masque, *The Siege of
Rhodes*, "The Ethic of Will," heroic plays, and three
other melodramas: Settle's *The Empress of Morocco*,
Dryden's *Aurenge-Zebe*, Lee's *Lucius Junius Brutus*.   The
appendices include notes on the visual aspects of the
masque, Jonson and Jones' *Oberon*, John Ford, and "The
Ethic of Will in *Tyrannic Love* and *The Conquest of
Granada*."

784.   Reyher, Paul. *Les Masques Anglais: Etude sur les
       ballets et la vie de cour en Angleterre
       (1512-1640)*....Rpt. New York: Benjamin Blom, [1964].
       Pp. x, 563.

                   See *1909*: Reyher.

785.   Ripley, J.D. "A Stage History of *Julius Caesar*
       1599-1934." Diss. Birmingham 1964.

786.   Shattuck, Charles. "Shakespeare Promptbooks of the
       17th and 18th Centuries." *Restoration and 18th
       Century Theatre Research*, 3 (May 1964), 9-11.

                   Shattuck requests information for his
       descriptive catalogue of professional theaters'
       Shakespeare promptbooks in the English language and he
       outlines where some promptbooks are published.

787.   Summers, Montague. *The Playhouse of Pepys*.   New York:
       Humanities Press, 1964. Pp. xv, 485.

                   See *1935*: Summers.

788.   Wilcox, John. *The Relation of Moliere to Restoration
       Comedy*. New York: Benjamin Blom, 1964. Pp. 240.

                   See *1938*: Wilcox.

                          1965

789.   Baier, Lee Stanley. "*Gondibert* and Its Debt to
       Hobbes." Diss. Columbia 1965. Pp. 177.

Beginning with the basic affinity of *Gondibert*
and *Leviathan*, both published in 1651, Baier closely
examines the poem according to the philosophic ideas
presented by Hobbes. After reviewing the scholarship
and summarizing the text of the poem, Baier establishes
the neoclassical doctrines that he finds in Hobbes and
applies them to Davenant's poem. Some of the
differences, however, are significant enough that Baier
suggests the poem is a "pre-Restoration ... anticipation
of sentimentalism."

790. Bertram, Paul. *Shakespeare and The Two Noble Kinsmen*.
New Brunswick: Rutgers Univ. Press, 1965. Pp. x,
306.

After tracing the theories of authorship,
Bertram accepts the position of Pope and De Quincey that
the play is by Shakespeare. He refers to Davenant's *The
Cruel Brother* and *The Just Italian* and to his treatment
of *Macbeth* more favorably than others such as Brooks and
Warren did in *Understanding Poetry*. See *1960*: Brooks.

791. Chase, Lewis Nathaniel. *The English Heroic Play: A
Critical Description of the Rhymed Tragedy of the
Restoration*. New York: Russell & Russell, 1965.
Pp. xii, 250.

See *1903*: Chase.

792. Dent, Edward. *Foundations of English Opera*. New
York: Da Capo, 1965. Pp. xv, ix, 241.

See *1928*: Dent.

793. Freehafer, John. "The Formation of the London Patent
Companies in 1660." *Theatre Notebook*, 20 (1965),
6-30.

Freehafer describes the efforts of Killigrew
and Davenant to gain control of the actors and to
establish their companies on stage after Charles II
granted their patents. He argues that the label "His
Majesty's Comedians" applies to Killigrew's company
alone and not to a joint company that might have
involved both Killigrew and Davenant. See *1971*: Itzin;
1979: Sorelius.

794.   Green, Adwin Wigfall. *The Inns of Court and Early English Drama*. New York: Benjamin Blom, 1965. Pp. xii, 199.

See *1931*: Green; *1968*: Green.

795.   Harrison, John, and Peter Laslett. *The Library of John Locke*. Oxford: Oxford Univ. Press, 1965. Pp. viii, 292.

The volume contains an essay on Locke and his books by Laslett and a catalogue of Locke's library edited by Harrison in which Davenant's works--plays and poetry--appear. See *1971*: Harrison.

796.   Hoffman, D.S. "Some Shakespearian Music, 1660-1900." *Shakespeare Survey*, 18 (1965), 94-101.

The article traces musical elements from Davenant's *Macbeth* to the late eighteenth century.

797.   Honnighausen, Lothar. *Der Stilwandel in dramatischen Werk Sir William Davenants*. Anglistische Studien, 3. Cologne: Bohlau Verlag, 1965. Pp. viii, 252.

The author discusses three major influences on Davenant's serious plays: Beaumont and Fletcher, the court, and love and honor. He considers the Shakespeare adaptations and the sentimental elements in Davenant's works. See *1963*: Honnighausen.

798.   Hunt, Hugh. "Restoration Acting." In *Restoration Theatre*. Eds. John Russell Brown and Bernard Harris. Stratford-upon-Avon Studies. New York: St. Martin's, 1965, pp. 179-92.

Hunt considers, among other things, Davenant's part in the developments that led to actresses and changing scenery becoming important features in Restoration theater. He gives special attention to the court masques, the Interregnum, and Restoration productions of *The Siege of Rhodes*.

799.   Kirsch, Arthur C. *Dryden's Heroic Drama*. Princeton: Princeton Univ. Press, 1965. Pp. 157.

Kirsch suggests that Dryden's heroic plays are still of interest because of the playwright's ability to

put his theories into practice. Of particular interest
is Dryden's relationship to Davenant and Davenant's
development of the heroic drama.

800. Melchionda, Mario. "Davenant, Hobbes, Sprat:
      Introduzione alla critica litteraria della
      Restaurazione." *Filologia e letteratura*, 11 (1965),
      317-36.

801. Mellers, Wilfrid. *Harmonious Meeting: A Study of the
      Relationship between English Music, Poetry and
      Theatre, c. 1600-1900*. London: Dobson, 1965. Pp.
      317.

          The Dryden-Davenant *Tempest*, Mellers finds,
      damages the Shakespeare play because of its insistence
      on realism. Purcell's music, he says, is more faithful
      to the design of Shakespeare.

802. Merchant, W. Moelyn. "Shakespeare Made Fit." In
      Restoration Theatre. Eds. John Russell Brown and
      Bernard Harris. Stratford-upon-Avon Studies. New
      York: St. Martin's, 1965, pp. 194-219.

          Merchant places Davenant in perspective with
      other adapters of Shakespeare's plays and demonstrates
      how Davenant altered the plays to suit the new
      conditions of the Restoration theater.

803. Muir, Kenneth. "Shakespeare's Imagery -- Then and
      Now." *Shakespeare Survey*, 18 (1965), 46-57.

          Muir examines the attitudes over the past
      three hundred years to Shakespeare's use of imagery. He
      notes that Davenant simplified Shakespeare's images in
      Macbeth.

804. Murrie, Eleanore (Boswell). *The Restoration Court
      Stage (1660-1702) With a Particular Account of the
      Production of Calisto*. New York: Benjamin Blom, 1965.
      Pp. xviii, 370.

          See *1930*: Murrie; *1932*: Murrie; *1966*:
      Murrie.

805. Myers, James P. "The Pre-Commonwealth Tragicomedies
      of Sir William D'Avenant." Thesis. Arizona 1965.

806. Orgel, Stephen. *The Jonsonian Masque.* Cambridge:
      Harvard Univ. Press, 1965. Pp. viii, 216.

         The work provides background that involves
      Davenant's early work on the masques as Jonson's
      replacement during the time of Charles I and on the
      productions of Inigo Jones.

807. Osborn, James M. *John Dryden: Some Biographical Facts
      and Problems.* Gainesville: Univ. of Florida Press,
      1965. Pp. 316.

         The book is a revised edition of an earlier
      work. See *1940:* Osborn.

808. Potter, L.D. "The Fop and Related Figures in Drama
      from Jonson to Cibber." Diss. Cambridge (Gerton)
      1965.

809. Righter, Anne. "Heroic Tragedy." In *Restoration
      Theatre.* Eds. John Russell Brown and Bernard Harris.
      Stratford-upon-Avon Studies, 6. New York: St.
      Martin's, 1965, pp. 135-58.

         Righter examines the differences between
      Restoration comedy and tragedy, traces the development
      of heroic tragedy, and cites the Earl of Orrery's *The
      General* (1661) rather than Davenant's earlier plays as
      the first English heroic play.

810. Sorelius, Gunnar. "The Rights of the Restoration
      Theatrical Companies in the Older Drama." *Studia
      Neophilologica,* 37 (1965), 174-89.

         The writer examines the production rights for
      Elizabethan and Jacobean plays and demonstrates that
      Killigrew's King's Men held them for all. In the course
      of the article, Davenant's situation is delineated. See
      also *1925:* Nicoll; and *1925:* Spencer.

811. Spencer, Christopher, ed. *Five Restoration
      Adaptations of Shakespeare.* Urbana: Univ. of Illinois
      Press, 1965. Pp. 475.

         In his introduction Spencer suggests that
      Davenant's *Macbeth* is better read as a new play rather
      than an adaptation. If readers would do so, they would

rank this *Macbeth* as one of the better plays of the
period. Along with four others, Davenant's *Macbeth* is
presented with careful textual work, useful notes, and
an informative introduction.

812. Sprague, Arthur Colby. *Beaumont and Fletcher on the
Restoration Stage.* New York: Benjamin Blom, 1965.
Pp. 229.

See *1926*: Sprague.

813. Thomas, Keith. "The Social Origins of Hobbes's
Political Thought." *Hobbes Studies.* Ed. K.C. Brown.
Oxford: Basil Blackwell, 1965, pp. 208-14.

For Thomas, Hobbes' remarks about his
indebtedness to Davenant included in his "Answer" should
"not be dismissed as airy compliments." Thomas states
that "Hobbes followed Davenant in regarding the moral
and political education of the aristocracy as the
essential task of government."

814. Van Lennep, William, ed. *The London Stage 1660-1800.*
Carbondale: Southern Illinois Univ. Press, 1965. I.
215-16.

In his discussion of the Davenant-Dryden
Tempest, discounts clear authorship or contributions to
the play.

815. Wilson, John Harold. *A Preface to Restoration Drama.*
Riverside Studies in Literature. Ed. Gordon N. Ray.
Boston: Houghton Mifflin, 1965. Pp. vii, 208.

The work is a brief, indexed introduction that
provides easy access to information on Davenant as
patentee and playwright-manager. See *1968*: Wilson.

816. Woodward, D.H. "The Manuscript Corrections and
Printed Variants in the Quarto Edition of *Gondibert*
(1651)." *Library*, 5th Ser., 20 (1965), 298-309.

Woodward carefully notes all the corrections
in the *Gondibert* quarto edition that seem to be in
Davenant's hand.

1966

817. Bartholomeusz, Dennis Stephen. "Macbeth and the
      Critics; a Critical Study of Players' Interpretations
      of the Roles of Macbeth and Lady Macbeth on the
      English Stage from 1611 to the Present. Diss. London
      1966. See *1967*: Bartholomeusz; *1969*: Bartholomeusz.

818. Cunningham, John E. *Literature in Perspective:*
      Restoration Drama. London: Evans Brothers, 1966.
      Pp. 160.

            Cunningham in his book, designed for the
      popular reader, provides a brief account of Davenant's
      introduction of Betterton and changing scenery to the
      English professional stage.

819. Elwin, Malcolm. *Handbook to Restoration Drama*. Port
      Washington, New York: Kennikat, 1966. Pp. 260.

            See *1928*: Elwin.

820. Evans, G. Blakemore. *Shakespearean Prompt-Books of*
      the Seventeenth-Century. Vol. 4. *The Smock Alley*
      Hamlet. Bibliographical Society of the University of
      Virginia. Charlottesville: Univ. Press of Virginia,
      1966. Pp. Pt. i, [iv], 48; Pt. ii, 730-60 (facs. of
      Hamlet, F3).

            Evans traces the similarities between the 1676
      Quarto, which he terms the Betterton *Hamlet*, and the
      Smock Alley *Hamlet*, which is a revision of the Third
      Folio edition of the play. The 1676 Quarto is believed
      to have been an alteration by Davenant.

821. Harbage, Alfred. *Conceptions of Shakespeare*.
      Cambridge: Harvard Univ. Press, 1966. Pp. viii,
      164.

            Originally a series of lectures given at
      various United States' universities during 1964, the
      book includes discussions of the actors, adaptations,
      and quality of Shakespeare's plays. Davenant's role in
      each element surfaces intermittently.

822. Hopkins, Kenneth. *Poets Laureate*. 1955; rpt.
      Carbondale: Southern Illinois Univ. Press, 1966. Pp.
      295.

In his chapter "Before the Laureateship:
Jonson and Davenant" (pp. 15-20), Hopkins surveys the
evidence for and against Davenant's having been poet
laureate and concludes that he and Jonson be termed
"traditional laureates" because the title was not
specifically mentioned in either of their patents.
Hopkins indicates that, when Davenant died in 1668,
Dryden was named to fill the position of poet laureate,
which had been vacated by Davenant.

323. Josten, C.H., ed. *Elias Ashmole (1617-1692): His
Autobiographical and Historical Notes, His
Correspondence, and Other Contemporary Sources
Relating to His Life and Works.* 5 vols. Oxford:
Clarendon, 1966.

The work provides authentic commentary on
people and events pertinent to the biography and
achievements of Davenant. See *1692:* Ashmole.

324. Loftis, John. "Exploration and Enlightenment:
Dryden's *The Indian Emperour* and Its Background."
Philological Quarterly, 45 (1966), 71-84.

Loftis' discussion includes the
Davenant-Dryden *Tempest* (1667), Davenant's
pre-Restoration operas *The Cruelty of the Spaniards in
Peru, The History of Sir Francis Drake,* and the five-act
play *The Play-house to be Let.* Dryden's play resembles
Davenant's in some details, as well as in its theme and
presentation.

325. McGee, Arthur R. "'Macbeth' and the Furies."
Shakespeare Survey, 19 (1966), 55-67.

McGee tries to present the supernatural
background of *Macbeth* "as if through Elizabethan eyes."
In doing so, he reviews Davenant's *Macbeth,* among
others, for evidence of witch trials and demonology.

326. Murrie, Eleanore (Boswell). *The Restoration Court
Stage (1660-1702) With a Particular Account of the
Production of Calisto.* London: George Allen and
Unwin, 1966.

See *1930:* Murrie; *1932:* Murrie; *1965:*
Murrie.

827. Odell, George C.D. *Shakespeare from Betterton to
      Irving.* With a new introduction by Robert Hamilton
      Ball. 2 vols. New York: Dover, 1966.

            See *1920*: Odell; *1963*: Odell.

828. Osborn, James M. "New Poems by Sir John Denham."
      Times Literary Supplement, 1 Sept. 1966, p. 788.

            The article includes a satirical elegy on
      Davenant that ends in a complimentary fashion. It was
      written by Denham on the flyleaf of his 1668 edition of
      Poems.

829. Presley, Horton Edward. "'O Showes, Showes, Mighty
      Showes': A Study of the Relationship of the
      Jones-Jonson Controversy to the Rise of Illusionistic
      Staging in Seventeenth-Century British Drama." Diss.
      Kansas 1966. Pp. 308.

            Presley examines Inigo Jones' theatrical
      methods and claims "the techniques used by Jones in
      staging the fantastic court masques of the early
      seventeenth century became the standard stage techniques
      of the Restoration stage," and he cites Davenant as the
      first public dramatist to use the innovations.

830. Rasco, Kay Frances Dilworth. "Supernaturalism in the
      Heroic Play." Diss. Northwestern 1966.

            Rasco studies the Restoration's attitudes
      toward the use of supernatural elements in the heroic
      plays. She is particularly concerned with five
      playwrights, among them Davenant.

831. Scouten, Arthur H. "Notes Toward a History of
      Restoration Comedy." *Philological Quarterly*, 45
      (1966), 62-70.

            The article notes differences between the
      comedy of the early Restoration and that of the 1690s.
      Scouten suggests that a history of Restoration comedy
      should consider more than just a few plays by the major
      dramatists.

832. Sorelius, Gunnar. *"The Giant Race Before the Flood":
      Pre-Restoration Drama on the Stage and in the*

Criticism of the Restoration. Acta Universitatis
Upsaliensis: Studia Anglistica Upsaliensia, No. 4.
Uppsala: Almquist and Wiksells, 1966. Pp. 227.

The work includes Davenant's plays in its
discussion of the theater's changing conditions, its
repertories and companies, and transitions from comedy
to tragedy. Sorelius covers Davenant's pre-Restoration
activities, his operas, heroic drama, and adaptations in
detail.

333. Spencer, Christopher. "'Count Paris's Wife': *Romeo
and Juliet* on the Early Restoration Stage." *Texas
Studies in Literature and Language*, 7 (1966), 309-16.

Spencer uses John Downes' comments on plays
performed at Lincoln's Inn Fields in the early 1660s,
and he argues that Davenant probably revised *Romeo and
Juliet* before James Howard made it into a tragicomedy.

334. Squier, Charles Le Barge. "Davenant's Comic Assault
on *Preciosite: The Platonic Lovers.*" *University of
Colorado Studies, Series in Language and Literature*,
10 (1966), 57-72.

Squier finds the play to be a "minor
masterpiece." He sees it is a burlesque of the court's
Platonism. He believes that the play has been
misunderstood because Davenant's parody is too close to
the original.

335. Summers, Montague. *Shakespeare Adaptations, The
Tempest, The Mock Tempest, and King Lear.* With an
Introduction and Notes. New York: Benjamin Blom,
1966. Pp. cviii, 282.

See *1922*: Summers.

336. Summers, Montague. *Shakespeare Adaptations, The
Tempest, The Mock Tempest, and King Lear.* With an
Introduction and Notes. New York: Haskell House,
1966. Pp. 282.

See *1922*: Summers.

837.   Bartholomeusz, Dennis. "The Davenant-Betterton
       Macbeth." *Komos*, 1 (1967), 41-48.

               Bartholomeusz considers the play to discover
       how Betterton acted it. After determining that Davenant
       reduced the complexity of Macbeth's character, refined
       and rationalized his speech, Bartholomeusz decides that
       Betterton did not present a "fully tragic Macbeth." See
       1966: Bartholomeusz; *1969*: Bartholomeusz.

838.   Brooke, Tucker, and Matthias A. Shaaber. *The
       Renaissance (1500-1660)*. Book II in *A Literary
       History of England*. Albert C. Baugh, ed. 2nd ed.
       New York: Appleton-Century-Crofts, 1967. Pp. 315-696,
       supplementary bibliography, [315-696].

               The book reprints the 1948 text along with a
       bibliographic supplement that adds items published
       through 1965. See *1948*: Brooke.

839.   Colby, Elbridge. *English Catholic Poets: Chaucer to
       Dryden*. Freeport, N.Y.: Books for Libraries, 1967.
       Pp. xlx, 208.

               See *1936*: Colby.

840.   Collins, Howard S. *The Comedy of Sir William
       Davenant*. Studies in English Literature 24. The
       Hague: Mouton, 1967. Pp. 179.

               Collins provides first a brief biography of
       Davenant and then he studies the comic elements and
       techniques in Davenant's plays. He defines comedy in
       view of the age's attitude toward humor, intrigue, and
       manners, and he analyzes *The Witts* and *News from
       Plymouth* according to his definition. He includes in
       the analysis eight Caroline tragedies and tragicomedies
       as well as other Restoration plays. See *1960*: Collins.

841.   Davis, Joe Lee. *The Sons of Ben: Jonsonian Comedy in
       Caroline England*. Detroit: Wayne State Univ. Press,
       1967. Pp. 252.

               Davis discusses *Gondibert, The Wits, News from
       Plymouth,* and *The Platonick Lovers* as contributions to

the development of the comedy of wit and as part of "a somewhat heterogeneous group." The book is well indexed and has informative notes and references.

342.   Deane, Cecil Victor. *Dramatic Theory and the Rhymed Heroic Play*. 1931; Rpt. London: Cass, 1967. Pp. vi, 235.

      See *1929*: Deane; *1931*: Deane.

343.   Gibbs, A.M. "A Davenant Imitation of Donne?" *Review of English Studies*, 18 (1967), 45-48.

      Gibbs presents a previously unpublished poem of twelve lines (Bodleian MS. Ashmole 36/37). The poem, Gibbs finds, is "clearly based on a poem by Donne," suggesting a "special allegiance" to Donne that Douglas Bush, for one, denied. The poem is in a collection bound in a folio volume bearing Ashmole's escutcheon in a gathering that Gibbs dates before 1645. The poem (fol. 22^V) begins:

      Search all the world about
      Seeke for Nile's concealed head....

Attribution is in Ashmole's hand. See *1962*: Bush.

344.   *The Great Assises Holden in Parnassus By Apollo And His Assessours at Which Sessions are arraigned Mercurius Britanicus*. London: E. Husbands, 1645. Sigs. A-F4, G1. New York: Burt Franklin, [1967]. Pp. 50.

      See *1645: The Great*.

345.   Harbage, Alfred. *Thomas Killigrew*. New York: Benjamin Blom, 1967. Pp. 256.

      See *1930*: Harbage.

346.   Johnson, Samuel. *Lives of the English Poets*. Ed. George Birkbeck Hill. 3 vols. New York: Octagon, 1967.

      See *1905*: Johnson.

347.   Nethercot, Arthur H. *Sir William D'Avenant: Poet Laureate and Playwright-Manager*. New York: Russell & Russell, 1967. Pp. 488, [7].

The book is a reprint of the 1938 work with
corrections and notes added. See *1938*: Nethercot.

848. Nilan, Mary Margaret. "The Stage History of *The
Tempest*: A Question of Theatricality." Diss.
Northwestern 1967.

The dissertation traces approaches to the play
beginning with 1667. Nilan places considerable emphasis
on the adaptations which held the stage from 1667-87.

849. Pendlebury, Bevin John. *Dryden's Heroic Plays: A
Study of the Origins*. New York: Russell & Russell,
1967. Pp. 138.

See *1923*: Pendlebury.

850. Sherburn, George, and Donald F. Bond. *The Restoration
and Eighteenth Century*. Book III of *A Literary
History of England*. Ed. Albert C. Baugh. 2nd ed. New
York: Appleton-Century-Crofts, 1967. Pp. 699-1108;
supplementary bibliography, [699-1108].

The book reprints the 1948 text along with a
bibliographic supplement that adds items published
through 1965. See *1948*: Sherburn.

851. Spencer, T.J.B., ed. *Salmacida Spolia*. Inigo Jones
and Sir William Davenant. In *A Book of Masques: In
Honour of Allardyce Nicoll*. Cambridge: Cambridge
Univ. Press, 1967. Pp. xv, 448.

The masque (pp. 337-70) is edited by Spencer
who has provided an introduction, an explanation of the
text, and a commentary. Thirteen other masques are
included in the volume, each edited by a different
scholar.

852. Stamm, Rudolf. *The Shaping Powers at Work: Fifteen
Essays on Poetic Transmutation*. Heidelberg: Carl
Wenter, 1967. Pp. 320.

The second chapter is "Sir William Davenant
and Shakespeare's Imagery" (pp. 85-129).

853. Taylor, Aline MacKenzie. "Dryden's 'Enchanted Isle'
and Shadwell's 'Dominion.'" *Essays in English*

*Literature of the Classical Period Presented to
Dougald MacMillan.* Eds. Daniel W. Patterson and
Albrecht P. Strauss. Chapel Hill: Univ. of North
Carolina Press, 1967, pp. 39-53.

Taylor identifies an allusion to Shadwell's
operatic version of *The Tempest,* and she suggests that
the new version was prompted by new interest in the West
Indies and that Davenant and Dryden saw Prospero's
island as Barbados.

354. Wilson, John Harold. *The Influence of Beaumont and
Fletcher on Restoration Drama.* New York: Benjamin
Blom, 1967. Pp. 156.

See *1928*: Wilson.

1968

355. Downes, John. *Roscius Anglicanus.* Ed. Montague
Summers. New York: Benjamin Blom, 1968. Pp. xiii,
286.

See *1929*: Downes.

356. Freehafer, John. "Brome, Suckling, and Davenant's
Theatre Project of 1639." *Texas Studies in Literature
and Language,* 10 (1968), 367-83.

Freehafer attributes Davenant's failure to
produce Brome's plays in the 1660s to the 1639 conflict
that stemmed from Brome's attack in *The Court Beggar*
(1640) on those powers at court who granted theatrical
privilege to Davenant and Suckling.

357. Freehafer, John. *"The Italian Night Piece* and
Suckling's *Aglaura." Journal of English and Germanic
Philology,* 67 (1968), 249-65.

After examining other playwrights, among them
Davenant, Freehafer dismisses them as writers of *The
Italian Night Piece* or *Italian Night Masque.* He focuses
attention, however, on Sir John Suckling and his work
Aglaura, noting a number of associations between the two
plays.

858.   Fujimura, Thomas H. *The Restoration Comedy of Wit*.
       New York: Barnes and Noble, 1968. Pp. vii, 232.

            See *1952*: Fujimura.

859.   Gosse, Sir Edmund. *From Shakespeare to Pope; An
       Inquiry into the Causes and Phenomena of the Rise of
       Classical Poetry in England*. New York: Kraus, 1968.
       Pp. x, 298.

            See *1885*: Gosse.

860.   Green, Adwin Wigfall. *The Inns of Court and Early
       English Drama*. New York: Benjamin Blom, 1968.

            See *1931*: Green; *1965*: Green.

861.   Hamilton, Walter. *The Poets Laureate of England;
       Being a History of the Office of Poet Laureate,
       Biographical Notices of its Holders, and a Collection
       of the Satires, Epigrams, and Lampoons Directed
       against them*. Detroit: Gale Research, 1968. Pp. xxv,
       308.

            See *1879*: Hamilton.

862.   Hayley, William. "Epistle The Third." In *An Essay on
       Epic Poetry; in Five Epistles to the Rev^d. Mr. Mason*.
       London: Dodsley, 1782. Facs. Introd. Sister M.
       Celeste Williamson, SSJ. Gainsville, Fla.: Scholars
       Facsimiles and Reprints, 1968, pp. 43-67.

            In his critical survey of the continental and
       English epic, in Epistle Three, Hayley wrote of
       Davenant:

            Poor DAVENANT march'd before with nobler aim,
            His keen eye fixt upon the palm of Fame,
            But cruel Fortune doom'd him to rehearse
            A Theme ill-chosen, in ill-chosen Verse. (p. 66)

863.   Holmes, H. D. "A Study of the Plays of Sir William
       Davenant, with Special Reference to His Position as
       Link Between the pre-Commonwealth and Restoration
       Theatre." Thesis Nottingham 1968.

864.   Langhans, Edward A. "The Vere Street and Lincoln's
       Inn Fields Theatres in Pictures." *Educational Theatre
       Journal*, 20 (1968), 171-85.

Using twenty-five illustrations, Langhans supports his thesis that Davenant and Killigrew established the structure of playhouses and staging practices of English public playhouses that continue still.

65. Macey, Samuel L. "Duffett's *Mock Tempest* and the Assimilation of Shakespeare During the Restoration and Eighteenth Century." *Restoration and 18th Century Theatre Research*, 7 (1968), 44-52.

Macey's explanation of Duffett's attitudes toward the theater incorporates Davenant's earlier role. *The Mock Tempest* satirizes Shadwell's opera of 1674 that derives from the Davenant-Dryden version of 1667.

66. Nicoll, Allardyce. *English Drama: A Modern Viewpoint.* London: Harrap, 1968. Pp. vi, 184.

The volume provides a survey of stage presentations. Listed for Davenant is a 1963 performance of *The Wits.*

67. Novak, Maximillian E. "Elkanah Settle's Attacks on Thomas Shadwell and the Authorship of the 'Operatic Tempest.'" *Notes & Queries*, 213 (1968), 263-65.

Novak recounts Downes' and Reggio's evidence as support for Shadwell's authorship of *The Tempest.* He adds to it Elkannah Settle's comments that ascribe the final masque to Shadwell.

68. Palmer, David John. *Shakespeare: The Tempest. A Casebook.* Casebook Series. Ed. A. E. Dyson. London: Macmillan, 1968. Pp. 271.

The book provides a view of *The Tempest* over the centuries. It begins with the Dryden-Davenant version, "a poor thing" because it "coarsened and vulgarized the original." The first chapter prints Act II, Scene ii, of the Davenant play.

69. Parker, William Riley. *Milton: A Biography.* 2 vols. Oxford: Clarendon, 1968.

The first volume traces Milton's life; the second contains documentation and discussion. The

relationship of Davenant and Milton is traced through al
the known sources--Aubrey, Wood, Richardson,
Harbage--and it is finally presented in terms that are
speculative. See II, 1017.

870. Stockwell, La Tourette. *Dublin Theatres and Theatre
Customs (1637-1820)*. New York: Benjamin Blom, 1968.
Pp. xviii, 406.

See *1936*: Stockwell; *1938*: Stockwell.

871. Wilson, John Harold. *A Preface to Restoration Drama*.
Cambridge: Harvard Univ. Press, 1968. Pp. vii, 208.

See *1965*: Wilson.

1969

872. Ashton, Robert, ed. and introd. *James I by His
Contemporaries: An Account of His Career and Character
as Seen by Some of His Contemporaries*. London:
Hutchinson, 1969.

The book contains a useful commentary on the
background of the period that immediately preceded
Davenant's first plays. In particular it highlights the
activities of James I and provides insights into some of
Davenant's characters in *Albovine* and *The Cruel
Brother*.

873. Bartholomeusz, Dennis. *Macbeth and the Players*.
London: Cambridge Univ. Press, 1969. Pp. xv, 302.

The book deals with the stage history of
Macbeth in England in chronological order and it
includes Davenant's Restoration adaptation. See *1966*:
Bartholomeusz; *1967*: Bartholomeusz.

874. Bernet, John William. "Toward the Restoration Heroic
Play: The Evolution of Davenant's Serious Drama."
Diss. Stanford 1969. Pp. 462.

The dissertation examines Davenant's early
career as court poet and poet laureate, and his
developing ethic through his early drama, his epic poem
Gondibert and its preface, and his experience in the
Civil War as a Royalist general. Bernet traces

Davenant's growing "political didactisism addressed by a
Cavalier dramatist to a Stuart monarch, his courtiers,
and his commanders." Davenant's didacticism develops
into Royalist celebration and reinforces the heroic play
as "the expression of an aristocratic ideal."

75. Broadus, Edmund Kemper. *The Laureateship: A Study of
the Office of Poet Laureate in England with Some
Account of the Poets.* Freeport, N.Y.: Books for
Libraries, 1969. Pp. vi, 239.

     This is a reprint of the 1921 edition. See
1921: Broadus.

76. Cavendish, Margaret. Princess, The Lady Marchioness
of Newcastle. *CCXI Sociable Letters.* General Series,
Vol. 113. Menston: Scolar, 1969. Pp. 473.

     See *1664*: Cavendish.

77. Denham, John. *The Poetical Works of Sir John Denham.*
Ed. with notes and intro. by Theodore Howard Banks.
Hamden, Conn.: Archon, 1969. Pp. xviii, 362.

     See *1928*: Denham.

78. Guffey, George Robert, ed. *After the Tempest: The
Tempest, or, The Enchanted Island (1670): The Tempest,
or The Enchanted Island (1674): The Mock-Tempest, or
The Enchanted Castle (1675): The Tempest. An Opera
(1756).* Los Angeles: Augustan Reprint Society,
William Andrews Clark Memorial Library, 1969. Pp.
xxiv, facsimiles.

     Guffey provides in his book four versions of
Shakespeare's play, one of which is the 1670 version by
Davenant and Dryden. In his introduction to the work,
Guffey analyzes the editorial problems he faced and he
also indicates how much of Shakespeare remained through
the years.

79. Martz, Louis L. *The Wit of Love: Donne, Crashaw,
Carew, Marvell.* Univ. of Notre Dame Ward Phillips
Lectures in English Language and Literature, vol. 3.
Notre Dame: Univ. of Notre Dame Press, 1969. Pp. xv,
216.

In his examination of the four poets, Martz includes Davenant and his works. In particular he discusses, quotes, and illustrates Davenant's masque *Salmacida Spolia* and reprints his "Song" ("The Lark now...") in relationship to the wit, drama, and poetry of love.

880. McManaway, James G. "The 'Lost' Canto of *Gondibert*." In *Studies in Shakespeare, Bibliography, and Theater*. Ed. Richard Hosley, Arthur C. Kirsch, and John W. Velz. New York: Shakespeare Association of America, 1969, pp. 35-54.

      See *1940*: McManaway.

881. Mitch, Albert Eugene. "A Study of Three British Dramas Depicting the Conquest of Peru." Diss. Northwestern 1969. Pp. 160.

      Mitch's discussion of Davenant's *The Cruelty of the Spaniards in Peru* includes comment on its anti-Spanish sentiments, its role in circumventing Puritan objections to dramatic production, and its revolutionary stagecraft.

882. Spencer, Christopher. "*Macbeth* and Davenant's *The Rivals*." *Shakespeare Quarterly*, 20 (1969), 225-29.

      The article offers evidence that Davenant's *The Rivals* contains in its first scene imitations from *Macbeth* and some others from Davenant's own adaptation of Shakespeare's play. See *1973*: Wood.

883. Sutherland, James. *English Literature of the Late Seventeenth Century. Oxford History of English Literature*, Vol. VI. Ed. Bonamy Dobree and Norman Davis. Oxford: Oxford Univ. Press, 1969. Pp. vii, 589.

      While suggesting through sporadic comments that Davenant is in the mainstream of the seventeenth century's drama, court, and poetic developments, Sutherland devotes little comment to Davenant except, in passing, to highlight a point or fill a development with significant names. The concluding segment on Davenant is a narrative bibliography that precedes the index to the book. Bibliographic entries for Davenant cover three brief paragraphs and include important primary and secondary materials.

84. Winter, William. *Shakespeare on the Stage.*   3rd Ser. New York: Benjamin Blom, 1969.   Pp. 538.

       The volume is a reprint of the 1916 edition. See *1916*: Winter.

1970

885. Baier, Lee. "An Early Instance of 'Daydream.'" *Notes & Queries*, 17 (1970), 409.

Baier identifies Davenant's *Gondibert* (II.vii.47) as an earlier (1650) instance of the "daydreams" allusion that occurs in Dryden's translation of Lucretius (III.266-67), published in 1685. Baier also notes that Davenant's use of the illusory daydream as something exemplary may derive from Hobbes' sanction of daydreams.

886. Bode, Robert F. "A Study of the Development of the Theme of Love and Duty in English Comedy from Charles I to George I." Diss. South Carolina 1970. Pp. 149.

Beginning with Davenant, Bode traces the theme of love and honor through the comedies of Dryden, Etherege, Wycherley, Vanbrugh, Congreve, and Steele. He concludes that the theme changes into that of love and duty in the eighteenth century.

887. Collier, J. Payne. *The History of English Dramatic Poetry to the Time of Shakespeare; and The Annals of the Stage to the Restoration.* 3 vols. 1831. Rpt. New York: A.M.S., 1970.

See *1831*: Collier.

888. Darby, J. E. "An Examination of Some Restoration Versions of Shakespeare's Plays." Thesis Manchester 1970.

889. Elze, Karl. "Sir William Davenant." In *Essays on Shakespeare.* Trans. Dora Schmitz. Port Washington: Kennikat, 1970, pp. 316-67.

See *1869*: Elze.

890. Evans, G. Blakemore. *Shakespearean Prompt-Books of the Seventeenth-Century.* Vol. 5. *The Smock Alley Macbeth.* Bibliographical Society of the University of Virginia. Charlottesville: Univ. Press of Virginia, 1970. Pp. Pt. i, [iv], 36; Pt. ii, 711-29 (facs. of *Macbeth*, F3).

Evans examines the extent to which the Smock Alley prompt-book for *Macbeth*, which is a revision of the Third Folio edition, followed Davenant's 1674 edition of the play.

891. Gurr, Andrew. *The Shakespearian Stage: 1574-1642.* Cambridge: Cambridge Univ. Press, 1970. Pp. ix, 192.

In his survey of the characteristics of the early English theater, Gurr draws on Davenant's works and experience in the discussions of the acting companies (Beeston's Boys), the playhouse (the new masquing-house), and the audiences (the Blackfriars). See *1980*: Gurr.

892. Hamilton, Walter. *The Poets Laureate of England: Being a History of the Office of Poet Laureate, Biographical Notices of its Holders, and a Collection of the Satires, Epigrams, and Lampoons Directed against them.* New York: Ben Franklin, 1970. Pp. xxv, 308.

See *1879*: Hamilton.

893. Hume, Robert D. *Dryden's Criticism.* Ithaca: Cornell Univ. Press, 1970. Pp. xvii, 236.

In a discussion of Dryden's critical theory, Hume refers to Davenant. In the discussions of heroic plays, digression, the theme of love and honor, literary chronicles or annals, cultural relativism, the function of the epic, and the veneration of Shakespeare, Hume repeatedly refers to Davenant as a forerunner, though lesser light, of some of Dryden's practices and critical perceptions.

894. James, E. Nelson. "Drums and Trumpets." *Restoration and 18th-Century Theatre Research*, 9 (1970), 46-55; 10 (1971), 54-57.

James traces the use of noisy action on stage in the Restoration's heroic play including Davenant's *Siege of Rhodes, Parts I* and *II*. He concludes from his analysis of Davenant's and Dryden's heroic plays that the study explains the action of other such plays and reinforces Spingarn's thesis that these plays are primarily love stories.

895. Lefkowitz, Murray, introd. *Trois Masques a la Cour
      De Charles Ier D'Angleterre: The Triumph of Peace, The
      Triumphs of the Prince d'Amour, Britannia Triumphans.*
      Paris: Du Centre National De La Recherche
      Scientifique, 1970. Pp. 355.

          After presenting a list of eleven masques
      staged at the court of Charles I, plus details on the
      poets, designers, and composers, Lefkowitz proceeds in
      his introduction to discuss the form of the masque and
      its evolution, the songs and dances, the musicians, and
      the scenery and costumes. The introduction,
      commentaries, and documentation are in French, the
      masques in English.

896. Muir, Kenneth. "Introduction." *The Rivals: William
      Davenant 1668.* Facs. ed. 1668; London: Cornmarket,
      1970, [pp. iii-iv].

          Muir provides a brief background of the play's
      first production in 1664 and its publication four years
      later. He compares the text with Shakespeare and
      Fletcher's *The Two Noble Kinsmen* and finds Davenant's
      play inferior.

897. Nethercot, Arthur H. "Scribblings in a Copy of
      D'Avenant's *Gondibert.*" *Notes & Queries,* 17 (1970),
      249-51.

          Nethercot's copy of the 1651 *Gondibert*
      contains Davenant's writings. It also has writings by
      others of interest to Nethercot including Charles
      Boynton, who added corrections to the text. Nethercot
      suggests Boynton had access to a manuscript copy.

898. Novak, Maximillian E., and George Robert Guffey, eds.
      The Tempest, or The Enchanted Island. In *The Works of
      John Dryden.* Vol. X. Berkeley: Univ. of California
      Press, 1970, pp. 1-104.

          The editors present a full commentary on
      details surrounding the play, which include stage
      history, the relationship between Dryden and Davenant,
      and alterations to the play. The editors also provide
      detailed notes with the text.

899. Pepys, Samuel. *The Diary of Samuel Pepys.* Eds.
      Robert C. Latham and William Matthews. 11 vols.
      Berkeley: Univ. of California Press, 1970-83.

The work is an invaluable guide to Davenant's
public life from 1660-1669, the years of Pepys' entries.
Pepys in many instances is our only source of
information concerning productions, actors and
actresses, and events that involved Davenant. Pepys
provides a good account of Davenant's funeral.

900. Saintsbury, George. *A History of Elizabethan
      Literature*. New York: Russell & Russell, 1970. Pp.
      xii, 472.

              See *1887*: Saintsbury.

901. Saunders, J. W. "The Social Situation of
      Seventeenth-Century Poetry." *Metaphysical Poetry*.
      Stratford-upon-Avon Studies 11. Eds. Malcolm Bradbury
      and David Palmer. London: Edward Arnold, 1970, pp.
      237-59.

              Saunders examines the publication of poetry
      during the seventeenth century. His examination
      includes details from Davenant's career.

902. Smith, A. J. "The Failure of Love: Love Lyrics after
      Donne." *Metaphysical Poetry*. Stratford-Upon-Avon
      Studies 11. Eds. Malcolm Bradbury and David Palmer.
      London: Edward Arnold, 1970, pp. 41-71.

              In his explanation of love poetry, Smith
      discusses and quotes Davenant's "Song" (The lark...).

903. Wedgwood, C[icely] V[eronica]. *Seventeenth-century
      English Literature*. London: Oxford Univ. Press, 1970.
      Pp. 186.

              This is the revised second edition of an
      earlier work. See *1950*: Wedgwood.

                        1971

904. Bentley, Gerald Eades. *The Profession of Dramatist in
      Shakespeare's Time, 1590-1642*. Princeton: Princeton
      Univ. Press, 1971. Pp. ix, 329.

              Bentley cites Davenant's *The Playhouse to be
      Let* as evidence for dramatists' benefit performances.
      He also surveys Endymion Porter's successful

intercession with Charles I when Sir Henry Herbert
censored Davenant's *The Witts*.

905. Cairns, Edward Alan. "Charles Gildon's *Measure for
      Measure, or Beauty the Best Advocate*: A Critical
      Edition." Diss. Denver 1971. Pp. 234.

           The dissertation studies Gildon's "conglation
      of the First Folio *Measure for Measure* and Sir William
      Davenant's *Law Against Lovers* (1662)" as an accomodation
      to the "taste of the town." The dissertation offers
      an edition of the play with a critical introduction.

906. *Certain Verses Written by Severall of the Authours
      Friends: to be Reprinted with the Second Edition of
      Gondibert. With Hero and Leander, the mock poem.*   In
      Sir William Davenant's Gondibert. Ed. David F.
      Gladish. Oxford: Clarendon, 1971, pp. 272-86.

           See *1653: Certain*.

907. Cowley, Abraham. "To Sir William D'Avenant, Upon his
      two first Books of *Gondibert*, Finish'd before his
      Voyage to *America*." In *Sir William D'Avenant's
      Gondibert*. Ed. David F. Gladish. Oxford: Clarendon,
      1971, pp. 270-71.

           See *1651*: Cowley.

908. Dillon, George L. "The Seventeenth-Century Shift in
      the Theory and Language of Passion." *Language &
      Style*, 4 (1971), 131-43.

           Restoration adaptations of Shakespeare changed
      the diction of the tragedies in order to fit their
      attitudes toward passion and character. A number of
      Davenant's adjustments in *Macbeth* are explained, along
      with others, as being, "neither better ('more expressive
      or more dramatic') nor worse than the Elizabethan mode;
      it is simply different."

909. Evans, Herbert Arthur, ed. *English Masques*. Freeport,
      N.Y.: Books for Library Presses, 1971. Pp. lxiii,
      245.

           See *1897*: Evans.

910. Forrester, Kent A. "Supernaturalism in Restoration
      Drama." Diss. Utah 1971. Pp. 191.

            In his examination of the changes in attitudes
      toward the supernatural, Forrester considers in his
      third chapter the Restoration adaptations of
      Shakespeare's plays that contain supernatural elements.
      Among others, he considers Davenant's versions of *The
      Tempest* and *Macbeth*. He blames Davenant's poor taste
      for his treatments of the supernatural that led to
      burlesques.

911. Gladish, David F., ed. *Sir William Davenant's
      Gondibert*. Oxford: Clarendon, 1971. Pp. xlv, 312.

            A companion to A.M. Gibbs' volume of
      Davenant's other poetry, Gladish's volume contains the
      1651 edition of the poem, the "Preface," Hobbes'
      "Answer," "The Seventh Canto," the commendatory poems by
      Waller and Cowley, *Certain Verses*... by the court wits
      (1653), and Charles Cotton's poem to Davenant. See
      1962: Gladish; *1972*: Gibbs.

912. Harbage, Alfred. *Sir William Davenant, Poet Venturer,
      1606-1668*. New York: Octagon, 1971. Pp. 317.

            See *1935*: Harbage.

913. Harrison, John, and Peter Laslett. *The Library of
      John Locke*. 2nd ed. Oxford: Clarendon, 1971. Pp.
      xxi, 313.

            Although the work is much like the edition
      published in 1965 by the Oxford Bibliographical Society
      this has appendices on the division of the library and a
      subject index of it that are new. Entries 923-924a list
      Platonick Lovers (1636), *The Siege of Rhodes* (1656), and
      Gondibert (1651); two of the twenty-one books on drama
      are Davenant's and one of the twenty-three of poetry.
      The taste of Locke and the reputation of Davenant are
      served by the volume. See *1965*: Harrison.

914. Haun, Eugene. *But Hark! More Harmony: The Libretti of
      Restoration Opera in English*. Ypsilanti: Eastern
      Michigan Univ. Press, 1971. Pp. xxi, 232.

            Haun examines the development of dramatic
      opera and Davenant's contribution to it. See *1954*:
      Haun.

915. Hughes, Leo. *The Drama's Patrons: A Study of the
      Eighteenth-Century London Audience.* Austin: Univ. of
      Texas Press, 1971. Pp. ix, 209.

          The book examines the audiences from Dryden to
      Sheridan and, in the process, outlines audience
      response, morality, sensibility, and class structure;
      the size of the house, the play-bills, and the theatre
      structures themselves are also examined. Davenant's
      influence on the theater--its plays, staging, and
      managing--is placed in perspective with the subsequent
      age.

916. Itzin, Catherine. *"Macbeth* in the Restoration."
      Theatre Quarterly, 1 (1971), 14-18.

          Itzin agrees with Freehafer that Davenant was
      bound by law to revise *Macbeth* before producing it, but
      she cites other factors, as well, such as the politics
      of the time, the taste of the audience for language, and
      the introduction of actresses. See *1965*: Freehafer.

917. King, T.J. *Shakespearean Staging, 1599-1642.*
      Cambridge: Harvard Univ. Press, 1971. Pp. xiv, 163.

          King presents a "systematic survey of
      theatrical requirements for 276 plays, first performed
      by professional actors" from 1599 through 1642, in order
      to clarify how Shakespeare's plays were produced.
      Included are early plays by Davenant that contain stage
      directions.

918. Langbaine, Gerard. *An Account of the English
      Dramatick Poets (1691).* Introduction by John Loftis.
      2 vols. Augustan Reprint Society, V. Los Angeles:
      William Andrews Clark Memorial Library, Univ. of
      California, 1971.

          The work is a two-volume reprint of the 1691
      edition. See *1691*: Langbaine, *An Account.*

919. Loofbourow, John W. "Robinson Crusoe's Island and the
      Restoration *Tempest.*" *Enlightenment Essays*, 2 (1971),
      201-07.

          Loofbourow suggests that the setting of
      Davenant's play may have been the model for Defoe's
      landscape of Crusoe's island.

920.   Miles, Dudley Howe.   *The Influence of Moliere on
       Restoration Comedy.*   New York: Octagon, 1971.   Pp. xi,
       272.

              See *1910*: Miles.

921.   Miner, Earl.   *The Cavalier Mode from Jonson to Cotton.*
       Princeton.   Princeton Univ. Press, 1971.   Pp. xxv,
       333.

              Miner includes frequent references to Davenant
       and prints entirely the song from *News from Plymouth*, "O
       thou that sleep'st like pig in straw" as an example of
       Cavalier freshness and wit singularly of its time and
       place.

922.   Mitchell, Eleanor Rettig.   "Pronouns of Address in
       English, 1580-1780: A Study of Form Changes as
       Reflected in British Drama."   Diss. Texas A and M
       1971.   Pp. 165.

              A computer study, the dissertation examines
       changes in the pronouns of address used in English drama
       over a period of two hundred years.   Among the
       dramatists used in the study is Davenant.

923.   Smith, John Harrington.   *The Gay Couple in Restoration
       Comedy.*   New York: Octagon, 1971.   Pp. xi, 252.

              See *1946*: Smith; *1948*: Smith.

924.   Waith, Eugene Mersereau.   *Ideas of Greatness: Heroic
       Drama in England.*   Ideas and Forms in English
       Literature Series.   London: Routledge & Kegan Paul,
       1971.   Pp. xii, 292.

              Fitting the series' aims, the volume explores
       the literary tradition of the heroic drama and those
       ideas that influenced it.   Waith traces heroic drama
       from the emergence of the ideals of chivalry to the
       Restoration where Davenant explains the mode as the
       expression of "ideas of greatness and virtue pleasing
       and familiar."   The first portion of chapter 4 discusses
       in detail Davenant, his ideas, and his plays.

925.   Waller, Edmund.   "To Sr. Will D'Avenant, upon his two
       first Books of *Gondibert*, Finish'd before his Voyage

to America." In *Sir William D'Avenant's Gondibert*.
Ed. David F. Gladish. Oxford: Clarendon, 1971, pp.
269-70.

See *1651*: Waller.

1972

926.   Bone, Quentin. *Henrietta-Maria: Queen of the
       Cavaliers*. Urbana: Univ. of Illinois Press, 1972.
       Pp. x, 287.

            The book clarifies Davenant's relationship to
       the court through the queen. Not only are his court
       poems, plays, and masques placed in perspective but also
       Davenant's function as the queen's messenger to the king
       during the Civil War.

927.   Casanave, Don Sheldon. "Shakespeare's *The Tempest* in
       a Restoration Context: A Study of Dryden's *The
       Enchanted Island*." Diss. Michigan 1972. Pp. 214.

            The dissertation is in two contradictory
       parts. The first is based on the premise that "though
       William D'Avenant is supposedly co-author, the work [*The
       Enchanted Island*] largely belongs to Shakespeare and
       Dryden." All subsequent discussion omits Davenant as
       author of the play. The second part of the dissertation
       is not mentioned in the abstract and corrects the error
       of the play's authorship by acknowledging that Davenant
       was the major writer of the play.

928.   Crino, Maria, ed. *News from Plymouth*. Verona:
       Fiorini, 1972.

            The play is printed in parallel
       English-Italian texts, but the introduction is in
       Italian.

929.   DiLorenzo, Ronald Eugene, ed. *Three Burlesque Plays
       of Thomas Duffett*. Iowa City: Univ. of Iowa Press,
       1972. Pp. xxx, 289.

            In the introduction, DiLorenzo discusses
       burlesques, among them Davenant's *Playhouse to Be Let*
       which contains in the fifth act a burlesque of Katherine
       Philips' *Pompey*. DiLorenzo suggests that Duffett may

have been inspired by Davenant's play, and he proceeds
to compare the two playwrights' works. Focusing on
Duffett's *The Empress of Morocco*, DiLorenzo notes that
Davenant provided in *Playhouse* an inversion of values
that Duffett may have used, and, in Davenant's *Macbeth*,
the witches' songs that Duffett burlesqued in *Empress*.

930. Gibbs, A. M., ed. *Sir William Davenant: The Shorter
      Poems, and Songs from the Plays and Masques*. Oxford:
      Clarendon, 1972. Pp. xciii, 477.

          Gibbs' biographical, critical, and textual
introduction and notes are among the most informative
and useful on the poetry of Davenant. The edition
contains all the known poems and songs by Davenant
except for *Gondibert*. The poems are divided into the
following sections: *"Madagascar; with other poems"*;
"Restoration Panegyrical Poems"; *"Poems on Several
Occasions"*; "Songs from the Plays and Masques"; "Poems
from Manuscript"; "Poem from Song Book"; "Poems and
Songs of Doubtful Authorship"; the 1656 text of "The
long Vacation"; and "Musical Settings," which has been
edited by Judy Blezzard.

931. Levison, William S. "Restoration Adaptations of
      Shakespeare as Baroque Literature." Diss. Illinois
      1972. Pp. 154.

          The work tries to show "that the versions of
Shakespeare's plays by such writers as Dryden, Davenant,
Shadwell, and Tate can be viewed as manifestations of
the prevalent baroque style." Included are Davenant's
Macbeth and *Tempest*.

932. Maxwell, J.C. "William Davenant." *Times Literary
      Supplement*, 25 August 1972, 997.

          Maxwell provides a gloss of "Written, when
Collonell Goring was believ'd slaine, at the siege of
Breda."

933. Parsons, Philip. "Restoration Tragedy as Total
      Theater." In *Restoration Literature: Critical
      Approaches*. Ed. Harold Love. London: Methuen, 1972,
      pp. 27-68.

          Parsons sees Davenant's tragedies as plays of
ideas which are revealed through moral and emotional
encounters.

934. Ridpath, George. *The Stage Condemn'd.* 1698. Rpt.
      Ed. Arthur Freeman. New York: Garland, 1972. Pp.
      6, 216.

              See *1698*: Ridpath.

935. White, Eric Walter. *The Rise of English Opera.* New
      York: DaCapo, 1972. Pp. vi, 335.

              In the brief commentary of Davenant's role in
      developing the first English opera, White provides some
      illustrations from Davenant and others involved in the
      early productions.

                          1973

936. Elze, Karl. *William Shakespeare, A Literary
      Biography.* Trans. L. Dora Schmitz. New York: AMS,
      1973. Pp. 587.

              See *1888*: Elze.

937. Fleay, Frederick Gard. *A Biographical Chronicle of
      the English Drama, 1559-1642.* 2 vols. New York: Lenox
      Hill, 1973.

              See *1891*: Fleay.

938. Gussow, Mel. Rev. of *The Tempest*, by William
      Shakespeare. *New York Times*, 13 Oct. 1973, p. 26,
      col. 1.

              Gussow reviews the Yale Repertory Theatre's
      production of the musical version of *The Tempest* which
      featured music by Purcell and song lyrics by Davenant
      among others.

939. Hedback, Ann-Mari. "The Printing of *The Siege of
      Rhodes.*" *Studia· Neophilologica,* 45 (1973), 68-79.

              The article offers background on the
      complicated printing history of *The Siege of Rhodes* from
      the first setting from the manuscript of the 1656
      edition to the resetting for the 1659, to the two
      versions of Part I in the 1663 edition of Parts I and
      II, and finally to the 1670 and 1673 editions of both
      parts. Hedback uses a proof-sheet bound into the Folger

copy of the 1656 edition, and she suggests that Davenant
may have supervised the printing.

940. Hedback, Ann-Mari, ed. *Sir William Davenant: The
      Siege of Rhodes, A Critical Edition.* Acta
      Universitatis Upsaliensis: Studia Anglistica
      Upsaliensia, No. 14. Uppsala: 1973. Pp. lxxviii,
      121.

            The documented and annotated edition contains
      an introduction in two parts: "Textual" and "Historical
      and Literary." It also contains the play in a text that
      retains the old spelling and is accompanied by critical
      commentary. In its appendices the edition offers
      extracts from Knolles' *Generall Historie of the Turkes*
      (1603), Fuscon's preface to the opera *Amore Innamorato*
      (1642), and a bibliography.

941. Highfill, Philip H., Jr., Kalman A. Burnim, and
      Edward A. Langhans. *A Biographical Dictionary of
      Actors, Actresses, Musicians, Dancers, Managers &
      Other Stage Personnel in London, 1660-1800.*
      Carbondale: Southern Illinois Univ. Press, 1973--.

            The multi-volume set offers information on
      much that touched the life and career of Davenant.
      Basic information on Davenant, his theater, and his
      casts is to be found in the work, particularly in volume
      4.

942. Jackson, MacD. P. "Three Unidentified Play Titles of
      the Early Seventeenth Century." *Notes & Queries.* 20
      (1973), 465-66.

            Jackson states that *The Tragedy of Heildebrand*
      is the alternate title for *The Unfortunate Lovers.*

943. Langbaine, Gerard. *An Account of the English
      Dramatick Poets. Or, Some Observations and Remarks on
      the Lives and Writings, of All Those That Have
      Publish'd Either Comedies, Tragedies, Tragi-Comedies,
      Pastorals, Masques, Interludes, Farces, or Opera's in
      the English Tongue.* Pref. by Arthur Freeman. New
      York: Garland, 1973.

            A reprint of the 1691 edition, the volume
      provides some of the earliest written material on

Davenant and his work and is a biographical source.
Langbaine reviews the life of Davenant (pp. 32ff) and
some of the plays. See *1691*: Langbaine.

944. Langbaine, Gerard. *Momus Triumphans; Or, The*
Plagiaries of the English Stage, and The Lives and
Characters of the English Dramatick Poets. Pref. by
Arthur Freeman. New York: Garland, 1973. Pp. 7, 182
[208].

Volume 19 of the Garland Series *The English*
Stage, Attack and Defense 1577-1730, the work is a
reprint of Langbaine's 1687 publication *Momus Triumphans*
and The Lives and Characters of the English Dramatick
Poets, 1699. Freeman identifies Langbaine's work as the
"earliest scholarly or critical attempt to classify the
English drama, and to identify its sources." Davenant
is listed among others. See *1687*: Langbaine; and *1691*:
Langbaine.

945. Leacroft, Richard. *The Development of the English*
Playhouse. London: Methuen, 1973. Pp. xiii, 354.

The elaborate, illustrated book contains
precise information--sketches, dimensions, plays--from
Davenant's productions and theaters to document chapter
4, "The Elements of a Developing Play House."

946. Loftis, John. *The Spanish Plays of Neoclassical*
England. New Haven: Yale Univ. Press, 1973. Pp.
xiii, 263.

The book examines one of the more important
dramatic motifs of the Restoration period. The book
includes discussions of Davenant's *The Cruelty of the*
Spaniards in Peru, A Playhouse to Be Let, and *The Man's*
The Master.

947. Orgel, Stephen, and Roy Strong. *Inigo Jones: The*
Theatre of the Stuart Court. 2 vols. London: Sotheby
Parke Bernet, 1973.

Magnificently illustrated, the text describes
the designs for the plays and masques of the seventeenth
century. The work traces the relationship of Jones and
Jonson, the role of Davenant in collaboration with
Jonson, and Davenant after the Restoration as theater-
manager and innovator with scenes and machines.

948.   Wood, James O. "Lost Lore in *Macbeth*." *Shakespeare
        Quarterly*, 24 (1973), 223-26.

            Wood argues that many of the songs that
        Davenant used in his *Macbeth* may have been Shakespeare's
        and that two of the songs in *The Witch* originally came
        from *Macbeth*. See *1969*: Spencer.

                              1974

949.   Blattes, Robert. "Elements parodiques dans *The Wits*
        de Sir William Davenant." *Caliban*, 10 (1974),
        127-40.

            The article, in French, closely examines
        parody in *The Wits*, arguing against the idea that the
        court demanded little satire in its drama in the 1630s.

950.   Broadbent, John, ed. *Signet Classic Poets of the 17th
        Century*. The Signet Classic Poetry Series. Gen. Ed.
        John Hollander. New York: New American Library, 1974,
        pp. 207-11 and 237-49.

            Broadbent mentions Davenant in several of his
        eleven commentaries; however, in number six, "Civil War
        and Commonwealth, 1642-1660: Casualties and Survivors,"
        he focuses on the masques as heralds of the coming war
        and upon *Gondibert* with its Jonsonian techniques and
        anticipation of Pope's "crammed antitheses."
        Broadbent's brief selections from the masques, the
        plays, and *Gondibert* seem to support the ideas.

951.   Brownstein, Oscar L. "The Duke's Company in 1667."
        Theatre Notebook, 28 (1974-75), 18-23.

            The article describes where Davenant and his
        wife lived at the time of his death. The information
        comes from the St. Bride's parish offices, 1677.

952.   Forrester, Kent. "Decay of the Literary Supernatural
        during the Age of Dryden." *Enlightenment Essays*, 5
        (1974), 57-64.

            The article considers "traditional
        supernatural creatures of England--the witches, demons,
        fairies, ghosts, and assorted bogies of popular
        superstition"--and finds that before 1660 they played

"significant, dignified roles in English literature."
With the ascension of Charles II and the founding of the
Royal Society, "the clear light of reason" took over.
Forrester cites in progress the Davenant adaptations of
the *Tempest* and *Macbeth*, which support the writer's view
of the Restoration and its failure "to complete the
picture [of man's relationship to man] because it
ignored or denigrated the dark side of the soul."

953. Hobbs, Mary. "Robert and Thomas Ellice, Friends of
      Ford and Davenant." *Notes & Queries*, 21 (1974),
      292-93.

            The article identifies the Ellices as brothers
      who were friends of Davenant during the Inns of Court
      days.

954. Lee, Sidney. *Pepys and Shakespeare: A Paper at the
      Sixth Meeting of the Samuel Pepys Club, on Thursday,
      November 30, 1905.* Folcraft, Pa.: Folcroft Library,
      1974. Pp. 40.

            See *1906*: Lee.

955. Miner, Earl. *The Restoration Mode.* Princeton:
      Princeton Univ. Press, 1974. Pp. xxiv, 587.

            Focusing upon Milton, Dryden, and Butler,
      Miner discusses major and minor poets, among them
      Davenant. All share, according to Miner, a growing
      tendency toward narrative poetry. The lengthy volume
      opens with a quote from Davenant's *Gondibert* which is
      then discussed at length in a number of passages in the
      book.

956. Schmitt-von Muhlenfels, Franz. "Die Rettung Miltons
      durch Davenant: Eine Anekdote als Opernstaff
      Spontinis." *Archiv fur das Studium der Neueren
      Sprachen und Literaturen*, 211 (1974), 382-91.

            The article discusses the Milton-Davenant
      relationship.

957. Vickers, Brian, ed. *Shakespeare: The Critical
      Heritage. Vol. I: 1623-1692.* London and Boston:
      Routledge and Kegan Paul, 1974. Pp. xi, 448.

The first of the six-volume set offers
excerpts from the Shakespeare adaptations by Davenant,
among others. Vickers suggests that Shakespeare
adaptations are keys to the taste of an age.

958. Werner, Doris Cecilia. "The Neoclassic Epic as a
      Genre (1650-1700), Exemplified by Five Representative
      Poems." Diss. Bowling Green State 1974. Pp. 206.

      The dissertation discusses five epics, one of
which is Davenant's *Gondibert*.

1975

959. Davies, H. Neville. "Davenant, Dryden, Lee, and
      Otway." In *English Drama (Excluding Shakespeare):
      Select Bibliographical Guides*. Ed. Stanley Wells.
      London: Oxford Univ. Press, 1975, pp. 150-72.

      Davies provides an essay that includes
Davenant and a two-page bibliography of works by and
about the poet-playwright-manager.

960. Day, Cyrus Lawrence, and Eleanore Boswell Murrie.
      *English Song-Books 1651-1702: A Bibliography with a
      First Line Index of Songs*. Folcroft, Pa.: Folcroft
      Library, 1975. Pp. xii, 439.

      This is a reprint of the 1940 work. See *1940*:
Day.

961. Gordon, Donald James. "Roles and Mysteries."
      *Renaissance Imagination: Essays and Lectures by D. J.
      Gordon*. Ed. Stephen Orgel. Berkeley: Univ. of
      California Press, 1975, pp. 3-23.

      The essay examines *Salmacida Spolia* as an
expression of the tragedy of Charles I's autocracy.
Gordon balances the function of the masque with the
function of Rubens' ceiling in the Banqueting House,
Whitehall, which were expressions of the triumph of
Charles' autocracy. He finds both are allegorical and
symbolic of the glory of Caroline rule and expressions
of European Renaissance thought.

962. Marshall, Geoffrey. *Restoration Serious Drama*.
      Norman: Univ. of Oklahoma, 1975. Pp. xx, 247.

Marshall examines the artificial language of Restoration drama. He occasionally cites Davenant's *Siege of Rhodes* for evidence.

963. Over, William Earl. "*The Rehearsal* and Its Place in the Development of English Burlesque Drama in the Seventeenth Century." Diss. Ohio State 1975.

Over provides historical and formal investigations of burlesque drama. In process, he discusses Davenant's *Playhouse to Be Let*.

964. Schoenbaum, S. *William Shakespeare: A Documentary Life*. New York: Oxford Univ. Press, 1975. Pp. xiv, 273.

The handsome volume offers a "straightforward account of Shakespeare's life" with facsimiles "faithfully reproduced, of the documents and records which comprise the biographers' materials." The Davenant-Shakespeare story is addressed in a number of places, but most fully on pages 164-66.

965. Visser, Colin. "The Anatomy of the Early Restoration Stage: *The Adventures of Five Hours* and John Dryden's Spanish Comedies." *Theatre Notebook*, 29 (1975), 56-69, 114-18.

Visser examines "one of Davenant's greatest successes": his production of Tuke's play at Lincoln's Inn Fields, Thursday, January 8, 1663. Questioning some of Southern's analyses of the play in *Changeable Scenery*, Visser suggests that the proscenium had a scenic function in Davenant's production and that the practice was used by Dryden and others. Visser returns to the 1663 folio edition as well as the 1671 edition that Southern used to elaborate his interpretation. The first part of the article stops with the reminder that this is all conjecture. The second part begins with Dryden's 1664 play *The Rival Ladies*. Visser concludes "that Davenant had established in his production of Tuke's play ... the form and preoccupations of 'Spanish' comedy." He affirms Davenant's achievement in bringing forth the prototype of all theaters in the Restoration.

1976

966. Bateson, Frederick Wilse, and Harrison T. Meserole.
      "An Augustan Reading List, 1650-1800." *A Guide to
      English and American Literature*. 3rd ed. London and
      New York: Longman, 1976. Pp. 111-37.

           The work is a brief guide to major secondary
      studies of Augustan literature and individual authors,
      Davenant included.

967. Bence-Jones, Mark. *The Cavaliers*. London: Constable,
      1976. Pp. xii, 206.

           The book examines the court in the 1630s.
      Chapter 8, "'Stone Walls do not a Prison Make': The
      Cavalier Poets," is devoted to Davenant, Suckling,
      Lovelace, and Waller, whose lives and works present a
      fuller portrait of the court in the 1630s.

968. Bordinat, Philip. "William Davenant and the Caroline
      Masque." *Bulletin of the West Virginia Association of
      College English Teachers*, 3 (1976), 1-18.

           The article describes the masque and
      Davenant's part in its development.

969. Cohn, Ruby. *Modern Shakespeare Offshoots*. Princeton:
      Princeton Univ. Press, 1976. Pp. xi, 426.

           Cohn examines the adaptations of Shakespeare
      commenting that we may laugh today at Davenant's
      Macbeth, but, she writes, "our century's *Macbeth*
      offshoots reflect our taste, as his reflected that of
      the Restoration." Cohn also discusses Davenant's
      Tempest, writing, "After the English Civil War,
      Shakespeare's play was displaced by the Davenant-Dryden
      adaptation, which then became the basis of an opera by
      Purcell. The Davenant-Dryden adaptation was the most
      popular play on the Restoration stage."

970. Gellert, J. H. "Sir William Davenant's *The Law
      Against Lovers*." Diss. Birmingham 1976.

971. Hamilton, Elizabeth. *Henrietta Maria*. New York:
      Coward, McCann & Geoghegan, 1976. Pp. 290.

This biography of the wife of Charles I offers
a clear picture of Davenant's relationship to both
monarchs.

72. Hume, Robert D[avid]. *The Development of English
     Drama in the Late Seventeenth Century.* Oxford:
     Clarendon, 1976. Pp. xvii, 525.

          Postulating that "the drama of this period is
     vastly varied and complex in type, and further that the
     different types change and interact on an almost
     season-by-season basis," Hume examines hundreds of plays
     from the period noting passing fads, fashions, and other
     social changes. He examines the famous writers and
     their plays "as they originally appeared--variably
     successful in the midst of a prolific, unstable, and
     rapidly changing theatre world" (p. ix). Through the
     course of his examination, Hume has many occasions where
     he cites Davenant, his plays, his poetry, his theories,
     and his considerable importance to the development of
     English drama in the late seventeenth century.

73. Kishler, Thomas C. "Hobbes's 'Answer' to Davenant:
     Some Aspects of the Style." *Language & Style*, 9
     (1976), 130-38.

          The article focuses on the philosopher's
     response to the poet's "Preface" and analyzes a style
     that possesses confidence, repetition, and figurative
     illustrations.

74. Penninger, Frieda Elaine, ed. *English Drama to 1660
     (Excluding Shakespeare): A Guide to Information
     Sources.* Vol. 5. The American Literature, English
     Literature, and World Literatures in English
     Information Guide Series. Detroit: Gale Research,
     1976. Pp. xix, 370.

          Equipped with a foreword, notes, and index,
     the volume is essentially a categorized bibliography of
     works dealing with the non-Shakespearean English drama
     up to the Restoration. About 150 pages are devoted to
     "Individual Authors" where Davenant is listed.
     Additional entries are listed and helpfully labelled in
     the index.

75. Rathke, Cornelia Ratliff. "The Career of Thomas
     Betterton as a Shaping Force in the Restoration

Playhouse and in the Restoration Drama." Diss. Tulane
1976.   Pp. 360.

The dissertation examines Betterton's career
and, in process, highlights Davenant, his career, and
his impact on Betterton.

976. *The Revels History of Drama in English*. Vol. V:
      1660-1750. Gen. ed. T. W. Craik. London: Methuen,
      1976.

Davenant is/ reviewed as a critic by John
Loftis in Chapter I, "The Social and Literary Context,"
as a stage innovator by Richard Southern in Chapter II,
"Theatres and Actors," and as a theater manager by
Marion Jones in the second half of the same chapter,
"Actors and Repertory," as an adaptor of Shakespeare and
inventor of the English opera by A. H. Scouten in
chapter III, "Plays and Playwrights."

977. Treglown, Jeremy. "Rochester and Davenant." *Notes &*
      Queries, N. S.   12 (1976), 554-59.

Emphasizing Rochester's basic genius, Treglown
notes repeatedly that the poet picked up and used
others' words and ideas. Davenant was one of
Rochester's favorite sources; he used poems,
particularly *Gondibert*, and songs from the plays and
operas. The point seems to be that Rochester's sources
may have been more popular than intellectual.

978. Visser, Colin. "John Dryden's *Amboyna* at Lincoln's
      Inn Fields, 1673." *Restoration and 18th Century*
      Theatre Research, 15 (May 1976), 1-11.

Visser notes that Davenant's plays *The Cruelty*
of the Spaniards in Peru and *The History of Sir Francis*
Drake influenced the design of Dryden's play because the
scenery of the earlier plays was still at Lincoln's Inn
Fields in 1673 where it was left by the King's Company
after their theater had burned in 1672.

1977

979. Bachorik, Lawrence Lee. "Davenant's Shakespeare,
      1660-1668." Diss. McGill, Canada 1977.

Countering the notion that Davenant merely
mutilated the plays, Bachorik argues that Davenant's
productions of Shakespeare have been misunderstood and
that "they were tempered by his experience, by the
theatrical situation, and by the social and political
condition of the Restoration" and that they reveal a
clear artistic design.

80. Kavenik, Frances Mary-Michele. "The Restoration
    Repertory Theatre: 1659-1668." Diss. Wisconsin 1977.
    Pp. 317.

The dissertation examines the audience appeal
of plays as it is demonstrated by the records in *The
London Stage*. It includes a close examination of three
comedies, one of them Davenant's *The Tempest*, to "show
the use of the repertory approach in analyzing
Restoration plays."

81. Luckett, Richard. "Exotick but Rational
    Entertainments: The English Dramatick Operas." In
    *English Drama: Forms and Development. Essays in
    Honour of Muriel Clara Bradbook*. Ed. Marie Axton and
    Raymond Williams. Introd. Raymond Williams.
    Cambridge: Cambridge Univ. Press, 1977, pp. 123-31.

Focusing upon Restoration works, the essay
defines and traces the development of English opera with
frequent references to Davenant and his dramatic,
operatic achievements. Luckett offers details
concerning musicians, instruments, and singers.

82. Nagy, Deborah Karen. "Who Was Shakespeare's Dark
    Lady? A Survey and Critical Analysis of the
    Theories." Thesis Stephen F. Austin State 1977.
    Pp. 230.

83. Plausevskaja, E. V. "Uil'jam Davenant i ege meste v
    anglijskoj literature XVII veka." *Filologiceskie
    Nauki*, 19 (1977), 34-44.

Through comment on the plays and poems, with
special attention to *Gondibert*, this introductory
article discusses Davenant and his place in
seventeenth-century English literature.

84. Plomley, S. "Dryden as Critic and Adapter of
    Shakespeare in the Context of Seventeenth Century
    Dramatic Criticism." Diss. Leicester 1977.

1978

985.   Ashton, Robert. *The English Civil War: Conservatism and Revolution, 1603-1649*. London: Weidenfeld and Nicolson, 1978. Pp. x, 453.

   Ashton sees the masque as epitomizing "the ethos and aspirations of the Stuart Court." In his discussion, he presents brief descriptions of *The Temple of Love* and *Salmacida Spolia*.

986.   Capelle, Alex. "William Davenant et le Genre Heroique." Thesis 1978.

   Defense of thesis reported in XVII-XVIII: *Bulletin de la Societe d'Etudes Anglo-Americanies des XVIIe et XVIIIe Siecles*, 6 (1978), 111.

987.   DePorte, Michael V. "William Davenant." In *The Later Jacobean and Caroline Dramatists: A Survey and Bibliography of Recent Studies in English Renaissance Drama*. Eds. Terence P. Logan and Denzell S. Smith. Lincoln: Univ. of Nebraska Press, 1978, pp. 192-209.

   The seventeen-page chapter on Davenant contains: reviews of general scholarship including the works on Davenant's biography, the plays, and *Gondibert*; reviews of criticism of individual plays and the current (1975) state of scholarship; and reviews of the canon, both collected and individual editions. Useful and informed commentary accompanies each review except for the last section ("See Also," pp. 208-09), which lists twenty-eight works that do not fit easily under other headings.

988.   Fischer, Hermann. "Thematische Strukturen im Vergleich: Shakespeares *Measure for Measure*. Davenants *The Law Against Lovers*. Gildons *Measure for Measure, or, Beauty the Best Advocate*." *Deutsche Shakespeare-Gesellschaft West Jahrbuch* (1978/79), 244-57.

989.   Fordyce, Rachel. *Caroline Drama: A Bibliographic History of Criticism*. Boston: G.K. Hall, 1978.

   Forty-five entries of the bibliography that deal with "major critical issues related to Caroline

Drama" refer in some way to Davenant and are important
in a study of the playwright.

90. Grabes, Herbert. "Figurenknostitution und historisch
wechselnder Sinn: Über die Veranderung der
Hauptfiguren von *Measure for Measure* bei Davenant,
Gildon, Kemble und Brook." *Deutsche
Shakespeare-Gesellschaft West Jahrbuch* (1978-79),
231-43.

91. McCarthy, William. "Davenant's Prefatory Rhetoric."
Criticism, 20 (1978), 128-43.

    The article argues that Davenant tries to
establish in his "Preface" to *Gondibert* an aesthetic
that is original for *Gondibert*, but the poet's effort
leads to contradictions. McCarthy states that the
"Preface" captures "the form of Hobbes without the
substance," and that the essay is an attempt to rid the
poet of the influence of the ancients and Hobbes.

92. Milhous, Judith. "The Duke's Company's Profits,
1675-1677." *Theatre Notebook*, 32 (1978), 76-88.

    Milhous discusses the Duke's Company's profits
and concludes that Davenant's company, some years after
his death, continued to be a "solidly profitable
operation."

93. Rosenberg, Marvin. *The Masks of Macbeth*. Berkeley:
Univ. of California Press, 1978. Pp. xiv, 802.

    The book deals with the stage history of
Macbeth, following through the play, line by line, the
various interpretations over the centuries. Rosenberg
ignores Davenant's *Macbeth*, except to call it an
"abortion."

94. Saslow, Edward L. "Dryden as Historiographer Royal,
and the Authorship of His Majesties Declaration
Defended." *Modern Philology*, 75 (1978), 261-72.

    After reviewing the scholarship, Saslow
disagrees with the conclusion that the document is
Dryden's. Saslow reviews also the laureateship and its
conditions under Davenant, especially the changes after
the Restoration when the pension was not renewed.

995. Zimbardo, R[ose] A. "Imitation to Emulation:
      'Imitation of Nature': From the Restoration to the
      Eighteenth Century." *Restoration: Studies in English
      Literary Culture, 1660-1700*, 2 (1978), 2-9.

          In her discussion that "the conception
      'imitation of nature' undergoes crucial changes from
      1660 to about 1730, that these changes affect all forms
      of literature but are most readily observable in the
      drama and in speculation about the drama, and that in
      large measure the change which occurs in the conception
      results in the novel's replacing the drama," Zimbardo
      begins with "the very influential Davenant" and two of
      his Caroline comedies.

1979

996. Capelle, Alex. "Une Image idealisee de la monarchie
      Stuart." *Bulletin de la Societe d'Etudes
      Anglo-Americaines des XVIIe et XVIIIe Siecles*, 9
      (1979), 43-63.

          The article examines Davenant's heroic imagery
      as it relates to the monarchy and Hobbes' attitudes.

997. Dyson, Peter. "Changes in Dramatic Perspectives: From
      Shakespeare's *Macbeth* to Davenant's." *Shakespeare
      Quarterly*, 30 (1979), 402-07.

          Dyson argues that, though some of Davenant's
      alterations can be explained by changed dramatic
      conditions, others involve his making the meaning more
      explicit at the cost of connotative values. Dyson
      examines the "kind of play the Davenant *Macbeth* is in
      relation to the Shakespeare."

998. Gellert, James. "Sir William Davenant's *The Law
      against Lovers*: Shakespeare's Problem Comedy and the
      Restoration Heroic Tradition." *Cahiers Elisabethains:
      Etudes sur la Pre-Renaissance et la Renaissance
      Anglaises*, 16 (1979), 27-43.

          Gellert considers *Law Against Lovers* as having
      developed from the popular Restoration tragicomedy and
      heroic drama. He thus explains Davenant's alterations
      of Angelo and Isabella from Shakespeare's
      psychologically ambiguous studies into characters in the
      heroic mode.

99.   Holland, Peter. *The Ornament of Action: Text and Performance in Restoration Comedy.* Cambridge: Cambridge Univ. Press, 1979. Pp. xii, 284.

       Holland's thesis is that aspects of a dramatic representation other than the text may be essential to the play's meaning. Beginning with the patents, Holland surveys Davenant's company, his use of scenery, and his need for plays. Holland describes the success of *The Siege of Rhodes* and its "Ornament." Davenant becomes for Holland the resource for basic evidence of the non-real scenery and the link with the masque tradition of symbolic scenes that will lead to the *Tempest*.

000.   Kalitzki, Judith Ann. "'Great Wits and Great Braves': The Relationship of Restoration Comedy to Heroic Drama." Diss. Univ. of Washington 1979. Pp. 177.

       The dissertation compares Tuke's *The Adventures of Five Hours* with a number of plays including *The Siege of Rhodes* in order to discover "innovations on Tuke's treatment of character, plot, and theme." Davenant's *The Man's the Master* is also cited. The dissertation demonstrates "how self-consciously aware these plays are of the affinity of comic and heroic values and conventions."

001.   Milhous, Judith. *Thomas Betterton and the Management of Lincoln's Inn Fields 1695-1708.* Carbondale: Southern Illinois Univ. Press, 1979. Pp. xvi, 287.

       To meet her objective "to show the importance of theatre management policy and company history to English drama in the pivotal years 1695-1708," Milhous begins with Betterton's mentor Davenant. In the first chapter, she explains the patent grants and the competition between Killigrew and Davenant. Leading up to the problems that Betterton encountered in 1695, Milhous delineates the actor-manager's debt to Davenant. She notes that Betterton may have been applying his early lessons to a theater that was now filled with aging players and problems that differed from those encountered earlier in the Restoration.

002.   Phelps, Wayne H. "The Second Night of Davenant's 'Salmacida Spolia.'" *Notes & Queries*, 224 (1979), 512-13.

Citing a letter from William Hawkins to the
Earl of Leicester, Phelps establishes Shrove Tuesday
February 18, 1639/40, as the date for the second
performance of Davenant's *Salmacida Spolia*. The
brief article reviews the significance of the masque
court documents, and events.

1003.   Price, Curtis A. *Music in the Restoration Theatre:
with a Catalogue of Instrumental Music in the Plays,
1665-1713*. Studies in Musciology, No. 4. Ann Arbor
Univ. of Michigan Research Press, 1979. Pp. xxi,
302.

Emphasizing the importance of music in the
drama of the late seventeenth century, Price
categorizes the music and surveys the types of each
category. He discusses the musicians and the abuses
and remedies during the period. In one of the two
appendices, Price gives a 100-page catalog of
instrumental music in the plays, giving both sources
and the musical requirements of the plays listed, and
also a list of music published by John Walsh from
1701 through 1710. Davenant, his operas, and plays
from 1656 are included in the discussion and the
lists.

1004.   Raddadi, Mongi. *Davenant's Adaptations of
Shakespeare*. Acta Universitatis Upsaliensis: Studia
Anglistica Upsaliensia, No. 36. Stockholm: Almquist
& Wicksell, 1979. Pp. 181.

The "dissertation is a study of Davenant's
adaptations of Shakespeare--*Hamlet, The Law Against
Lovers, Macbeth*, and *The Tempest, or the Enchanted
Island*--not only as adaptations but also as plays
independent of their Shakespearian models. Emphasis
is laid on the linguistic, dramatic, and theatrical
reasons underlying the alterations in the parts taken
over from Shakespeare."

1005.   Sorelius, Gunnar. "The Early History of the
Restoration Theatre: Some Problems Reconsidered."
Theatre Notebook, 33 (1979), 52-61.

The writer argues against Freehafer's
position that Killigrew was more important than
Davenant in setting up the joint Cockpit Company and

that Davenant's alterations of certain plays arose
not from compulsions contained in the patents but
from an adjustment to the new tastes of the times.
See *1965*: Freehafer.

006. Staves, Susan. *Players' Scepters: Fiction of
      Authority in the Restoration.* Lincoln: Univ. of
      Nebraska Press, 1979. Pp. xviii, 361.

      Staves examines the changes in the late
seventeenth century toward the "fictions of
authority" in England. She begins with the
Interregnum and its impact on the rest of the period,
looking at "common cultural experiences" for
evidence. Davenant enters early as a royalist poet,
illustrating special problems he faced. His
imprisonment, appeals, and release seem preliminaries
to his revival of English drama and its relationship
to the Stuart masque.

9.   1980 - 1985

1980

007.   Arundel, Dennis. *The Critic at the Opera:*
Contemporary Comments on Opera in London Over Three
Centuries. DaCapo Reprint Series. New York: DaCapo,
1980. Pp. xiii, 424.

The work is a reprint of the 1957 work. See
1957: Arundel.

008.   Cogan, Stephen Lawrence. "Wisdom and Idolatry in the
Seventeenth-Century Masque." Diss. Columbia 1980.
Pp. 476.

The study, which argues that a causal
relationship exists between the Caroline world view and
the decline of the poetry of the masque, involves a
chronological reading of the genre with Davenant
discussed in the latter part.

009.   Gurr, Andrew. *The Shakespearean Stage*: *1574-1642.*
2nd ed. Cambridge: Cambridge Univ. Press, 1980. Pp.
263.

See *1970*: Gurr.

010.   Hume, Robert D., ed. *The London Theatre World,*
1660-1800. Carbondale: Southern Illinois Univ.
Press, 1980. Pp. xix, 394.

Hume in this festschrift to A. H. Scouten has
collected twelve articles which constitute a "systematic
assessment" of the London theater world from 1660-1800.
Judith Milhous describes the monopoly granted to
Davenant and Killigrew after the Restoration, the
contracts between Davenant and his actors, and other
financial arrangements for management of the Duke's
Company. Colin Visser outlines the physical
arrangements of Davenant's stages at Rutland House and
Lincoln's Inn Fields, through the staging of *The Siege*
of Rhodes and *The Adventures of Five Hours*. Calhoun
Winton relates the details of the conflict between
Killigrew and Davenant, on the one hand, and Sir Henry
Herbert, Master of the Revels, on the other, concerning
the control of dramatic activities after the
Restoration. Finally, Joseph Donohue presents the
pertinent facts from the patents granted by Charles II
to Killigrew and Davenant.

1011. Laurie, Margaret. "Davenant, Sir William." In *The
       New Grove Dictionary of Music and Musicians*. Ed.
       Stanley Sadie. 20 vols. London: Macmillan, 1980,
       V, 259.

              Unlike the fifth edition in which there was no
       entry on Davenant, *The New Grove Dictionary* has a
       separate article on Davenant which surveys the
       playwright's contributions to music through his
       librettos to five masques, three entertainments, and *The
       Siege of Rhodes*, the first English opera. In another
       entry on the masque, Murray Lefkowitz mentions Davenant
       frequently (Vol. XI). Davenant is also mentioned in the
       entries on opera and on the musicians William and Henry
       Lawes, Matthew Locke, George Hudson, Charles Coleman,
       and Henry Cooke. See *1955*: Groves.

1012. Levin, Richard A. "Shakespeare's Bastard Son."
       Notes & Queries, 27 (1980), 177-79.

              Levin reviews Aubrey's questionable
       statements that suggest Davenant was Shakespeare's
       illegitimate son. He argues that it may have been a
       literary joke that Davenant guaranteed would be
       identified because of his play *Albovine* in which he
       alludes to King John. Levin suggests that Davenant was
       drawing a parallel between himself and the bastard,
       Philip Faulconbridge.

1013. Lyday, Jo Wilkinson. "'Timotheus' Varied Lays':
       Dryden and Music." Diss. Houston 1980. Pp. 495.

              Lyday discusses Dryden's poetry for musical
       setting in an effort to determine how the poet acquired
       "knowledge of the concepts of word-music peculiar to
       Renaissance humanists." In the discussion, Davenant is
       cited as an early influential collaborator.

1014. Orrell, John. "Filippo Corsini and the Restoration
       Theatre." *Theatre Notebook*, 34, No. 1 (1980), 4-9.

              Orrell compares two diaries of visitors to
       London in 1669 and finds that both describe the Duke's
       Theatre in Lincoln's Inn Fields, which seemed to have an
       almost circular plan. Lorenzo Malotte visited London in
       1669. He attended "the Theatre Royal on 15 April old
       style, the Duke's on 20 April, the Theatre Royal on 10

May and finally the Theatre Royal again on 24 May." So
too did Filippo Corsini. The comments and description
suggest that Davenant's theater was circular rather than
rectangular.

1015. Ripley, John. *Julius Caesar on Stage in England and
       America, 1599-1973.* Cambridge: Cambridge Univ.
       Press, 1980. Pp. xiii, 370.

        Ripley examines the stage history of *Julius
Caesar*, and he admits having no information of the
acting version used from 1660-82. Killigrew's company
had rights to the play, and after the union in 1682
Betterton acted it. The play continued to be popular,
and Ripley cites the Dryden-Davenant 1719 edition as the
likely text for the eighteenth-century performances.

1016. Treglown, Jeremy. "Scepticism and Parody in the
       Restoration." *Modern Language Review*, 75 (1980),
       18-47.

        The writer discusses parodies from the
Restoration miscellanies, citing some of *Gondibert* and
its *Preface.*

1017. Treglown, Jeremy. "Shakespeare's *Macbeth*'s:
       Davenant, Verdi, Stoppard, and the Question of
       Theatrical Text." *English*, 29 (1980), 95-113.

        After reviewing works by Waith (see *1959*:
Waith), Rosenberg (*1978*: Rosenberg), and Bartholomeusz
(*1967*: Bartholomeusz), Treglown reviews qualities of
Davenant's *Macbeth* retained by Verdi and German translations, and then he examines in detail some of the
changes such as his clarifications and the expansions,
correlating them with Verdi's opera.

1018. Venute, Lawrence Michael. "The Cavaliers in Love:
       Erotic Poetry at the Court of Charles I." Diss.
       Columbia 1980.

        Davenant is a part of the discussion of
poetry and court politics.

1981

1019. Bordinat, Philip, and Sophia B. Blaydes. *Sir William Davenant*. Twayne's English Authors Series, No. 303. Boston: Twayne, 1981. Pp. 188.

       Following the Twayne format, the book has a chronology, biographical chapter, and then discussions of Davenant's early plays, masques, nondramatic poetry, and the drama of the Interregnum and Restoration. Basic to the book's thesis is the statement "To know William Davenant is to know much of the seventeenth century. More than most writers Davenant was a man of his world, reflecting the Royalists' political and social activity as well as their intellectual and literary tastes."

1020. Brown, Laura. *English Dramatic Form, 1660-1760: An Essay in Generic History*. New Haven: Yale Univ. Press, 1981. Pp. xvi, 240.

       Using conventional classifications of dramatic form, Brown traces heroic tragedy, social satire, tragedy, and comedy, particularly in the first four chapters on representative works of Restoration dramatists including Davenant, in order to examine interpretive and generic problems in an historical context. She examines *The Siege of Rhodes* for its simple aesthetic and ideology, and she explains the artificiality in the historical context of Caroline court drama, the Interregnum, and the Restoration period.

1021. Desai, Meena. "Metadramatic and Metatheatrical Elements in Restoration Comedy: A Structuralist-Semiotic Approach." Diss. Houston 1981. Pp. 269.

       The dissertation examines the self-conscious elements in the drama of Davenant, Buckingham, Dryden, Etherege, Shadwell, Tuke, and Wycherley. In particular, the study examines *The Play-House To Be Let* as one of the self-conscious plays that draw attention to the physical condition of the Restoration theatrical scene.

1022. Langhans, Edward A. *Restoration Promptbooks*. Carbondale: Southern Illinois Univ. Press, 1981. Pp. xxvii, 535.

In the book's first section, "Acting
Companies and Their Promptbooks," the third chapter is
devoted to the Duke's Company, 1660-1682, and Davenant's
role as its manager. In Appendix E, Langhans reprints a
portion of a play that had been prepared for performance
by the Duke's Company in late 1662.

023. Parry, Graham. *The Golden Age restor'd: The*
      Culture of the Stuart Court, 1603-42. Manchester:
      Manchester Univ. Press, 1981. Pp. xi, 276.

         In his discussion of the Caroline masque,
Parry surveys Davenant's development as Inigo Jones'
collaborator on these royal entertainments, which depict
Charles I as "a refined, virtuous, philosophic
sovereign."

024. *The Revels History of Drama in English. Vol. IV:*
      1613-1660. Gen. ed. Lois Potter. London: Methuen,
      1981. Pp. lvii, 337.

         Davenant is considered as a manager by Philip
Edwards in "Chapter I. Society and the Theatre," as the
"resuscitator of English Drama" by Gerald Eades Bentley
in "Chapter II. The Theatres and the Actors," as the
expressor of Platonic love and the exponent of decorum
by Kathleen McLuskie in "Chapter III. The plays and the
Playwrights: 1613-42," and as a reformer by Lois Potter
in "Chapter IV. The Plays and the Playwrights:
1642-60."

025. Tadie, Andrew, and James P. Mesa. "A Problem of
      Audience: A Semiotical Approach to the Deistic
      Elements in *The Siege of Rhodes*." In *Semiotic*
      Themes. Ed. Richard T. DeGeorge. Lawrence: Univ.
      of Kansas, 1981, pp. 109-31.

         The chapter applies the semiotic theories of
Charles Sanders Peirce to *The Siege of Rhodes*.

                        1982

026. Davison, Peter. *Popular Appeal in English Drama to*
      1850. Totowa, New Jersey: Barnes & Noble, 1982.
      Pp. xi, 221.

         Davison discusses the antimasque and the
sense of improvisation found in *Play-House To Be Let*,

and its relationship to the compendium plays of the late
sixteenth and early seventeenth centuries, to the
rehearsal plays, and to burlesque plays that followed.

1027.   Gewirtz, Arthur David. *Restoration Adaptations of
        Early Seventeenth-Century Comedies.* Washington,
        D.C.: Univ. Press of America, 1982. Pp. xxiii,
        190.

                The book covers the most influential adapters
        of early seventeenth-century plays during the
        Restoration. Davenant is cited as the most prolific and
        ultimately the most influential because of Betterton who
        continued to present work by Davenant at the Dorset
        Garden. Discussing Davenant's "variety" in the first
        chapter, Gewirtz uses the playwright to support his
        thesis that the "relatively unified Jacobean-Caroline
        world" contrasts with the varied Restoration world that
        was comprised of a society "at odds with itself, a
        society of warring factions who live within its rules
        not because they wish to but because they must."

1028.   King, Bruce. *Seventeenth-Century English Literature.*
        History of Literature Series, ed. A.Norman Jeffares.
        New York: Schocken, 1982. Pp. xiii, 295.

                In a volume that offers biographical,
        political, and social background of literature and
        literary figures of the seventeenth century, King
        devotes a few pages to Davenant, his life and his work,
        both in the Caroline and Restoration periods.

1029.   Maus, K. E. "Arcadia Lost: Politics and Revision in
        the Restoration *Tempest.*" *Renaissance Drama*, 13
        (1982), 189-209.

                After affirming that the Davenant-Dryden
        Tempest was the most popular play of the Restoration,
        Maus compares Shakespeare's Prospero with that of the
        revisers and concludes that the former reflects James
        I's view of a paternalistic monarch of the kind revealed
        in his tracts on kingship while the latter reflects
        Charles I's views of a politically conservative monarchy
        guided by rigidly enforced laws designed to curb immoral
        chaos.

1030.   Murray, Christopher. "Philip's *The Revengeful Queen*,
        Davenant's *Albovine*, Middleton's *The Witch* and the

Kinship of Sources." *Notes & Queries*, 29 (Dec. 1982), 525-26.

Murray reviews the information contained in Philips' "Epistle Dedicatory" in which the playwright claims his source was Machiavelli's *Florentine History*, not, as suggested by others, Davenant's *Albovine*. On the basis of an examination of the *History*, Murray concludes that Philips is correct and that Davenant, who later used Middleton's *The Witch* for parts of the alteration of *Macbeth*, probably used it for *Albovine*, as well. Thus, Davenant, not Philips, may have "reflected the works of others."

1983

1031. Brooks-Davies, Douglas. *The Mercurian Monarch: Magical Politics from Spenser to Pope*. Manchester: Manchester Univ. Press, 1983. Pp. viii, 228.

The "magical politics" study takes Brooks-Davies to the masques of Davenant. Included are discussions of Davenant's pre-war masques and *The Tempest*. The study emphasizes the magical, mercurial elements in theme, characterization, and production.

1032. Butler, Martin. "Entertaining the Palatine Prince: Plays on Foreign Affairs 1635-37." *English Literary Renaissance*, 13 (1983), 319-44.

According to Butler, the arrival in London of the youthful Charles Louis, exiled Count Palatine, was designed to gain England's support for the recovery of German lands lost in recent wars against Catholic Austria and Spain. The plays and masques attended by the count as guest of the English monarchs were to convince Charles I of the need to renew aggression against Spain. Among the entertainments was Davenant's *The Triumphs of the Prince d'Amour*, which Butler analyzes in terms of his argument. He also mentions in relation to these political events the unrealized plan for the count's brother Rupert to conquer Madagascar, a non-event celebrated by Davenant in the courtly-heroic poem "Madagascar," which Butler also discusses in detail.

1033. Capelle, Alex. "The Misadventures of *Julius Caesar*." *Cahiers Elisabethains: Etudes sur la Pre-Renaissance et la Renaissance Anglaises*, 24 (1983), 33-45.

The article discusses adaptations of *Julius Caesar*. Among them is Davenant and Dryden's 1719 revision.

1034.   Carlton, Charles.   *Charles I: The Personal Monarch*.
        London: Routledge & Kegan Paul, 1983.   Pp. xiii,
        426.

                In an effort to present a portrait of Charles
        I and his time, Carlton uses all materials available and
        places Davenant, among others, in perspective.   Of
        particular interest are Davenant's masques, his military
        activity, his use of poetry in the conflict, his
        activities in exile, and his appeal to the king on the
        queen's behalf to deny the Anglican religion.

1035.   Helgerson, Richard.   *Self-Crowned Laureates: Spenser,
        Jonson, Milton and the Literary System*.   Berkeley:
        Univ. of California Press, 1983.   Pp. ix, 292.

                After identifying the laureate's task as
        making "of a gentleman's toy something of unspeakable
        profit," Helgerson reviews poets of renown.   Chapter 4
        has segments devoted to Davenant and other Caroline
        courtiers, "Orpheus Sons" as the poet called them.
        Pages 204-14 are devoted to Davenant, his self-mocking
        poetry, lyrics, and epic.

1036.   Johnson, Jeffrey Lawson Laurence.   "Sweeping up
        Shakespeare's Rubbish."   *Eighteenth Century Life*, 8,
        No. 3 (1983), 14-25.

                Johnson uses the 1676 Davenant edition of
        Hamlet, among several versions, in his discussion of
        Garrick's condensation of the play.

1037.   Maguire, Nancy Klein.   "Origins and Development of
        Serious Drama in the 1660's."   Diss. Northern
        Illinois 1983.   Pp.   316.

                The dissertation examines the development of
        the heroic play and tragicomedy after 1660.

1038.   Sawday, Jonathan.   "The Leiden Anatomy Theatre as a
        Source for Davenant's 'cabinet of death' in
        Gondibert."   *Notes & Queries*, 30 (1983), 437-49.

Sawday denies Gladish's suggestion that Davenant's "cabinet of death" was based on the anatomy theater at Leiden University, pictured in a catalogue. Sawday notes that the catalogue was printed in 1691, not 1591. He suggests that the sources might have been two prints of the anatomy theater, 1609 and 1610, conversations with Doctors Thomas Cademan and Gideon Delaune, both friends of Davenant, or that Davenant saw the laboratory on one of his trips to the continent.

1039.   Tierney, James E.   "Recent Studies in Eighteenth-Century Drama." *Philological Quarterly*, 62(1983), 335-52.

In his description of the Pedicord-Bergmann edition of Garrick's plays, Tierney mentions Davenant briefly with Garrick's adaptations of *The Rehearsal* and *Macbeth*.

1984

1040.   Bentley, Gerald Eades. *The Profession of Player in Shakespeare's Time, 1590-1642*. Princeton: Princeton Univ. Press, 1984. Pp. xiv, 315.

Bentley refers frequently to Davenant, especially his replacement in 1640 of Beeston at the Cockpit in Drury Lane.

1041.   Butler, Martin. *Theatre and Crisis 1632-1642*. Cambridge: Cambridge Univ. Press, 1984. Pp. xii, 340.

The book examines the drama that was written and produced just before the Civil War. It includes discussions of Davenant's *Albovine, The Fair Favorite, The Just Italian, Luminalia, Madagascar, Salmacida Spolia, The Temple of Love, The Triumphs of the Prince d'Amour, The Unfortunate Lovers*, and *The Wits*. Butler suggests that the drama offers evidence that the Caroline court was neither as frivolous nor as oblivious of the political forces that were antagonistic to Charles I.

1042.   Guffey, George R.   "Politics, Weather, and the Contemporary Reception of the Dryden-Davenant Tempest." *Restoration: Studies in English Literary Culture, 1660-1700*, 8 (1984), 1-9.

Finding The *Tempest* adaptation by Davenant
and Dryden to have been "generally maligned" during the
last eighty years, Guffey returns to the Restoration
audiences' own assessments. He observes that the play
is itself a "Restoration" comedy of the Duke of Milan
who was restored to his throne; a statement on the
relations between France, Spain, and England, which
explains the added and substituted characters; and a
response to the public excitement caused by severe,
damaging storms, cited as "tempests" in the *Gazette*.
Guffey states, "When Pepys and the Court attended the
first performance of the Dryden-Davenant *Tempest* on 7
November 1667, they witnessed, then, a play that, in
their view, reflected the realities of recent domestic
and foreign history." The play is, as Pepys noted,
"innocent" and, Guffey concludes, a "more substantial
and responsible creation than most of its
twentieth-century critics have thought it to be."

1043. Hammond, Paul. "Did Dryden Write the Prologue to
'Julius Caesar'?" *English Studies*, 65 (1984),
409-19.

Hammond rejects the various arguments that
Dryden wrote the Prologue to *Julius Caesar* which was
published apart from the play in *Covent Garden drolery*
(1672). Among the arguments discussed is that of Bolton
Corney who noted the Davenant-Dryden alteration of the
play. See *1854*: Corney.

1044. Jose, Nicholas. *Ideas of the Restoration in English
Literature 1660-71*. Cambridge: Harvard Univ. Press,
1984. Pp. xvi, 205.

Citing Davenant's panegyrics to Monck and
Charles II, his association with Milton, and his "naive"
poems and masques, Jose includes the poet in a study of
the "emergence of the modern world."

1045. Prescott, Anne L. "The Stuart Masque and
Pantagruel's Dream." *English Literary History*, 51
(1984), 407-30.

Prescott's purpose is to demonstrate the
influence on the Stuart masque of the Rabelaisian *Les
songes drolatiques*, a collection of grotesque figures
attributed to Francois Despres. She traces the

influence in the works of Inigo Jones and his
collaborators. She closes with the argument that Jones'
grotesque figures in *Salmacida Spolia* were copied from
Les songes.

046.   Robinson, Randal F. *Hamlet in the 1950s: An
        Annotated Bibliography of Criticism.* The Garland
        Shakespeare Bibliographies, William Godshalk,
        general ed. New York: Garland, 1984. Pp. xxvi,
        383.

            Davenant appears in only one item in the
bibliography and that because of George C. Branam's
1956 study of Davenant's adaptation of *Hamlet.* (See
1956: Branam). When all of the twentieth-century
volumes of *Hamlet* scholarship are published and when all
of the Garland Shakespeare Bibliographies are completed,
those interested in Davenant would benefit from looking
at each of the volumes.

047.   Vander Motten, J. P. "Iago at Lincoln's Inn Fields:
        Thomas Porter's *The Villain* on the Early Restoration
        Stage." *Studies in English Literature,* 24 (1984),
        415-28.

            In the discussion of the "third most popular
play of its day"--Davenant's *Siege of Rhodes* and Samuel
Tuke's *Adventures of Five Hourse* are the others--Vander
Motten explains Davenant's need for plays in 1660, and
he suggests that *The Villain* deliberately echoed
Othello, a play not granted to Davenant and his company.
The Villain, Vander Motten explains, was a new play
"badly needed to fill out Davenant's meager repertory."
Davenant may have encouraged Porter, the son of
Endymion, to write it and may have provided "a
well-timed presentation" as well.

048.   Vince, Ronald W. *Renaissance Theatre: A
        Historiographical Handbook.* London: Greenwood, 1984.
        Pp. xi, 204.

            The purpose of this work is to identify
sources of Renaissance theater history. The material on
Davenant is brief but significant with references to
ground plans, elevations, and scene and costume designs
for *Salmacida Spolia, Britannia Triumphans,* and *The
Siege of Rhodes.*

1985

1049.   Lindley, David, ed. *The Court Masque*. Manchester: Manchester Univ. Press, 1985. Pp. [vii], 196.

In his introduction to this collection of essays by authorities on the court masque, Lindley briefly surveys Davenant's *Salmacida Spolia* as a reflection of the political tenor of the times and of Inigo Jones' artistic achievements in that form. Other authorities mention Davenant, usually in relation to Jones or to the antimasque.

1050.   Orrell, John. *The Theatres of Inigo Jones and John Webb*. Cambridge: Cambridge Univ. Press, 1985. Pp. 218.

In his discussion of the English court theater of the seventeenth century, Orrell describes both the Cockpit at Whitehall Palace and the Cockpit in Drury Lane. Although not a court theater, the Cockpit in Drury Lane was remodelled in 1616, probably with the help of Inigo Jones. Since plays by Davenant were acted at both theaters and since Davenant was theater-manager from 1640 to 1642 of the Cockpit in Drury Lane, Orrell's study of the theater illuminates an important part of Davenant's activities.

1051.   Smith, A. J. *The Metaphysics of Love*. Cambridge: Cambridge Univ. Press, 1985. Pp. ix, 349.

In a work that traces the "prolonged debate about the spiritual worth of love," Smith mentions Davenant's Caroline love lyrics and his political activism in chapter 4, "*Among the Wastes of Time*: seventeenth-century love poetry and the failure of love." The work emphasizes Dante, Milton, Spenser, Shakespeare, Donne, and Vaughan.

1867

1052.   Hazlitt, W. Carew. *Handbook to the Popular,*
Poetical, and Dramatic Literature of Great Britain,
From the Invention of Printing to the Restoration.
London: John Russell Smith, 1867. Pp. xii, 701.

Hazlitt presents a twenty-five item primary
bibliography which lacks among other works *Luminalia*
and the adaptations of Shakespeare. For about half of
the entries, he reprints the full title-pages; otherwise he lists title, date, and format.

1888

1053.   Knight, Joseph. "Davenant, Sir William." *Dictionary*
of National Biography [*DNB*]. 64 vols. Ed. Leslie
Stephen. London: Smith Elder, 1888, XIV, 108.

The essay contains a brief but important
bibliographical paragraph.

1893

1054.   *The Grolier Club's Catalogue of Original and Early*
Editions of Some of the Poetical and Prose Works of
English Writers from Langland to Prior. 4 vols. in
1. 1892-1905; rpt. London: Holland, 1964.

Davenant's work appears in volume 2, called
the first, on pages 211 to 214. The purpose of the
listing is to present to collectors descriptions of
rare and valuable books in order to inform before
purchase. Literary value is not the issue here. Items
243-48 are devoted to Davenant's poetry, *Madagascar* and
Gondibert in particular. See *1964: The Grolier Club.*

1909

1055.   Tupper, James W., ed. *Love and Honour and The Siege*
of Rhodes. Belles-Lettres Series, Sec. III. *The*
English Drama. New York: D. C. Heath, 1909. Pp.
xlvii, 362.

The volume contains a four-page bibliography
on Davenant (pp. 350-54).

1911

1056. Jaggard, William. *Shakespeare Bibliography. A Dictionary of Every Known Issue of the Writings of Our National Poet and of Recorded Opinion Thereon in the English Language*. Stratford-on-Avon: Shakespeare Head, 1911. Pp. xxi, 729.

Jaggard lists Davenant's Shakespeare adaptations chronologically to 1911.

1916

1057. Bartlett, Henrietta Collins, and Alfred W. Pollard. *A Census of Shakespeare's Plays in Quarto, 1594-1709*. New Haven: Yale Univ. Press, 1916. Pp. xli, 153.

The work contains an annotated, alphabetical list of the plays and a chronological list of the editions according to their titles.

1920

1058. *Annual Bibliography of English Language and Literature*. Modern Humanities Research Association. Cambridge: Bowes and Bowes, 1920 --.

Entries on Davenant are listed annually in the seventeenth-century section under his name.

1922

1059. Bartlett, Henrietta C. *Mr. William Shakespeare: Original and Early Editions of His Quartos and Folios, His Source Books and Those Containing Notices*. New Haven: Yale Univ. Press, 1922. Pp. xxviii, 217.

The chief value of Bartlett's bibliography to the Davenant scholar is the information in the entries and commentaries on the adaptations of Shakespeare's *The Tempest* and *Macbeth*.

1923

1060. Palmer, George Herbert. *A Catalogue of Early and Rare Editions of English Poetry Collected and*

Presented to Wellesley College. Boston: Houghton Mifflin, 1923. Pp. xii, 613.

The value of the bibliography is that the reader will find these rare editions at Wellesley. Among Davenant's works are first editions of *Madagascar, Gondibert, The Seventh and Last Canto to the Third Book of Gondibert,* and *Works, 1673.*

1926

1061. "English Literature, 1660-1800: A Current Bibliography." *Philological Quarterly,* 5-55 (1926-1975).

The bibliography appeared in the April number, 1926-1948, and in the July number, 1949-1975. Since 1976 the bibliography has been published for the American Society for Eighteenth-Century Studies; see *1975 B: The Eighteenth Century.* Beginning with Volume 55 (1976) the journal issues one number on Restoration and eighteenth-century literature including review articles. Material pertinent to Davenant is listed under his name and under material cross-referenced. See *1950B:* Landa; see also *1975B: The Eighteenth Century; 1976B: Philological Quarterly.*

1062. Spencer, Hazelton. "Improving Shakespeare: Some Bibliographical Notes on the Restoration Adaptations." *Publications of the Modern Language Association,* 42 (1926), 727-46.

Spencer gives bibliographies of Restoration alterations and first editions of altered versions.

1934

1063. Summers, Montague. *A Bibliography of the Restoration Drama.* London: Fortune, [1934]. Pp. 143.

Summers offers an alphabetical list of "plays, acted and unacted, printed and unprinted, belonging to the Restoration Theatre." Davenant's plays are included.

1935

1064.   Harbage, Alfred. "Bibliography." In *Sir William
        Davenant, Poet Venturer, 1606-1668*. Philadelphia:
        Univ. of Pennsylvania Press, 1935; rpt. New York:
        Octagon, 1971. Pp. 288-303.

            Harbage provides a bibliography in two major
        divisions: I. "Davenant's Works," that has three
        subdivisions, "Collections" (pp. 288-89), "Editions
        of Individual Works" (pp. 289-93) and "Addenda"
        (pp. 293-94); II. "Materials: Biographical, Critical,
        Etc." (pp. 294-303). See *1971B*: Harbage.

1939

1065.   MacDonald, Hugh. *John Dryden: A Bibliography of
        Early Editions and of Drydeniana*. Oxford: Clarendon,
        1939. Pp. x, 358.

            MacDonald lists and describes seven editions
        of *The Tempest, or the Enchanted Island* between 1670
        and 1701. He surveys the arguments concerning the
        relative contributions of Davenant, Dryden, and later
        Shadwell (pp. 101-03). MacDonald also lists and
        describes the 1719 edition of *Julius Caesar* as
        "alter'd" by Davenant and Dryden, although there is no
        "confirmatory evidence for the statement." See *1966B*:
        MacDonald.

1066.   Steible, Daniel Joseph. "Bibliography." "A Critical
        Edition of Sir William Davenant's *The Temple of Love*
        and *The Platonic Lovers*." Diss. Cincinnati 1939.
        Pp. 152-62.

            The ten-page bibliography is one single
        alphabetized list of works relating to Steible's
        study.

1940

1067.   Day, Cyrus Lawrence, and Eleanore Boswell Murrie.
        *English Songbooks, 1651-1702: A Bibliography, With a
        First-Line Index of Songs*. London: Bibliographical
        Society at the Univ. Press, Oxford, 1940 (for 1937).
        Pp. xxi, 439.

The book lists, describes, and indexes almost all the secular songbooks published in England and Scotland between 1651 and 1702. The bibliography of books runs about 160 pages and is followed by indexes of first lines, composers, authors, singers and actors, tunes and airs, sources, song-books, and printers, publishers, and booksellers. Easily accessible are references to Davenant, his songs, and the books where they appeared. See *1975B*: Day.

1941

1068. Bateson, F. W. *The Cambridge Bibliography of English Literature.* 4 vols. New York: Macmillan, 1941. Also, vol. 5: Supplement: A.D. 600-1900. Ed. George Watson. New York and London: Cambridge Univ. Press, 1974.

In volume I, the bibliography covers the years 600-1660, and it encompasses material on primary and secondary sources by or relating to Davenant during the pre-Restoration years. Pages 453 through 455 contain: Davenant's collected works; his poems, collected and individually published; his prose works; his plays and masques; his separately published works; and Davenant biography and criticism. See *1966B*: Watson; *1974B*: Watson; *1981B*: Watson.

1069. Bentley, Gerald Eades. *The Jacobean and Caroline Stage.* 7 vols. Oxford: Clarendon, 1941-68.

In volume III, pages 193 through 225, Bentley provides a narrative as well as a bibliography of Davenant's primary works. He includes biographical, interpretative, and historical studies of Davenant and his individual works.

1945

1070. Woodward, Gertrude L., and James G. McManaway. *A Check List of English Plays, 1641-1700.* Chicago: Newberry Library, 1945. Pp. x, 155.

The compilers list Davenant's plays published during the Commonwealth and Restoration periods, along with indications of the libraries where the various editions can be found. See *1949B*: Bowers.

1949

1071. Baer, Elizabeth, comp. *Seventeenth Century Maryland: A Bibliography.* Baltimore: John Work Garrett Library, 1949. Pp. xxix, 219 [209 facs. of title pages].

Item 38, which includes a bibliographic description, an explanatory note, and a facsimile of the title page, is in the New York Public Library. The title page reads, "THE LORD BALTEMORE'S CASE, Concerning the Province of Maryland.... With full and clear Answers to all material Objections, touching his Rights, Jurisdiction, and Proceedings there.... Unto which is also annexed, a true Copy of a Commission from the late King's Eldest Son, to Mr. William Davenant, to dispossess the Lord Baltemore of the said Province, because of his adherence to this Common-Wealth. London. Printed in the Yeare, 1653." The commission to Davenant from the exiled King Charles II challenged the legitimacy of the Governorship of Maryland and forced Lord Baltimore to defend his position.

1072. Bowers, Fredson. *A Supplement to the Woodward & McManaway Check List of English Plays 1641-1700.* Charlottesville: Bibliographical Society of the Univ. of Virginia, 1949. Pp. 22.

The *Supplement* provides Davenant scholars with additional libraries where the plays may be found. See *1945B*: Woodward.

1950

1073. Landa, Louis, et al. *English Literature 1660-1800: A Bibliography of Modern Studies.* 6 vols. Princeton: Princeton Univ. Press, 1950-1972.

The volumes are a collection of the articles "The Eighteenth Century: A Current Bibliography" that were published annually in *Philological Quarterly* from 1925 through 1960. The six volumes provide access to materials on Davenant through their alphabetical listing of authors and topics and through their indexes given in volumes 2, 4, and 6. See *1926B*: "English Literature"; see also *1975B*: *The Eighteenth Century*; see also *1976B*: *Philological Quarterly*.

1952

1074. Nicoll, Allardyce. "Handlist of Restoration Plays." In *Restoration Drama, 1660-1700*. Cambridge: Cambridge Univ. Press, 1952. Pp. 400-02.

> Nicoll includes Davenant's Commonwealth and Restoration plays in this annotated list, which is comprised chiefly of the operas and the adaptations.

1954

1075. Wikelund, Philip. "Restoration Literature: An Annotated Bibliography." *Folio*, 19 (1954), 135-55.

> Wikelund surveys what was available by and about Davenant in 1954.

1962

1076. Bush, Douglas. "Bibliography." *English Literature in the Earlier Seventeenth Century, 1600-1660*. 2nd ed. rev. *The Oxford History of English Literature*. Vol. V. F. P. Wilson and Bonamy Dobree, eds. New York: Oxford Univ. Press, 1962. Pp. 461-668.

> The bibliography is divided into six parts: General Biographies and Works of Reference; General Collections and Anthologies; General Literary History and Criticism; Special Literary Studies and Literary Forms; The Background of Literature; and the Individual Authors. On page 560, Bush provides a narrative bibliography of Davenant's poetry, biography, and interpretive material from Davenant's career prior to 1660.

1077. Northup, Clark Sutherland. *A Register of Bibliographies of the English Language and Literature*. New York: Hafner, 1962. Pp. 507.

> Originally published in 1925, the work reprints material that is divided into general and individual authors and topics. It contains additions and corrections as well. The material relating to Davenant is limited but good.

1078. "Restoration and 18th Century Bibliography." *Restoration and 18th Century Theatre Research*. 1962--.

The journal contains an annual bibliographic
article of items that relate to the drama of the
Restoration and eighteenth century. Studies of
Davenant are included.

1963

1079. "Theses and Dissertations in Restoration and 18th
Century Theatre." *Restoration and 18th Century
Theatre Research.* 1963--.

The journal carries occasional lists of theses
and dissertations in the field that includes Davenant
and his work.

1964

1080. *The Grolier Club's Catalogue of Original and Early
Editions of Some of the Poetical and Prose Works of
English Writers from Langland to Prior.* 4 vols. in
1. London: Holland, 1964.

See *1893B*: *The Grolier.*

1081. Parsons, Philip E. "*The Siege of Rhodes* and
Restoration Tragedy: An Interpretation of Some Formal
Developments in the Serious Drama of the
Restoration." Diss. Cambridge (King's and Christ's)
1964. Pp. 409-18.

The dissertation contains source material
directly related to the topic and a list of critical
and useful works.

1966

1082. MacDonald, Hugh. *John Dryden: A Bibliography of
Early Editions and of Drydeniana.* 1939; rpt. London:
Dawsons of Pall Mall, 1966. Pp. x, 358.

See *1939B*: MacDonald.

1083. Stratman, Carl J., ed. *Bibliography of English
Printed Tragedy 1565-1900.* Carbondale and
Edwardsville: Southern Illinois Univ. Press, 1966.
Pp. xx, 843.

In the "bibliography of 6852 numbered entries are 1483 English tragedies, of which 103 are anonymous works, and the remaining 1380 represent plays by 769 authors" (p. x). Included are Davenant's tragedies. "For each entry the following information is given: 1) the author; 2) the complete title of the play; 3) the imprint; 4) the major pagination; 5) the library symbols; 6) whatever notes or commentaries seem necessary" (p. xi).

1084. Watson, George, ed. *The Concise Cambridge Bibliography of English Literature.* 2nd ed. Cambridge: Univ. Press, 1966. Pp. xi, 270.

First published in 1958, the bibliography came out in a second edition in 1965. This particular paperback edition was a reprint of the 1965 edition. It contains a brief but useful survey of English literature devoting about fifty pages to the period labelled "The Restoration to the Romantics (1660-1800)." Davenant is listed under the section "The Renaissance to the Restoration (1500-1660)," page 65. Some of the primary and secondary works are listed, taking about 1/2 a page. See *1941B*: Watson; *1974B*: Watson; see also *1981B*: Watson.

1967

1085. Collins, Howard Stuart. *Comedy of Sir William Davenant.* Studies in English Literature, vol. 24. The Hague: Mouton, 1967. Pp. 176-79.

The bibliography includes separate lists of primary and secondary sources that relate generally and specifically to Collins' study.

1969

1086. Crum, Margaret C., ed. *First-Line Index of English Poetry, 1500-1800, in Manuscripts of the Bodleian Library, Oxford.* 2 vols. Oxford: Clarendon, 1969.

The work contains more than twenty items that refer either to Davenant's poems or to poems about Davenant that are in the manuscripts of the Bodleian Library.

1087. "Sir William Davenant."   In *The New Cambridge
       Bibliography of English Literature*.   Cambridge:
       Cambridge Univ. Press, 1969.

            The major entry on Davenant (I, 1208-10),
       which is located under "Jacobean and Caroline Poetry,"
       lists collections, individual works, and biographical
       and critical studies.   Shorter entries are found under
       "University Plays" (I, 1766) and "Literary Criticism"
       (I, 2319).

1088. Stratman, Carl J., ed.   *Restoration and 18th Century
       Theatre Research 1961-1968*.   Compiled by Edmund A.
       Napieralski (1961-1968) and Jean E. Westbrook
       (1961-1966).   Troy, New York: Whitson, 1969.   Pp. ii,
       241.

            In part a compilation of *Restoration and 18th
       Century Theatre Research* bibliographies, the volume
       presents alphabetically and under headings, including
       both topics and authors, works published within a
       seven-year span.   Davenant is covered on pages 43 and
       44, items 227-35, and in eight other "See also" items.
       Each item is annotated.

1089. Sutherland, James.   "Bibliography."   *English
       Literature of the Late Seventeenth Century*.   *The
       Oxford History of English Literature*.   Vol. VI.   Ed.
       F. P. Wilson and Bonamy Dobree.   New York and Oxford:
       Oxford Univ. Press, 1969.   Pp. 442-578.

            The bibliography contains, in addition to the
       general bibliographies, collections, general histories,
       special literary studies and forms, background of
       literature, and sections on individual authors.   The
       section on Davenant (pp. 519-20) offers in narrative
       form   a paragraph of primary works, another on
       biographical studies, and a third on reprints,
       discussions, and critical comment.

                              1970

1090. Bond, Donald Frederick.   *The Age of Dryden*.   New
       York: Appleton-Century-Crofts, 1970.   Pp. xii, 103.

            Designed for graduate and advanced
       undergraduate students, the book is a convenient

bibliography of significant scholarship on English
literature of the Restoration period, 1660-1700.
Twelve items on Davenant published from 1925 to 1967
are included.

091. *MLA International Bibliography: British, American,
      Australian, English-Canadian, New Zealand, and
      English-Caribbean Literatures.* Vol. 1. New York:
      Modern Language Association, 1970--.

           Actually available from 1922, not 1970, the
      MLA International Bibliography was published prior to
      1970 as a part of *PMLA.* The more recent volumes,
      1981--, offer in addition to the listings under
      Davenant's name some brief descriptive notes and
      indexes that enable the researcher to find additional
      information on related topics more easily.

                          1971

092. Gladish, David F. "Introduction: The Text of the
      'Preface' and 'Answer.'" In *Sir William Davenant's
      Gondibert.* Oxford: Clarendon, 1971. Pp.
      xxix-xxxiv.

           Gladish describes three modern texts and then
      establishes the copy text for the "Preface" and
      "Answer." He also gives manuscript corrections,
      cancels, press-variants, and the text of the "Seventh
      Canto."

093. Harbage, Alfred. "Bibliography." In *Sir William
      Davenant, Poet Venturer, 1606-1668.* New York:
      Octagon, 1971. Pp. 288-303.

           See *1935B*: Harbage.

094. Stratman, Carl J., David G. Spencer, and Mary
      Elizabeth Devine, eds. *Restoration and Eighteenth
      Century Theatre Research: A Bibliographical Guide,
      1900-1968.* Carbondale and Edwardsville: Southern
      Illinois Univ. Press, 1971. Pp. ix, 811.

           The bibliography of more than six-thousand
      entries includes studies and editions of plays
      published between 1900 and 1968. It is divided into
      780 subject headings in alphabetical order. Those

headings include all people associated with the theater
as well as topics such as audiences, marriage, and
wits. Under each heading the items are placed in
chronological order. Davenant appears in a section
headed with his name (pp. 177-82) that is subdivided
into his works, plays, poems, individual plays,
biography, and criticism.

1973

1095.   Hedback, Ann-Mari, ed. *Sir William Davenant: The
        Siege of Rhodes, A Critical Edition*. Acta
        Universitatis Uppsaliensis: Studia Anglistica
        Upsaliensia, No. 14.   Uppsala: 1973.   Pp. lxxviii,
        121.

           The work contains a useful bibliography that
        focuses on *The Siege of Rhodes*.

1096.   Howard, Patsy C., ed. *Theses in English Literature
        1894-1970*. Ann Arbor: Pierian, 1973. Pp. xix, 387.

           The book contains 9000 entries "drawn from
        listings ... at many southwestern, southern and eastern
        colleges and universities during the summer of 1970."
        The work indicates by author and subject in
        alphabetical arrangement the theses written within the
        76 years noted in the title. Davenant appears on page
        83 in entries 2365 through 2374. The editor has also
        provided two Davenant items from other categories.

1974

1097.   Watson, George. *The New Cambridge Bibliography of
        English Literature*.   5 vols.   Cambridge: Cambridge
        Univ. Press, 1974.

           This is an update of *1941B*: Bateson.   See also
        1941B: Watson; *1966B*:   Watson.

1975

1098.   Davies, H. Neville.   "10. Davenant, Dryden, Lee, and
        Otway."   In *English Drama (Excluding Shakespeare):
        Select Bibliographical Guides*.   Ed. Stanley Wells.
        London: Oxford Univ. Press, 1975.   Pp. 150-72.

Of the 22 pages, only pp. 150-55 of the text
and pp. 168-69 of the bibliography itself are devoted
to Davenant. Yet, the commentary is useful and the
list identifies the most reliable sources and primary
works.

099. Day, Cyrus Lawrence, and Eleanore Boswell Murrie.
*English Song-Books, 1651-1702: A Bibliography, With a
First Line Index of Songs.* Folcroft, Pa.: Folcroft
Library Series, 1975. Pp. xxi, 439.

This is a reprint of the 1940 work. See
1940B: Day.

100. *The Eighteenth Century: A Current Bibliography.* N.S.
1, 1975. American Society for Eighteenth-Century
Studies.

The series was previously published by
Philological Quarterly, 1926-1974. The volumes provide
annotated items, alphabetically listed. Material
pertinent to Davenant is under his name and under
material cross-referenced by the editors. See *1926B:*
"English Literature"; *1950B:* Landa; *1976B: Philological
Quarterly.*

1976

101. Bateson, Frederick Wilse, and Harrison T. Meserole.
"An Augustan Reading List, 1650-1800." *A Guide to
English and American Literature.* 3rd ed. London and
New York: Longman, 1976. Pp. 111-37.

The work is a brief guide to major secondary
studies of Augustan literature and individual authors,
Davenant included.

102. Latt, David J., and Samuel Holt Monk, eds. *John
Dryden: A Survey and Bibliography of Critical
Studies, 1895-1974.* Minneapolis: Univ. of Minnesota
Press, 1976. Pp. xv, 199.

Those interested in Davenant will find that
bibliographies such as this provide useful information.
Dryden's career overlapped Davenant's, and this
particular bibliography is testimony to that. Davenant
is listed only in the index, but there are fifteen to

twenty such entries and some entries on Shakespeare are
also pertinent to him.

1103.   Link, Frederick M., ed. *English Drama, 1660-1800: A
        Guide to Information Sources*. Vol. 9. The American
        Literature, English Literature, and World Literatures
        in English Information Guide Series. Detroit: Gale
        Research, 1976. Pp. xxii, 374.

        The volume contains a preface, an index of
names and another of play titles, a general
bibliography, and more than 200 pages of lists devoted
to individual authors listed alphabetically. Davenant
has two pages of materials presented in two paragraphs
rather than alphabetical lists. The index provides
nine other pages that mention Davenant. See *1976*:
Penninger.

1104.   Penninger, Frieda Elaine. *English Drama to 1660:
        (Excluding Shakespeare): A Guide to Information
        Sources*. Vol. 5. The American Literature, English
        Literature, and World Literatures in English
        Information Guide Series. Detroit: Gale Research,
        1976. Pp. xvii, 370.

        A companion to the Link volume (see *1976 B*:
Link), the bibliography contains lists of general works
such as bibliographies, editions, availability and
prices, *festschriften* and other collections, general
literary histories, general studies of the drama,
studies of medieval drama, studies of Tudor and Stuart
drama, playlists, records, theater and stagecraft and
biographical notes and studies of more than one figure
The second part, beginning on page 199, lists
thirty-four individual authors including Davenant, who
has five entries on two pages. The book has an index
that is conveniently labelled so that under Davenant we
have items according to "biography" and "masques."

1105.   *Philological Quarterly*, Volume 55, No. 4 (1976--).

        PQ provided a six-volume bibliography that
encompassed scholarship published from 1925 through
1970. From 1971 through 1974, the annual bibliography
for the eighteenth century was published at the
University of Iowa for *Philological Quarterly* as the
third or fourth number of volumes 51-54. With volume

55 (1976) the bibliography was published by the AMS
Press as *The Eighteenth Century: A Current
Bibliography*. Davenant appears as he does in the other
volumes in the series, under his own name and
cross-referenced to other listed items. Almost all of
the entries have annotations. See *1926B*: "English
Literature"; *1950B*: Landa; *1975B*: *The Eighteenth
Century*.

1978

1106.   DePorte, Michael V. "William Davenant." *The Later
Jacobean and Caroline Dramatists: A Survey and
Bibliography of Recent Studies in English Renaissance
Drama*. Ed. Terence Logan and Denzell S. Smith.
Lincoln: Univ. of Nebraska Press, 1978. Pp.
192-209.

The bibliography on Davenant is divided into
four parts: Part I, "General" has three
subdivisions--"Biographical," "General Studies of the
Plays," and "Works at Large"; Part II, "Criticism of
Individual Plays" including *The Siege of Rhodes, I* and
*II, The Wits, The Platonic Lovers, Macbeth, The
Tempest, or The Enchanted Island, The First Day's
Entertainment at Rutland House*, and *The Man's the
Master*, and a section on the "State of Scholarship";
Part III, offers the "Canon" that includes first the
"Plays in Chronological Order," then "Uncertain
Ascriptions; Apocrypha," a "Critique of the Standard
Edition," "Single Work Editions" and the "Nondramatic
Works." The final section, "See Also," lists
twenty-eight additional references of significance to a
study of Davenant. The bibliography is helpful and
good.

1107.   Fordyce, Rachel, ed. *Caroline Drama: A Bibliographic
History of Criticism*. A Reference Publication in
Literature. Ed. Lawrence S. Thompson. Boston,
Mass.: G.K. Hall, 1978. Pp. xix, 203.

The work contains hundreds of entries under
the labels: "General Reference and Bibliographies"
(1-145 entries), "Textual Considerations" (146-193),
"Major Caroline Dramatists" (194-463), "Lesser Caroline
Dramatists" (464-593), "Individual Studies and
Comprehensive Works" (594-773), "Stage History"

(774-829). Those entries are followed by three
indexes: "Subject Index"; "Persons, Plays and Places";
and "Authors of Secondary Writings." The work is
"designed to survey the major critical issues related
to Caroline Drama as they have emerged over
approximately the last 100 years ..." (p. ix). Almost
fifty items related to the study of Davenant are listed
in the second index, and other works of some interest
to Davenant scholarship are found in the other
indexes.

1979

1108.   Raddadi, Mongi. *Davenant's Adaptations of
Shakespeare*. Studia Anglistica Upsaliensia, 36.
Stockholm: Almquist & Wiksall, 1979. Pp. 162-70.

The bibliography covers material pertinent to
the study.

1981

1109.   Bordinat, Philip, and Sophia B. Blaydes. *Sir William
Davenant*. Twayne's English Authors Series, 303.
Boston: Twayne, 1981. Pp. 171-80.

The volume contains a selected bibliography of
bibliographies, primary sources, and secondary sources
that are divided into critical studies, dissertations,
and theses.

1110.   Watson, George, ed. *The Shorter New Cambridge
Bibliography of English Literature*. Cambridge:
Cambridge Univ. Press, 1981. Pp. xiv, 1622.

The volume provides an abbreviated list of the
entries in the five-volume set. See *1941B*: Watson;
1966B: Watson; *1974B*: Watson.

INDEX

References are to numbers preceding the items in the bibliography. The letter n indicates that the reference is to the note of the numbered item, and the letter B indicates that the reference is to the last section, *Bibliographies*.

311

DATE DUE
